DATE DUE

Why People Cooperate

Why People Cooperate

THE ROLE OF SOCIAL MOTIVATIONS

Tom R. Tyler

PRINCETON UNIVERSITY PRESS

PRINCETON AND OXFORD

Library of Congress Cataloging-in-Publication Data

Tyler, Tom R.
Why people cooperate : the role of social motivations / Tom R. Tyler.
  p.   cm.
Includes bibliographical references and index.
ISBN 978-0-691-14690-4 (hardcover : alk. paper)
1. Motivation (Psychology)—Social aspects. I. Title.
BF503.T955 2010
302´.14—dc22   2010005109

British Library Cataloging-in-Publication Data is available

This book has been composed in Bodoni

Printed on acid-free paper. ∞

Printed in the United States of America

10 9 8 7 6 5 4 3 2

Contents

Illustrations

Acknowledgments

The preparation of this volume was facilitated by talks given at the Program on Negotiation at Harvard University, the Department of Sociology at the University of Washington, the Ethics Center at Stanford University, the Society for Experimental Social Psychology, and the Woodrow Wilson School at Princeton University. I thank the many people who contributed to the volume by making comments on drafts; these include John Darley, Jeffrey Fagan, and Dale Miller as well as several anonymous reviewers. The collection of the panel data on employees was supported by the Alfred P. Sloan Foundation Program in Business Organizations. I thank Gail Pesyna for her support on that project. The panel data on community residents of the police was supported by grants from the National Institute of Justice and the Law and Social Science Program of the National Science Foundation. The Afrobarometer data on political evaluations in Africa was collected as part of a joint enterprise of Michigan State University, the Institute for Democracy in South Africa, and the Centre for Democracy and Development in Ghana. For more information on the Afrobarometer, see www.afrobarometer.org.

Why People Cooperate

Overview

W hat connects people to groups, organizations, and societies? Why do people under some conditions throw their lot in with others and act on behalf of collectivities rather than pursuing their personal self-interest, while in other situations it is difficult or even impossible to motivate such cooperative efforts and people intently pursue their personal self-interest? In other words, what are the reasons that people have for cooperating with others when they are in a group, organization, community, or society? Answering this question is central to all of the social sciences.

A natural tendency, widely found in social psychology as well as in sociology, political science, economics, management, law, and public policy, is to view people as primarily relating to groups instrumentally—that is, cooperating to the degree that others are seen as potential sources of material rewards and/or material costs. Rewards and costs can potentially be thought of in many ways, but are frequently framed in terms of the type of rewards and costs associated with monetary gains or losses. Closely associated to this framing of rewards and costs are the physical pleasures associated with obtaining material rewards or the pain of experiencing material losses. One reason for joining with others in groups is to be better able to obtain rewards and avoid costs and to the extent that people are motivated in this way their relationship is linked to the degree to which they view their potential resource exchanges with others as personally beneficial.

This book argues that the core motivation shaping people's relationships with others is not of this material type. While not denying the importance of material rewards and costs, it is argued that for most people, most of the time, the connections dominating their relationship with others are related to social links. And, in particular, it is suggested that the extent to which people are motivated to act on behalf of others, cooperating with groups, organizations, and societies, rather than pursuing self-interested objectives, is defined by the nature and strength of people's social connections to others.

What are the social links that connect people to others? They are long-term connections to groups that are based upon attitudes, emotional connections, shared identities, common values, trust in the character and motivations of others, and a joint commitment to using fair procedures to exercise authority and make decisions. All of these connections share a linkage based upon social ties and are distinct from concerns about personal material gains and losses. Of course, material gains and losses are also important. However, it will be argued that the core factors shaping cooperation, especially voluntary cooperation, are social. Because of the centrality of social motivations to cooperation it will be further argued that the viability of groups, organizations, and societies is linked to the ability of groups to create and sustain supportive social motivations among their members.

While I argue that social links underlie people's behavior across all types of social settings, the strength of that motivation is often most obvious in situations in which people cooperate when that cooperation makes little sense in terms of the personal rewards and costs they are facing. When the risks of cooperation are high and the likelihood of gains seems remote, it is hard to understand people's willingness to act on behalf of collectivities.

Consider a common problematic situation, risking injury or death to fight for one's country. Although coercion in the form of conscription is common in such situations, and in conflict situations there are risks associated with shirking from battle, as well as with fighting, it is striking how often people are motivated by their social connections to their group to take risks for their group. As an example, in his well-known book about the American revolution David McCullough describes George Washington's efforts to hold the American army together in the face of seemingly overwhelming odds of defeat by the British. Washington did so by appealing to identity and values, arguing that if the soldiers would stay they would "render that service to the cause of liberty, and to your country, which you can probably never do under other circumstance" (McCullough 2005, 286). Similarly, in *Henry V*, William Shakespeare imagines the king, prior to the Battle of Agincourt, appealing to common identity, saying "we few, we happy few, we band of brothers—for whoever sheds his blood with me today shall be my brother" (act 4, scene 3).

Efforts to inspire voluntary commitment of the type outlined are important because the "only obedience worth soliciting and maintaining [from soldiers] is one born of love not fear. It is not money, legislation, or conscription . . . but the people's attachment to their government from the sense of the deep stake they have in such a glorious institution." This type of obedience is "freely given and inspired by love of country" (Samet 2004, 7). Consequently, it is valuable to the group, which does not have to—and in these dire moments cannot—create incentives or credible punishments sufficient to motivate desired behavior. As McCullough makes clear, the revolutionary soldiers who were inspired by Washington's plea well understood that they faced great risks and hardships that many anticipated (correctly) they would not survive. A rational actor would not have stayed. This emphasis on socially motivated commitment and on the willing exercise of voluntary initiative in fighting ("taking risks") for one's country that exists in democratic culture is generally credited with the superior military effectiveness of democratic armies (Reiter and Stam 2002).

Of course, we do not need to focus upon such extreme settings to see the virtue of social motivations. Even the mundane tasks associated with fast food restaurants are difficult to motivate with money. Rather, managers look for "people who can be instructed in the general goal . . . and let loose to achieve it" (Newman 1999, 176) rather than someone who is only motivated to do required tasks—that is, the work for which he is paid. The broad recognition of the value of such socially motivated cooperation is found in scholarly discussions of cooperation in groups, communities, organizations, and societies (Tyler 2000, 2009).

The idea that appeals to common identities and shared values underlie people's willingness to act on behalf of groups is not new. Classic writing in sociology, for example, recognizes the importance of such connections. The Baron Montesquieu (Shackleton 1961), one of the founders of modern sociology, discussed the human passions that underlie effective societies and, in the case of democracies, focused upon "virtue"—the willingness to put aside self-interest to act in ways that help one's society. He contrasted that virtue to fear, which he characterized as the passion underlying the success of despotic states. This focus upon values as a core linkage between people and their communities is also prominent within both Max Weber's writing upon legitimacy—the perception of obligation to obey legal authorities (Swedbert 2006; Tyler 2006a, 2006b; Weber 1968)—and Émile Durkheim's focus upon legal authorities as enforcers of shared moral values (Cotterrell 1999; Jackson and Sunshine 2007; Nisbet 1974). The writings of these sociologists, while different in many ways, share a focus upon the argument that the success of governmental authorities in democratic states is linked to their ability to call upon the people's values as a basis for their actions.

Within psychology a similar focus upon internalized values is central to the work of Sigmund Freud, who was concerned with the importance of the internalization of values—that is, a transformation after which societal norms were not viewed as "external, coercively imposed pressures to which they must submit" (Hoffman 1977, 85) but instead became part of a person's own value system and were followed even in the absence of external authority. Freud focused primarily upon moral values rather than social ties, but his work shares with sociologists the focus on the development of social motivations.

Social scientists have also recognized the centrality of internal values to regulation and governance (Tyler 2006a). As Herbert Kelman puts it, "It is essential to the effective functioning of the nation-state that the basic tenets of its ideology be widely accepted within the population.... This means that the average citizen is prepared to meet the expectations of the citizen role and to comply with the demands that the state makes upon him, even when this requires considerable personal sacrifice" (1969, 278). Political scientists refer to this set of values as a "reservoir of support" for government and society (Dahl 1956; Easton 1965, 1975), and writers in political science have also noted the importance of creating and maintaining legitimacy as a foundation for the authoritativeness of the state (Lipset 1959). Just as the law needs people to obey it, the state needs people to be willing to act on its behalf by paying taxes, fighting wars, and so on. All of these classic writings view shared social links as a key element shaping the ability of society and government to motivate cooperative actions on the part of the members of groups.

Within psychology the idea of social motivations was extensively elaborated in the work of Kurt Lewin (Gold 1999) and was central to the Research Center for Group Dynamics that came about after that research. In Lewin's classic studies the focus of concern was the behavior of groups of boys. Various types of behavior were considered, including the performance of group tasks (making theatrical masks) and aggression toward others in the group. In the studies, leaders sought to encourage/discourage these behaviors using a variety of styles of motivation, including authoritarian and democratic leadership.

Because his work was inspired by the events in Germany during World War II, Lewin was concerned with understanding when groups are hostile toward people or subgroups within them. Hence he focused his attention upon issues of aggression and scapegoating. In addition, and most relevant to this discussion, Lewin studied the performance of group tasks—in this case whether the boys being studied were engaged in their task of making theatrical masks. The focus on group performance carried forward as an important aspect of the agenda of the Research Center for Group Dynamics inspired by the work of Lewin and his students and it is this aspect of his early work that is reflected in the concept of cooperation as it is presented in this volume.

A key experimental distinction introduced in the Lewinian research approach was between behavior while the leader is present and behavior when the leader is absent. It was found that when the leader of an autocratic group left the room, the behavior of the boys changed (work dropped from occupying 52 percent to occupying 16 percent of the children's time). When the leader was democratic, this change did not occur (i.e., work only dropped from 50 percent to 46 percent of the children's time). So, when work was motivated by democratic means, children worked irrespective of whether there was an authority present to provide them with rewards and/or sanction shirking.

Lewin argues that democratic leadership, which is participatory, engages the internal motivations of the boys, so their behavior is no longer linked to the presence of the external forces represented by the leader. Instead, behavior flows from internal motivations—from what the boys want to do or feel that they ought to do. Further, and central to Lewin's concerns, the boys are not suppressing negative feelings in the presence of the democratic leader, so there is no motivation for them to be aggressive toward other boys when the leader leaves.

The first aspect of this Lewinian approach is the effort in field theory to identify two sources of motivation. The first is external, and reflects the contingencies in the environment. Lewin recognized that the environment shapes behavior by altering the costs and benefits associated with various types of behavior. The second type of behavior is internal, and is shaped by the traits, values, and attitudes of the person. These are the motivational forces developing from sources within the person and reflecting their own desires. In the terminology used in this volume, the motivations are social.

When external contingencies were strong, individual differences in behavior did not emerge in Lewin's groups. Conversely, in the absence of strong external pressures, behavior reflected people's attitudes and values. Hence, Lewin argued that there is a balance between these two types of motivation within any given situation.

As is the case in the Lewinian approach, the argument taken herein is that the engagement of internal, or social, motivations is especially key when the type of cooperation of concern is behavior that will occur outside of the surveillance of authorities. Such behavior is "voluntary" in the sense that it is not a reflection of the contingencies of the external environment. The leader is not present and cannot either reward or punish behavior. Hence, the behavior that occurs is a more direct reflection of the internal attitudes and values of the boys.

This analysis is broadly framed using the Lewinian field theory model in several ways. First, as is true with the work of Lewin, this analysis of people's actions views behavior as a reflection of two factors: external (instrumental) and internal (social) motivations. Second, and again as articulated by Lewin, the key issue is the mix of these motivations. Finally, this analysis distinguishes between those behaviors that are and those that are not voluntary—that is, behaviors that do and do not occur in settings in which behavior is being observed and those who engage in it are aware that the incentives and sanctions they receive will be shaped by their actions.

While the idea of social motivation has a rich history, in recent decades the focus of attention has shifted strongly toward instrumental motivations. Within the social sciences as well as in law, management, and public policy, discussions of organizations and organizational design have emphasized the use of incentives and sanctions as mechanisms for shaping behavior. Coincident with this focus a large and sophisticated literature on decision making has explored the many heuristics and biases that influence people's efforts to define and pursue their material goals. The argument presented herein will be for an expansion of the factors considered when efforts are made to understand the factors shaping behavior in social settings.

Further, it will be suggested that the additional social factors that emerge as important in such an examination point to a different approach to many social issues and societal problems. The reason to read this book and to adopt the perspective it advocates is that it provides a different approach to a number of societal issues than has dominated discourse in recent decades. That new approach is to focus on creating and maintaining social links between people and groups, and to base efforts to encourage cooperation on those links rather than seeking to motivate cooperation instrumentally through providing rewards or threatening punishments.

An instrumental approach involves the concentration of resources into the hands of authorities, who can then credibly reward and punish desired and undesired behavior. In contrast, an approach based upon social motivations focuses upon creating and sustaining social links between people and groups. This is a long-term strategy that begins with socialization into groups and continues with the exercise of authority in ways that support and enhance social ties.

In any given situation, instead of seeking to shape behavior by promises of reward or threats of punishment group authorities appeal to social motivations, including attitudes, identities, and values. In making these appeals the goal is to encourage people within groups to cooperate because of their own internal desires and feelings of appropriateness. When people do so, the group does not need to motivate them with promises of reward or monitor their behavior for deference to group needs. People want to do what benefits the group and do so willingly based upon their social links to the group.

In this volume I will argue that too little attention is currently paid to social motivations, which I suggest are more effective in motivating cooperation. I will present evidence to support this argument from studies in management, regulation, and governance. While it is generally true that social motivations are important, there has been a general shift in the type of behavior that we want from the members of groups that has heightened the value of a focus on social motivations. This shift is from compliance to cooperation. It is illustrated by the case of regulation. In the legal arena the traditional concern has been with motivating compliance with the law. When I wrote *Why People Obey the Law* (1990) the legal literature focused on one primary goal for the members of society: compliance with the law. This includes compliance in the context of the particular decisions made by legal authorities, such as judges and police officers, and compliance with the law in everyday life. In both cases, a key societal objective is to be able to bring people's behavior in line with the law (Tyler 2006b). A good citizen was viewed as someone who obeyed the law.

Today the view of what is desired from citizens is more complex. First, the problems of compliance have been more widely recognized. To gain compliance society must deploy resources toward surveillance to catch rule-breakers, and toward prisons to punish them. It is preferable to gain voluntary deference. Such deference is shaped by social motivations.

And these goals for citizens extend broadly. In the arena of crime it is viewed as desirable to have public cooperation in the production of social order. The police need the help of communities to identify criminals and report crimes and to help police communities. Neither of these forms of cooperation is effectively motivated by the risk of sanctions. For example, if a crime is occurring and citizens do not report it there is little realistic risk that they will ever be identified or sanctioned for this lack of cooperation. Similarly, failure to attend a neighborhood meeting about crime and community problems will typically go unnoticed. In other words, while compliance with rules is potentially motivated by the fear of detection through ongoing surveillance by legal authorities, such surveillance is not directed at—and is unlikely to be effective in—detecting the failure to voluntarily come forward when there are opportunities to help the police.

Because cooperation is important, a change is needed in the type of motivation that is the focus of regulatory efforts. It is important to have the type of motivation that leads to voluntary deference and cooperation, and that motivation is social. Social motivations lead not only to compliance but to voluntary deference to rules and to more general willing cooperation.

Changing our behavioral focus from compliance to voluntary acceptance and cooperation leads to a change in the type of motivation that we need to create among community residents. The old focus has been upon creating and maintaining a credible risk of being punished for rule-breaking behavior and/or demonstrating competence by controlling crime. The new focus needs to be upon the internal motivational forces that lead people to undertake voluntary actions without calculating the risks of punishment for wrongdoing or the potential personal gains for cooperation. People need to have an alternative basis for their actions. I will argue that social motivations are this alternative basis.

While this example has focused upon regulation and people's connections to the law and legal authorities, this volume considers three areas: work organizations and worker behavior (management), the law and law-related actions (regulation), and communities and activities related to political behavior (governance). Although these are not all the possible group settings, these areas are three key arenas in which people's willingness to cooperate is central to the effectiveness of relevant institutions. My overall argument, supported by data from studies in these three areas, is that in each social motivations are central to cooperation—especially to voluntary cooperation.

SECTION ONE

Introduction

CHAPTER ONE

Why Do People Cooperate?

A cross the social sciences there has been a widespread recognition that it is important to understand how to motivate cooperation on the part of people within group settings. This is the case irrespective of whether those settings are small groups, organizations, communities, or societies.[1] Studies in management show that work organizations benefit when their members actively work for company success. Law research shows that crime and problems of community disorder are difficult to solve without the active involvement of community residents. Political scientists recognize the importance of public involvement in building both viable communities and strong societies. And those in public policy have identified the value of cooperation in the process of policy making—for example, in stakeholder policy making groups.

Understanding *why* people are motivated to cooperate when they are within these group settings is a long-term focus of social psychological research. In particular, social psychologists are interested in identifying the motivations that are the antecedents of voluntary cooperation. The goal of this volume is to examine the psychology of cooperation, exploring the motivations that shape the degree to which people cooperate with others. In particular, this analysis focuses on the factors that influence voluntary cooperation. A better understanding of why people cooperate is essential if social psychology is to be helpful in addressing the question of how to motivate cooperation in social settings.

Cooperation in the Real World

The issue of cooperation is central to many of the problems faced by real-world groups, organizations, and societies (De Cremer, Zeelenberg, and Murnighan 2010; Van Lange 2006; VanVugt et al. 2000). As a result, the fields of management, law, and political science all seek to understand how to most effectively design institutions that can best secure cooperation from those within groups. Their efforts to address these issues are mainly informed by the findings of social psychological and economic research on dyads and small groups.

Work organizations encourage positive forms of cooperation, like working hard at one's job and contributing extra-role and creative efforts to one's work performance (Tyler and Blader 2000). They also seek to prevent personally rewarding, but destructive, acts such as sabotage and the stealing of office supplies by encouraging deference to rules and policies. For these reasons a central area of research in organizational behavior involves understanding how to motivate cooperation in work settings (Frey and Osterloh 2002).[2] Management is the study of motivation in work organizations.

Law is concerned with how to effectively shape behavior so as to prevent people from engaging in actions that are personally rewarding but damaging to others and to the group—actions ranging from illegally copying music and movies to robbing banks (Tyler 2006a; Tyler and Huo 2002). In addition, the police and courts need the active cooperation of members of the community to control crime and urban disorder by reporting crimes and cooperating in policing neighborhoods (Tyler and Huo 2002). And, of course, it is important that people generally support the government through actions such as the paying of taxes (Braithwaite 2003; Feld and Frey 2007). Hence, an important aspect of the study of law involves seeking to understand the factors shaping cooperation with law and legal authorities. Regulation explores how the law can shape the behavior of people in different communities.

Those who hold political office want people to cooperate by participating in personally costly acts ranging from paying taxes to fighting in wars (Levi 1988, 1997). Further, it is equally important for people to actively participate in society in ways that are not required, such as by voting, by maintaining their communities through working together to deal with community problems, and by otherwise helping the polity to thrive (Putnam 2000). For these reasons, understanding how to motivate cooperation is central to political scientists, leading to an interest in exploring why people do or do not have trust and confidence in the government (Levi and Stoker 2000). Governance involves the study of how to motivate desired political behaviors.

One aspect of governance involves studies of public policy, which are concerned with developing social policies that can effectively coordinate the actions of people within communities.[3] Such efforts focus on creating a procedure for developing and implementing policies and policy decisions, be they decisions about whether to go to war or where to site a nuclear power plant. The key to success in such efforts is to create policies that all of the people within a community are motivated to accept—that is, to be able to gain widespread rule adherence (Grimes 2006). And, as is true in the other arenas outlined, the value of cooperation in general is widely recognized. In particular, it is important that people not just do what is required. Many aspects of involvement in a community are voluntary, and it is especially important to motivate community residents to engage in voluntary acts such as voting and participating in community problem solving over issues such as environmental use (May 2005).

In a broader arena, regulation and governance involve international relations, questions of compliance with laws, and political relations among states (Simmons 1998). The question of what motivates states to follow international norms, rules, and commitments has been a long-standing concern of international relations (Hurd 1999). It is an issue that is of increasing centrality as the dynamics among states, multinational organizations, and nongovernmental organizations becomes more complex (Reus-Smit 1999). And underlying all of these forms of cooperation is the ability to motivate mass publics whose behavior plays a key role in the stability and viability of societies to both follow laws and accept agreements. Over the past decade, all of these issues have taken on a new urgency as terrorism has made clear the tremendous difficulties that the lack of public cooperation in the form of organized opposition across national borders can pose to institutional actors in the international arena.

The first goal of this volume is to test the range and robustness of one type of motivation—social motivation—in these types of settings. This volume does so by systematically exploring the importance of two aspects of social motivation: organizational policies and practices (procedural justice, motive-based trust) and dispositions (attitudes, values, identity). The importance of these motivations is compared to that of instrumental motivations involving the use of incentives and sanctions.

What perspective is advanced in this volume? The findings herein will show that people are motivated by a broader range of goals than is easily explained via material self-interest—that is, by people's concerns about incentives and sanctions. Across the five areas examined, social motivations are consistently found to explain significant amounts of variance that are not explained by instrumental factors. This suggests that broadening the motivational framework within which cooperation is understood will help to better explain how to motivate cooperation.

In fact, the results of this volume go further than simply arguing that social motivations have value. They suggest that cooperative behavior, especially voluntary cooperation, is better explained by such social motivations than it is by the traditionally studied impact of instrumental variables such as incentives and sanctions. When the magnitude of the influence of instrumental and social motivations is directly compared, social motivations are found to explain more of the variance in cooperation than can be explained by instrumental motivations. As a consequence, those seeking to best understand how to motivate cooperation should focus their attention upon social, as opposed to instrumental, motivations for behavior.

The results suggest that the influence of social motivations on voluntary cooperation is especially strong. Because organizations focus heavily upon motivating such voluntary behavior, social motivations become even more important to the study of how to obtain desired behaviors in groups, organizations, and communities.

A second purpose of this volume is to test the range within which social motivations are important. While it is not possible to test the model in all group settings, three distinct settings are examined. The first setting involves work organizations (management); employees are interviewed about their workplaces and their views are linked to their workplace cooperation. The second setting is community-based and looks at people's rule related behaviors (regulation); residents of a large metropolitan community are interviewed about their views concerning law enforcement, and their willingness to cooperate with the police is measured. The third setting is also community-based, but examines political participation using several studies of participation in governance within communities in Africa (governance). By comparing these three diverse settings an assessment can be made of the breadth of the influence of social motivation.

Finally, the third purpose of the volume is to test a psychological model of cooperation. That model argues that organizational policies and practices (procedural justice, motive-based trust) influence dispositions (attitudes, values, identity) and through them shape cooperation.[4] This model provides an organizing framework for understanding how the different social motivations are dynamically connected to one another. This psychological model provides guidelines concerning how to exercise authority in groups, organizations, and communities. It suggests that authorities should focus on acting in ways that encourage judgments that they are using just procedures when exercising their authority and that their intentions and character are trustworthy. Procedural justice and motive-based trust lead to favorable dispositions and, through them, motivate voluntary cooperation on behalf of groups.

Beyond Material Self-interest

Psychologists distinguish between motivations, which are the goals that energize and direct behavior, and people's judgments about the nature of the world used to make plans and choose when to take action and how to behave—that is, which choices to make. This book is about the nature of desired goals.

The issue of cognition or judgment and decision making involves choices that people must make about how to most effectively achieve desired goals. It explores how, once they have a goal, people make decisions about how and when to act so as to most likely achieve that goal. Motivation explores the issue of what goals people desire to achieve. Unless we know what goal people are pursuing, we cannot understand the intention of their actions. Of course, people may make errors that lead them to fail to achieve their desired goals. Nonetheless, their actions are guided by their purposes.

A simple example of the distinction between cognition and motivation is found in the instrumental analyses of action. The goal that energizes people within instrumental models is the desire to maximize their rewards and minimize their costs—for example, the punishments that they experience. To do so, people make estimates of the likely gains and losses associated with different types of actions. These judgments about the nature of the world shape the degree to which people engage in different behaviors in the pursuit of their goal of maximizing rewards and minimizing punishments.

Within the arenas of law, management, political science, and public policy, most discussions of human motivation are drawn from the fields of psychology and economics. The assumption that people are seeking to maximize their personal utilities—defined in material terms—underlies much of the recent theory and research in both psychology and economics. The argument is that people are motivated by this desire, but simplify their calculations when seeking to maximize their personal utilities by "satisficing" and using heuristics. Further, while motivated to maximize their utilities, people also have limits as information processors, making errors and acting on biases. In other words, people may be trying to calculate their self-interest in optimal ways, but lack the ability to do so well; so they are acting out of the desire to maximize their own material self-interest, but they do it imperfectly due to limits in their time, information, and cognitive abilities.

The Interface of Psychology and Economics

In the past several decades there have been tremendous advances in the connection between economics and psychology. Economists have drawn upon the research and insights of psychologists and have also conducted their own empirical research as part of the burgeoning field of behavioral economics. The goal of this volume is to further the connection between psychology and economics by showing the value of considering the range of motivations that are important in social settings.

A major area of psychology upon which economists have drawn in the last several decades is that of judgment and decision making. This area, characterized by the work of psychologists such as Amos Tversky and Daniel Kahneman (1974,

1981; see also Kahneman, Slovic, and Tversky 1982; Kahneman and Tversky 2000), focuses upon the cognitive errors and biases that shape the individual judgments of people seeking to pursue their material self-interest during decision making (Brocas and Carrillo 2003; Dawes 1988; Hastie and Dawes 2001; Hogarth 1980; Nisbett and Ross 1980; Plous 1993; Thaler 1991).

The literature on judgment and decision making is not primarily focused on issues of motivation but on cognition. It seeks to understand how people use their subjective knowledge of the world to make decisions, and assumes that a key motivation for such actions is the desire to maximize material gains and minimize material losses. However, an important message from social psychology is that both cognition and motivation are important. They act in tandem to shape behaviors such as cooperation (see Higgins and Kruglanski 2001). As a consequence, this analysis of decision making can profit from being combined with an expanded analysis of the motivations for action.

In terms of motivations, economists have generally operated on the assumption that people are motivated to maximize their own personal self-interest, a self-interest defined in terms of material gains and losses. No doubt, most psychologists and economists would acknowledge that people can be motivated by a broader range of motivations than material gains and losses, but these other motivations have not been the primary focus of this research. Similarly, the models of human motivation dominating law, management, political science, and public policy have not generally been broader in their focus than to consider the role of incentives and sanctions (Green and Shapiro 1994; Pfeffer 1994).[5]

While incentives and sanctions have dominated the study of motivation (Goodin 1996), there have been suggestions of the need for a broader focus (Zak 2008). In articulating such a broader vision of human motivation this work connects to the recent work of behavioral economists working in this area (see, among others, Falk and Kosfeld 2004; Fehr and Falk 2002; Fehr and Gächter 2002; Fehr and Rockenbach 2003; Frey 1997; Frey and Stutzer 2002; Stutzer and Lalive 2001). It does so by arguing for the potential benefits—of those involved in studying law, management, political science, and public policy—of considering a broader range of the motivations that can shape behavior in institutional settings.

While the experimental economics literature increasingly acknowledges social motivations, the use of experimental methodologies makes it difficult to compare their degree of influence to that of instrumental motivations. In contrast, the survey approach outlined here makes more explicit comparisons of relative influence in nature settings by providing an estimate of the amount of the variance in cooperation that is explained by a particular group of variables in a real-world setting. Such comparisons highlight the importance of social motivations.

In recent years there has been an increasing effort to empirically examine the internal dynamics of firms—for example, in the relational contract model (Baker, Gibbons, and Murphy 2002). The key argument of the relational contract model is that we need to move beyond the formal structure of organizations, recognizing that formal rules and contracts are incomplete and must be supplemented by an understanding of the more informal "relational contracts" that allow particular people to use their own detailed knowledge of their situation to adapt to new and unique contingencies. Relational contracts offer important advantages over formal contracts because they can be more flexibly linked to the realities of particular situations and people. But they are held in place by weaker organizational forces, making the likelihood of nonadherence a more serious problem for organizations that value relational contracts and want to facilitate their use.

The goal of organizational design, in other words, is to induce greater levels of rule adherence and high performance among the people in organizations by implementing the best possible relational contracts. The question is how to design groups or organizations so as to facilitate the maintenance of relational contracts—that is, to create conditions under which such contracts will be honored even in the face of temptation. In other words, the focus on social motivation in this volume coincides with the increasing focus by economists on interpersonal processes within groups and organizations (see, e.g., Gächter and Fehr 1999).

A similar concern with understanding how people behave in social settings underlies the recent efforts of experimental economists. A major recent effort is a fifteen-society study of cooperative behavior, one that seeks to identify the motivations shaping cooperation. The authors find that beyond seeking material payoffs, people have social preferences—that is, "subjects care about fairness and reciprocity, are willing to change the distribution of material outcomes among others at a personal cost to themselves, and reward those who act in a pro-social manner while punishing those who do not, even when these actions are costly" (Henrich et al. 2004, 8). These authors undertook an ambitious cross-cultural series of studies of cooperation and demonstrated that in none of their fifteen studies were people's behaviors consistent with a narrow material self-interest model. In each there was evidence of social motivations. Commenting on these cross-cultural studies, Colin Camerer and Ernst Fehr (2004) refer to these motivations as "social utility," and indicate that they are found throughout societies that differ widely in social, economic, and political characteristics (see also Gintis et al. 2005). The argument that people will accept personal costs to enforce fairness rules is also supported by more recent experimental research (Gürerk, Irlenbusch, and Rockenbach 2006).

The focus of much of this behavioral economic-based research is to understand how people feel about market situations. It is striking, therefore, that studies consistently find that people use fairness-based judgments in market settings. One approach that people are often found to use is to adjust their marketplace behavior to reflect justice norms (Kahneman, Knetsch, and Thaler 1986). Further, people will refuse to engage in market transactions when moral principles are being violated (Baron and Spranca 1997; Tetlock and Fiske 1997). Finally, people are found to consider issues of procedural justice when deciding on the suitability of markets as allocation mechanisms (Frey, Benz, and Stutzer 2004; Sondak and Tyler 2007) or when negotiating (Hollander-Blumoff and Tyler 2008).

A New Framework for Voluntary Cooperation

The goal of this volume is to build upon the suggestion that we need a better understanding of the factors that shape people's behavior in social settings—that is, to provide a better sense of what social motivations are and how they influence people's cooperative behavior. To do so this work will present an analysis of several studies and, through them, move toward a broader framework for understanding human motivation within social settings. That framework includes concern with costs and benefits, as well as issues such as "reputation" as defined by economists. As framed in economic analysis, these issues are instrumental and are linked to concerns about material gains and losses. The studies reviewed here suggest that social mechanisms that move beyond such reputational influences also help us to explain additional aspects of voluntary cooperation. These social mechanisms provide another set of goals or reasons that lead people to take the actions that they do when they are in social settings.

In this analysis I will identify several types of social psychological mechanisms that deal with issues relevant to cooperation and to test their importance in organizational settings of three types—managerial, legal, and political. This demonstration is based upon the premise that it is by showing that social motivations strongly influence cooperation that their value in social settings can best be demonstrated.

The core argument is that while people are clearly motivated by self-interest and seek to maximize their material rewards and minimize material deprivations, there is a rich set of other, more social motivations that additionally shape people's actions. These motivations have an important influence on behavior that is distinct from instrumental calculations but that has not received as much attention as have material gains and losses. The argument that social motives are important has implications for issues of the design of groups, organizations, and communities (Tyler, 2007, 2008, 2009). The primary implication is that there are a broader range of motivations that can be tapped to encourage desirable behaviors than is encompassed within traditional incentive and sanctioning models.[6]

The Myth of Self-interest

One of the reasons the issue of social motivations has organizational implications is that people are generally found to overestimate the centrality of self-interest and of material gains and losses to the motivation of their behavior. D. T. Miller uses "the myth of self-interest" to capture this idea—that people's own image of their motivation is skewed in the direction of viewing themselves and others as more strongly motivated by self-interest than is actually the case (see Miller 1999; Ratner and Miller 2001).

Central to this volume is the suggestion that these ideas about human motivation shape institutional designs. Of special concern is that theories can "win" in the marketplace of ideas, independent of their empirical validity (Ferraro, Pfeffer, and Sutton 2005, 8). In particular, the motivational assumptions of economics can be the key to the design of policies and practices within organizations, even when a broader conception of motivation might produce institutions more consistent with the factors actually shaping the behavior of people within organizations.

Two types of cooperation are considered in this volume: rule adherence (following organizational policies and rules) and performance (being productive and creating resources for the group). The starting point of this study is the recognition that people vary in how much effort they exert on behalf of the groups, organizations, and communities to which they belong. The members of most groups can point to examples of people who are always ready to step up and help their group—to volunteer and to take on responsibility for meeting the group's needs. They can also think of those who often seem to do little more than what is specifically required by their roles in the group, who never voluntarily take on any added obligations, and who are generally uninvolved in their groups. Finally, there are those who cannot even be expected to do what is required by their roles, preferring to shirk those tasks whenever possible.

What predicts these differences in people's behavior when they are in groups? Why are some people motivated to cooperate more fully with the groups to which they belong than are others? This study will contrast the role of two basic types of motivation in shaping the degree to which people cooperate with the groups, organizations, or communities of which they are members. These are instrumental and social motivations.

The issue of motivation is of concern because people usually have considerable latitude to determine the extent and nature of their efforts within the groups to which they belong. They may choose to expend a great deal of effort on promoting the goals and functioning of the group; or they may take a less active role, and do what they feel is required to get by.[7] The choices people make regarding their behavioral engagement with the group have important implications for the group's functioning and viability. The goal here is to understand the motivations that influence these choices.

Psychologists identify a wide variety of types of potential motivation. This volume will simplify that discussion and focus on the two basic types of motivations, instrumental and social. Instrumental motivations are linked to the connection between cooperation and material self-interest. Irrespective of whether they are motivated by the desire to gain material resources or the goal of avoiding material costs, these behaviors are responsive to people's calculations of short-term material gain and loss.

Cooperation as a Theoretical Issue

Social scientists generally recognize that people have mixed motivations when interacting with others. On the one hand, there are clear personal advantages to be gained by cooperation. On the other hand, people are often unable to maximize their pursuit of personal self-interest if they act in ways that simultaneously maximize the welfare of the group. So to some extent people are motivated to cooperate, and to some extent to act out of personal self-interest. People must balance between these two distinct motivations (i.e., act on "mixed motivations") when shaping their level of cooperative behavior. Social psychologists explore the psychological dynamics underlying cooperation in a wide variety of situations ranging from dyadic bargaining (Rusbult and Van Lange 2003; Thibaut and Kelley 1959) to group and community level social dilemmas (see Kopelman, Weber, and Messick 2002; Weber, Kopelman, and Messick 2004). Across all of these literatures, a common theme is the desirability of motivating individuals to act in ways that transcend their self-interest and serve the interests of their groups.

While social psychology is generally focused upon dyads and small groups, mixed-motive conflicts within institutions and communities have been studied most directly by social psychologists within the literature on social dilemmas (Baden and Noonan 1998; Ostrom et al. 2002). This literature asks how people deal with situations in which the pursuit of short-term self-interest by all the members of a group has negative implications for the group and, in the long term, for those people who are members of the group. Social dilemmas have two characteristics: "(a) at any given decision point, individuals receive higher payoffs for making selfish choices than they do for making cooperative choices, regardless of the choices made by those with whom they interact, and (b) everyone involved receives lower payoffs if everyone makes selfish choices than if everyone makes cooperative choices" (Weber, Kopelman, and Messick 2004, 94).

In situations with social dilemma–type characteristics, the interest of the group, organization, or society lies in motivating greater levels of cooperation from the individual. Because cooperation is central to this discussion it is important to clarify what is meant by the term *cooperation* in this volume. The term is used in various research areas of psychology, and is defined in a variety of ways. In this volume, cooperation will be defined as a decision about how actively to involve oneself in a group, organization, or community through taking actions that will help the group to be effective and successful. These actions may have long-term benefits for the individual, but they are not necessarily linked to immediate benefits or costs. In fact, they are often in conflict with people's immediate material self-interest.

As noted, the concept of cooperation being used here develops most directly from the literature on social dilemmas. That literature recognizes that there is a conflict between an individual's immediate personal or selfish interests and the actions that maximize the interests of the group (Komorita and Parks 1994). However, in the long term people have an interest in the well-being of the group. In other words, "social dilemmas can be defined as situations in which the reward or payoff to each individual for a selfish choice is higher than that for a cooperative one, regardless of what other people do; yet all individuals in the group receive a lower payoff if all defect than if all cooperate" (Smithson and Foddy 1999, 1–2). That is, the individual also loses if group resources are destroyed, since she benefits from those resources herself.

And, as in social dilemma situations generally, the individual has mixed motivations. On the one hand, if none of the members of the group cooperate, the group will fail, to the mutual loss of everyone. On the other hand, the individual's self-interest does not unambiguously lie in maximally cooperating. The individual would benefit if others in the group were to cooperate and she could simply "free ride" on the efforts of others. As Jonathan Baron notes, "each person benefits by consuming the fruits of others' labor and laboring himself as little as possible—but if everyone behaved this way, there would be no fruits to enjoy" (2000, 434).

In organizations, the benefits of membership depend, in the long term, upon maintaining the efficiency and effectiveness of the group. This requires cooperation from group members. Yet, each individual can easily imagine that others would do the work needed, leaving her free to pursue her own desired activities. Hence, the group urges the person to put aside her immediate concerns and to act on behalf of the group by cooperating. This is a public goods dilemma in the sense that people are tempted to let other group members take on the work of making the group successful but are also at risk if everyone takes this same attitude. If all take a "free ride," the group will not succeed.

The key issue in this volume is the degree to which people do, in fact, engage in cooperative behavior on behalf of their group. In this case, the people being interviewed are employees in various organizations or residents in a community. Those employees/residents have an interest in gaining the benefits of group membership, and as long as they are in a group, potentially gain when the group is effective and viable. On the other hand, it is often not in their immediate self-interest to follow group policies or to put extra effort into achieving group goals. People's self-interest can conflict with group interests, as when it is advantageous to steal office supplies, or employees can feel that they have little to gain from working when that work will not be observed and rewarded by management. Similarly, the residents of communities reasonably see risks associated with reporting criminals or otherwise aiding legal authorities.

What Types of Cooperation Influence Group Success?

Two types of cooperation are central to the viability of groups—rule adherence and performance. The aspect of cooperation examined in many experimental games is cooperation that occurs when people follow rules limiting their exercise of their self-interested motivations (Tyler and Blader 2000). People want to fish in a lake, but limit what they catch to the quantity specified in a permit. They want to exploit others in bargaining, but follow rules dictating fairness. They want to steal from a bank, but defer to the law. In all of these situations, people are refraining from engaging in behavior that would benefit their self-interest but is against the welfare of others and/or of their group. This area of research is referred to as regulation and involves limiting undesirable behavior. This aspect of cooperation involves rule adherence—following the rules groups develop to regulate the use of resources.

The other aspect of cooperation involves performance on behalf of the group to create resources or perform tasks for the group (Tyler and Blader 2000). Groups also want their members to actively engage in tasks that effectively deal with group problems. In work institutions these tasks involve job performance issues; in communities they involve working with neighborhood groups, meeting about community problems, and otherwise helping the larger community deal with its concerns. Governments rely upon their members to vote and participate in the political process. The performance of these behaviors encourages the effectiveness and viability of the group.

In sum, the distinction drawn between two functions of cooperative behaviors differentiates between those that proactively advance the groups' goals through performance of actions that help the group and those that limit behaviors that are obstacles to achieving the group's goals. What this suggests is that people cooperate with groups both by doing things that help the group in a positive, proactive manner and also by refraining from doing things that may hurt the group. This volume terms these types of behavior or nonbehavior *cooperation* since people make choices along each of these dimensions as to whether they are going to do things that help (or don't hurt, as the case may be) the group.

Voluntary Cooperation

Within both forms of cooperation this volume distinguishes between cooperating in required ways and voluntary cooperation. In the case of workplace productivity employees are required to engage in those behaviors that are linked to their job description. Such expected behaviors are the "in-role" behaviors that are defined by their job. For example, they are expected to be in the office during the working hours of 9:00 AM to 5:00 PM. In addition, employees may engage in extra forms of cooperation that are not required, ranging from helping others to coming up with new ideas about how the organization can be more effective. Such "extra-role" behaviors are not a required aspect of the job, and are thought of as voluntary in nature.

With policy adherence and rule-following, employees are expected to act in ways that are consistent with organizational policies and rules about appropriate conduct. Such compliance is part of appropriate behavior within the organization. In addition, employees may or may not follow rules willingly, deferring to them in the sense that they follow rules irrespective of whether their behavior is being observed by others. Such willing buy-in leads people to voluntarily accept the rules.

The focus on social motivations is especially relevant in situations in which the goal is to motivate voluntary cooperative behavior. Motivation is linked to the viability of a strategy of delivery. Employees motivated by incentives need a clear set of expected behaviors and a direct link between those behaviors and rewards. So, for example, coming to work on time and performing clearly specified tasks can be connected to rewards. Sanctions are similar, although they add the complexity that people try to hide their behavior, so there must be effective surveillance strategies in place to detect rule-breaking. In either case, people are not motivated to act in the absence of a link between their actions and a reward/sanction.

In many settings, however, it is desirable for people to engage in cooperation even when incentives and sanctions are not being effectively deployed. As has been noted, even when effective, there are problems with incentive- and/or sanction-based approaches. One way to win the support of employees is to provide them with benefits for themselves. However, it is usually difficult to give everyone all the benefits they want. Further, companies are least able to provide desired benefits during times of transition or economic downturn, when they are most in need to employee cooperation if they are to be viable. Hence, work organizations benefit when people will cooperate for noninstrumental reasons. This analysis labels such cooperation "voluntary" because it is shaped by social, rather than instrumental, motivations.

With sanctions the value of voluntary cooperation becomes even clearer. Sanction-based strategies are always costly to implement because they require the development and maintenance of credible sanctioning strategies. So, for example, it is clear that crimes, such as employee theft, can be deterred by sanctions, but only when management deploys sufficient resources to establish a credible connection between such behavior and the likelihood of being caught and punished. In this context it is clear that the authorities benefit when people cooperate for social, rather than instrumental, reasons. Again, such cooperation is "voluntary" in character.

Tom Tyler and Steven Blader (2000) differentiate between two forms of cooperative behavior: *discretionary* cooperative behavior and *mandated* cooperative behavior. Mandated cooperation occurs when people engage in behavior that is dictated or required by group rules or norms. The terms and guidelines of the behavior are prescribed by some rule or policy of the group.

In contrast, discretionary behavior is that which is not directly required by the rules or norms of group membership. Such behavior is "voluntary" in the sense that it is not specifically required by group rules or norms and is not directly linked to incentives or sanctions. Thus, this distinction between types of cooperative behavior involves the nature of the behavior involved. Mandated— that is, required—behaviors originate from external sources (group rules), while discretionary behaviors originate with the group members themselves. For example, carrying out the duties prescribed in one's job description can be considered mandated behavior. In contrast, picking up trash from the office floor or fixing paper jams in the photocopy machine is something that people may or may not do (unless they are part of a group of employees for whom these tasks are mandatory).

It is worth taking a moment to explain how it is that the performance of mandated behaviors can be cooperative in nature. What is cooperative about doing what one is required to do? One important issue is the quality of the performance of even required behaviors. As already noted, group members usually have considerable latitude in how they carry out their group-related tasks. This latitude includes some freedom in the energy they put into doing what is required and in the quality with which they carry out those tasks. So, for instance, employees can do their jobs in an adequate manner, carrying out their duties as specified without much emphasis on the quality of their work or the nature of the task.

Alternatively, people can perform the same mandated behaviors with an emphasis on high performance and with a concern that the tasks be completed in the best manner possible. Since people have the option of performing these mandated behaviors in either of these forms, cooperation with the group is a relevant concept to consider when examining mandated behaviors. People are cooperating with the groups they belong to when they perform mandated behaviors and especially when they do them with vigor and zeal rather than with a focus on what is merely sufficient.

The enthusiasm with which people engage in their jobs has been recognized to be important even in situations in which theirs are low-level jobs (Newman 1999). Even jobs that seem largely defined by rules and procedures depend heavily for their success on the motivations of employees. Managers cannot effectively supervise all aspects of job performance, or can only do so by investing large amounts of their time and effort in surveillance and instruction. As a consequence, it is important that employees be motivated to do their jobs. Katherine Newman's study is an excellent example because it focuses on fast food restaurants. Even in that setting, one of highly repetitive jobs and extensive safety regulations, she finds that managers view the willingness to voluntarily help as a highly desirable employee characteristic. This is not only true in work organizations. As has been noted, community cooperation is central to managing community tasks such as social order.

The distinction between two types of cooperative behavior—mandated and discretionary—is important because it is anticipated that mandated behavior is more strongly motivated by instrumental judgments and concerns. Instrumental judgments involve people's assessments of the likelihood that engaging in cooperative behavior will be rewarded and/or that failing to engage in cooperative behavior will be punished. In other words, there is some direct link between cooperation and people's material self-interest. In contrast, discretionary behavior is primarily motivated by people's attitudes and internal values. That is, people's

TABLE 1.1

Forms of Cooperative Behavior

Function	*Required/mandated*	*Voluntary/discretionary*
Rule adherence	Compliance	Deference
Performance	In-role	Extra-role

discretionary behavior is influenced by their sense of what it is desirable and/or right and appropriate to do.

One reason for predicting that mandated behaviors will be instrumentally motivated is that rewards and punishments are most typically linked to the degree to which people engage in the behaviors that are required by their group. For example, the salaries of employees are based upon whether and how well they do their job. The group monitors how well people perform their required tasks because those are the criteria that define the behaviors that the group expects from the individual person. Further, expectations are developed by the group member that doing one's job well will lead to rewards.

In contrast, discretionary behaviors are not specified by the group, and hence are not typically rewarded or punished by the group. The degree to which they are enacted, therefore, is likely to be more strongly dependent upon whether people feel some internal motivation to engage in such discretionary behaviors. These internal motivations develop from attitudes and values, such as feelings about the legitimacy of group authorities or about commitment to the group. These attitudes and values provide people with personal reasons for acting cooperatively, as opposed to extrinsic reasons like the possibility of gaining rewards or the risk of being punished. This is not to say that people's material self-interest is not affected by whether or not they cooperate. It may be. However, people are not deciding whether to cooperate by looking for a direct linkage between their cooperation and their material self-interest.

Taken together, the distinctions outlined lead to the four forms of cooperation outlined in table 1.1. Complying with rules is distinguished from deference by the expectation that people who defer to rules will do so even in the absence of external losses (sanctions). Similarly, extra-role behaviors are enacted without the anticipation of external gains (incentives). People engage in such behaviors even when they do not anticipate that others will know whether or not they have done so.

CHAPTER TWO

Motivational Models

Within social psychological theory two broad perspectives—instrumental and social—explore the connection between the person and the group.

Instrumental Motivations

The first model is the instrumental model, which argues that people engage in interactions to exchange material resources. That is, people's behavior is motivated by the availability of incentives for desired behavior, the threat of sanctions for undesired behavior, or both. There are a variety of such models. One model is a rational choice approach in which people are viewed as motivated by incentives and sanctions. Second, a more complex version of this approach is based upon resources invested in attaining one's position in a group, which is linked to the expectation of long-term gains. Third, an instrumental approach may focus on the dependence that people have on the resources they receive from their job and the consequent difficulty they would have if their resource-based connection to a group were to end. Fourth, instrumental models of justice are concerned with using distributive justice principles to maximize long-term outcomes when dealing with others. Finally, instrumental trust is concerned with expectations about the likely behavior of others—that is, about the future actions of others.

Sanctions/Incentives

People are often thought of as rational actors whose behavior is shaped by sanction-based risks and incentive-based gains. In the case of sanction-based risks, for example, one reason that people do not break rules is that they fear being caught and punished for wrongdoing. This is the instrumentally based deterrence motive that is central to many efforts to manage rule-following in institutions by creating a credible surveillance system that leads to reasonable risks of detection when rules are broken (see, e.g., Tenbrunsel and Messick 1999). Such instrumental approaches are important in work settings (Tyler and Blader 2000), where both sanctions and incentives are used to shape cooperation (Podsakoff et al. 2006).[1] The advantage of an organizational setting such as a work organization is that the authorities can not only threaten to punish wrongdoing but can also reward desired behavior.

Research suggests that incentives and sanctions frequently do shape the level of cooperative behavior that occurs in organizational settings (Nagin 1998; Tyler and Blader 2000; Yamagishi 1986; Yamagishi, Cook, and Watabe 1998). While such studies show that instrumental approaches can motivate cooperation, this literature also demonstrates that instrumental mechanisms are not an especially effective motivational strategy, since their impact is often marginal and they require a large commitment of organizational resources to achieve, at best, a small impact on behavior (MacCoun 1993; Podsakoff et al. 2006; Tyler and Blader 2000). For these and other reasons, the adequacy of instrumental approaches to motivating cooperation has been questioned within law (Tyler 2006a; Tyler and Huo 2002), political science (Green and Shapiro 1994), and management (De Cremer and Van Knippenberg 2002; Pfeffer 1994; Tyler and Blader 2000).

An instrumental model is also articulated in discussions of potential reasons for attitude and behavior change. Herbert Kelman labels instrumentally motivated change "compliance." When people comply with others—that is, when they change the way they express their views to accord with the desires of someone who controls resources that they value—they are shaping their attitudes and actions in response to the desires of others because those others have the ability to control their material self-interest via the provision of incentives or sanctions. As Kelman notes, "Compliance can be said to occur when an individual accepts influence from another person or from a group because he hopes to achieve a favorable reaction from the other." Kelman posits that the person "may be interested in attaining certain specific rewards or in avoiding certain specific punishments that the influencing agent controls" (Kelman 1961, 62).

Investment in Social Groups

One example of instrumental models is the social exchange model, which defines resources in varying ways but has the important common feature of viewing interpersonal cooperation as being rooted in material exchanges (Kelley et al. 2003; Rusbult and Van Lange 1996).[2]

The instrumental model focuses on the favorability of the outcomes obtained in group settings. However, expected gain and loss judgments in group settings are not only made about the immediate situation; rather, people have long-term relationships with groups and they make long-term judgments about the expected costs and benefits of group membership. In the context of ongoing groups, these more long-term judgments of expected rewards/costs guide people's behavior within their group. In making such long-term judgments about what types of behavior will be rewarding, people evaluate the overall quality of the outcomes they are receiving from the group, across situations and across time, as well as judge the degree to which they have already invested resources in the group.

An example of the application of long-term resource-based approaches to the study of behavior in groups is provided by the investment model (Rusbult and Van Lange 1996), which studies the factors shaping people's decisions to leave or remain within groups (their "loyalty" to the group). The investment model predicts that the key factor shaping personal decisions about whether to exit a group is how dependent individuals feel they are on the group for obtaining personally valued resources. Dependence judgments involve considerations of one's immediate and expected long-term reward level and the amount that one has invested in a group.

Studies based upon the investment model suggest that greater dependence on a group or relationship leads to heightened loyalty, with people less willing to leave groups that provide them with high levels of desired resources and/or in which they have already invested resources (Rusbult and van Lange 2003).

Instrumental Motivations for Work

Another instrumental approach focuses upon the degree to which people indicate that their relationship with their jobs is defined in terms of the money that they make. People may simply work because they need money and when at work may cooperate only when cooperation is rewarded. That is, people may be motivated to work because they need the resources they receive as pay and benefits and define the scope of their efforts in terms of what is materially rewarded or punished. And when working they may do those things that they feel are directly rewarded, but they may also not act voluntarily on behalf of their group.

Justice from an Instrumental Perspective

Theories of distributive justice argue that people's desire for justice is motivated by their concern about receiving favorable outcomes over time, a model that is instrumental in nature (Walster, Walster, and Berscheid 1978). To be effective in interacting with others so that they can maximize their outcomes over time, people follow principles of distributive justice, such as equity. Their motivation for following these justice rules is long-term gain for themselves across interactions with others and over time (see Baron 2000).[3]

The potential gain of following rules of distributive fairness is that they guide efforts to effectively exchange resources. If people had to "reinvent the wheel" every time they had an exchange with others by discussing the rules that ought to govern that exchange (equal allocation, allocation by need, allocation by effort and performance, etc.) their social exchanges would be slow, time-consuming, and conflictual, and potentially profitable relationships would never begin or would break down. By having set rules of exchange that are honored by all parties to exchanges, everyone ends up benefiting. Long-term self-interest is thus best met by short-term distributive justice.

Studies suggest that the psychology of distributive justice is complex. While theories of distributive justice have focused upon instrumental motivations for caring about receiving fair outcomes, research suggests that distributive justice has both instrumental and social elements (Tyler 1994b). However, for the purposes of this study, I will err on the side of caution and treat distributive justice as an instrumental motivation.[4]

Instrumental Trust

Finally, instrumental trust is linked to the ability to trust others (i.e., to make oneself vulnerable to others) because of expectations that people will behave as anticipated, based upon their promises, or upon our knowledge of their past behavior. For example, if you deliver something to another person and he gives you a check to pay for it, you expect that the check will be good and will not be rejected by the bank. I will refer to this as instrumental trust because it is linked to the ability that people believe that they have to predict what other people will do in the future—that is, whether or not people will act in ways that they have promised, or at least in ways that a person can anticipate. Trust as predictability is one type of trust. For example, Ronald Burt and Marc Knez define trust as linked to "anticipated cooperation" from others (1996, 70).

Roderick Kramer (1999) labels models that link trust assessments to the perceived ability to estimate others' future actions as "cognitive" approaches to trust because such approaches are linked to estimates about likely future behavior that people can factor into their decisions about how to maximize personal material self-interest. Attention to others' future actions illustrates a key aspect of calculation in social interaction—the element of risk assessment. When people interact with others their outcomes become intertwined with the outcomes of others—they become interdependent. This creates the possibility that another person's failure to act as agreed upon will hurt the interests of a person within a relationship. Each person must make estimates of the likelihood that others will keep their agreements and not act opportunistically (Bradach and Eccles 1989). Those estimates of likely future behavior are cognitive estimates of the "trustworthiness" of others.

The underlying premise is that people want to know that the situation is one that will lead the other person to act in ways that will benefit them. They want to be able to create a situation in which they can act so as to maximize their own outcomes by adjusting their own level of risk taking to fit with their estimates of the likelihood that the other person will reciprocate any cooperative efforts that they make. As a result, people feel that they are best behaving in ways that maximize their self-interest at whatever level they do cooperate with others—that is, they only cooperate as much as is reasonable given their estimate of the other person's likely behavior in response. So trust is linked to a heuristic judgment about "the likelihood that the trustee will undertake expected actions if trusted" (Scholz 1998, 137).

This cognitive model is consistent with the image of trust that emerges from the economics literature on rational choice (for a classic statement of this argument see Williamson 1993; for more recent work, see Kramer 1999). In this literature, trust is based upon the view that people are rational actors who judge the likely actions of others so that they can include those estimates into an overall model of likely costs and gain of possible future actions. From this perspective, "When we say we trust someone or that someone is trustworthy, we implicitly mean that the probability that he [or she] will perform an action that is beneficial or at least not detrimental to us is high enough for us to consider engaging in some form of cooperation" (Williamson 1993, 463). This probability is estimable, so rational calculations about the likely gains and losses associated with behaviors can be made.

Summary

In the previous section, a variety of types of instrumental motivation have been outlined. They are united in their view that people approach their behavior in groups with a desire to maximize their short-term or long-term gains when dealing with others. While it is not necessary to view such gains in material terms, discussions in this literature generally have focused primarily if not exclusively upon the desire to gain material resources and/or to avoid material losses.

Social Motivations

A contrasting type of motivation is social motivation. This volume identifies, measures, and shows the importance of five types of social motivations: attitudes, values, identity, procedural justice, and motive-based trust. In reviewing these social motivations, the general goal is to demonstrate the benefits of considering social motivations when explaining cooperation.

Attitudes: Commitment/Intrinsic Motivation

Attitudes are internal predispositions—part belief, part feeling—that motivate people to engage in actions that are personally fulfilling by approaching those objects, activities, or events toward which they have favorable beliefs and positive feelings and avoiding those about which their orientation is negative (Brief 1998). Attitudes reflect the behaviors that people *want* to engage in, while values reflect those actions that they feel they *ought* to engage in. Both attitudes and values are long-term predispositions that shape behavior in a manner that is distinct from the influence of the benefits and costs associated with immediate environments. The concept of attitudes has a long history within social psychology (McGuire 1969). As would be expected given both that long history and the breadth of the study of attitudes, there are many variations in how attitudes are defined and studied. Here attitudes will be thought of as general predispositions for or against a group or activity—predispositions acquired over time and expressed across situations (Brief 1998).[5]

Three types of attitude are especially relevant to motivation in group settings: satisfaction that is derived from the tasks being completed (intrinsic motivation), satisfaction that flows from the motivation to help a group to which one feels commitment or loyalty, and the affect/emotion associated with being in the group.

Attitudes about the Group, Organization, or Community

Psychologists recognize that people have positive connections to their organizations, reflecting an intrinsic motivation to do tasks that they find enjoyable and interesting. This recognition is linked to literatures on intrinsic motivation (Frey 1997). A key social motivation for cooperation is enjoyment of one's group tasks. When people find such tasks intrinsically fulfilling and enjoyable, working becomes internally rewarded. A large body of research in psychology shows the important role that intrinsic motivation plays in shaping behavior (Deci 1975, 1980). Cooperation may also be motivated by positive attitudes toward the group or organization for which a person is working. Such commitment to the group motivates involvement in group tasks, because people want their group to be successful.

Attitudes toward Tasks

People's views about the desirability of their assigned tasks and their experiences are often described as reflecting their task satisfaction (Brief 1998). Such task satisfaction is more obvious in work settings where people have a specific task to perform. Of course, satisfaction can be divided into many elements, and one key division is satisfaction with the social aspects of one's relationships within and to the organization and satisfaction with the tasks involved in performing one's role. This distinction forms the basis for the distinction between attitudes toward the group and toward tasks within the group that frames the conceptualization of attitudes within this volume.

The distinction between attitudes about one's group and attitudes toward group tasks fits nicely with the important literature on intrinsic motivation. Social psychologists have demonstrated that people develop attitudes of intrinsic motivation through which tasks become internally motivated because they are experienced as enjoyable and interesting. These internal motivations influence behavior even in the absence of incentives (Deci 1975, 1980; Frey 1997). People can enjoy their work, can enjoy involvement in government, and can enjoy working with others to manage social order in their community. Any of these tasks can be valuable in and of itself.

And, as noted, people also develop favorable dispositions toward the group and its members. They are motivated to act for the group because of loyalty to the group, and view group success as personally fulfilling. Such loyalty has also been referred to as cohesion—that is, "the number and strength of mutual positive attitudes among members of the group" (Lott and Lott 1965, 259). Cohesion can be horizontal and refer to ties among group members, or it can be vertical and refer to ties between group members and the leaders of those groups. This analysis focuses on vertical cohesion in the form of attitudes toward the group, organization, or society. In other words, the role of cohesion with coworkers or others in the community is not directly addressed.

Affect/Emotion

Psychologists also recognize that part of the idea of an attitude is a general affective or emotional predisposition toward an object or person. Such an emotional reaction is often linked to evolutionary models, because it is viewed as having adaptive value (Cosmides and Tooby 2000). While it is possible to differentiate among many types of emotions (Barrett et al. 2007; Scherer, Schorr, and Johnstone 2001), this analysis examines two: positive and negative. These dimensions emerge in studies of affect in social settings (Bradburn 1969; Bradburn and Caplovitz 1965).

Emotions are important because they motivate behavior in groups (Katz 1999). For example, emotions are a key issue in decisions about whether to break the law (Katz 1988). Studies of legal actors show that emotions shape law-related behavior (Maroney 2006), including decision making and behavior toward rules and institutions. Similarly, emotions shape whether people take actions such as helping the disadvantaged (Wakslak et al. 2007).

Values

A second literature involves values, and two are considered: legitimacy and morality. Several values are central to efforts to activate ethically motivated behavior. One is the responsibility to defer to legitimate rules and to obey legitimate authorities (legitimacy). Another is the personally felt obligation to follow one's own moral principles (moral value congruence). When organizational rules are congruent with those principles, this motivates cooperation.

Legitimacy

Cooperation might flow from people's feelings of obligation and responsibility to others. One example of an obligation-based judgment is the assessment of the legitimacy of a set of rules or authorities. Legitimacy is defined as "a property that a rule or an authority has when others feel obligated to voluntarily defer to that rule or authority. In other words, a legitimate authority is one that is regarded by people as entitled to have its decisions and rules accepted and followed by others" (National Research Council 2004, 297; see also Fagan 2008).

Modern discussions of legitimacy are usually traced to the writings of Max Weber (1968) on authority and the social dynamics of authority (Swedberg 2006; Zelditch 2001). Weber argued that successful leaders and institutions use more than brute force to execute their will. They strive to gain the consent of the governed so that their commands will be voluntarily accepted (Tyler 2006a). There are rules that people will voluntary obey, and authorities whose directives will be voluntarily followed, and the property that leads to these desirable consequences is legitimacy. Legitimacy, therefore, is a quality possessed by an authority, a law, or an institution that leads others to feel obligated to obey its decisions and directives. This feeling of responsibility reflects a willingness to suspend personal considerations of self-interest because a person thinks that an authority or a rule is entitled to determine appropriate behavior within a given situation or situations.

Herbert Kelman and V. Lee Hamilton refer to legitimacy as "authorization" to reflect the idea that a person authorizes an authority to determine appropriate behavior within some situation, and then feels obligated to follow the directives or rules that authority establishes. As they indicate, the authorization of the actions taken by authorities "seem[s] to carry automatic justification for them. Behaviorally, authorization obviates the necessity of making judgments or choices. Not only do normal moral principles become inoperative, but—particularly when the actions are explicitly ordered—a different type of morality, linked to the duty to obey superior orders, tends to take over" (Kelman and Hamilton 1989, 16).

One way to think about legitimacy is as a property of an institution. Studies of the legitimacy of legal authorities typically ask people to evaluate their general feelings of responsibility and obligation to obey the law and legal authorities (see Tyler 2006a). This focus on the importance of legitimacy reflects concern with the circumstances under which people follow the directives of social rules and social authorities. Legitimacy is important to the success of such authorities because they are enabled to gain public deference to a range of decisions by virtue of their social role (Tyler 2006a, 2006b).

Legitimacy can also be the property of a person. In early policing, for example, beat officers patrolled a particular area, an area in which they often lived. The officers developed personal relationships with the public—that is, people knew them. So they had legitimacy as individuals, and they built or undermined that legitimacy by the manner in which they exercised their authority. In modern police forces, which are rooted in police cars, the officers who step out of a car to respond to a particular situation are generally someone that the people involved do not know. These officers have institutional legitimacy, marked by a uniform, a cap, a badge. Their authority comes from the authority of the office, not from anything about them as particular people.

Legitimacy has been shown to be a predictor of rule-following behavior both in communities (Tyler 2006a; Tyler and Huo 2002) and in work organizations (Tyler 2005; Tyler and Blader 2005; Tyler, Callahan, and Frost 2007). Obligation is often studied in the context of rule-following, but people can also be motivated by their feelings of obligation to perform well on their assigned tasks, as well as to be loyal to their group.

Consider two specific examples of the influence of legitimacy. Building on the previous work of Tom Tyler (2006a), Jason Sunshine and Tom Tyler (2003) examined the antecedents of compliance and cooperation with the police among people living in New York City. The results of this analysis show that police legitimacy influences people's compliance with law and their willingness to cooperate with and assist the police. These findings also support the argument that legitimacy is a social value that is distinct from performance evaluations. They show that such values have both an important and a distinct influence on people's support for the police. This finding supports the arguments of Weber (1968) about the normative basis of public reactions to authority. It extends prior research findings (Tyler 2006a) by showing that cooperation, in addition to compliance, is influenced by legitimacy. People who view the police and the law as legitimate both comply with the law and cooperate with the police to fight crime (also see Tyler and Fagan 2008).

Tyler and Steven Blader (2005) examined the influence of legitimacy in two studies of employees focusing on people's values in relationship to the institutions for which they work. The findings support the argument that employees' ethical values—that is, their views about legitimacy—shape their rule-following behavior in work settings. The study suggests that companies benefit by fostering the ethical values in their employees that support rule-following. Those ethical values are a major motivation leading to employee compliance with company policies and rules. They also lead to lower levels of rule-breaking behavior on the part of employees. These results suggest that one promising way to bring the behavior of group members into line with codes of conduct is to activate their values. The study provides empirical support for this argument in a general sample of employees, as well as in a study of corporate bankers.

In another study, Tyler, Patrick Callahan, and Jeffrey Frost (2007) conducted a similar analysis with social control agents (the police, the army) and found similar results. When agents of social control view the rules of their organization as legitimate, they are more deferential to organizational rules. This volume provides a further link to organizational policies and practices, suggesting that when the procedures of an organization are fair, those within it view the rules and policies of the organization as legitimate.

Yet another study (Tyler, Sherman, et al. 2007) demonstrated a direct link between judgments of the legitimacy of the law and police-recorded rule-following by examining people who had been arrested for drinking and driving. These people were followed four years after their case was disposed. It was found that legitimacy ratings shaped subsequent adherence to the law, as reflected in both police records and self-reported behavior.

Moral Values

Of course, legitimacy is not the only social value upon which cooperation might potentially be based. A second form of obligation is the person's feeling of obligation to her own moral values—a desire to do what she feels is right. A large psychological literature argues that the motivation to act in accord with her values about what is morally right and wrong is an important human motivation.

Values reflect people's assessments of what is right or appropriate to do in a given situation. Another approach to social motivation is to activate the ethical motivations that lead people to adhere to group rules and to act on behalf of the group (Tyler 1990; Tyler and Huo 2002). Here the goal is to shape not what people want to do, but what they think is appropriate do to. Hence, people will not engage in behaviors that might be personally rewarding because they think it would be wrong to engage in those actions.

Paul Robinson and John Darley (1995) argue for the importance of congruence between moral values and rules in the context of law. A core element of moral values is that people feel a personal responsibility to follow those values, and feel guilty when they fail to do so. Hence, moral values, once they exist, are self-regulatory in character, and those who have such values are personally motivated to bring their conduct into line with their moral standards. Internalized moral values are self-regulating and people accept and act on the basis of values that produce respect for societal institutions, authorities, and rules. Robinson and Darley suggest that people are more likely to obey laws if they view those laws as consistent with their own moral values.

The Tyler and Blader study (2005) extends this argument to management settings and demonstrates that employees are also motivated by the assessment that their work organization acts in ways consistent with their moral values. Similarly, Tyler, Callahan, and Frost (2007) show that it applies to agents of social control (i.e., police officers and members of the armed forces).

The significance of morality is illustrated by research on punishment. Studies demonstrate that people's views about appropriate sentencing decisions in criminal cases are driven by moral judgments about deservingness rather than by instrumental judgments concerning how to deter future criminal conduct (Carlsmith, Darley, and Robinson 2002; Darley, Carlsmith, and Robinson 2000). People accept that a punishment is appropriate when it accords with their moral sense of what is appropriate given the level and type of wrong committed. More generally, research shows that people are more willing to comply with the law to the extent that they view it as consistent with their moral values (see, e.g., Robinson and Darley 1995; Tyler 2006a). As a consequence, an important question for the law is the degree to which it is congruent with the publics' moral values. If people correctly understand the law, and if the law truly reflects moral standards of the community, then the internalized sense of morality acts as a force for law-abidingness.

The distinction between legitimacy and morality is that, in the case of morality, legal authorities gain support for particular laws or decisions when those laws or decisions are in accord with people's personal morality. Hence, the motivation to behave in ways that are moral does not lead to support of the rule of law when the public thinks that the law is inconsistent with their morality—when moral values and legal rules are incongruent. To activate the motivation force of morality, legal authorities must pursue policies that are consistent with people's moral values (Sunshine and Tyler 2003).

Robinson and Darley (1995), for example, show gaps between law and public morality. To the extent that such gaps are widely known, they would undermine public compliance with the law. The law can enlist people's moral values as a motivational force supporting deference to the law by pursuing ends that people view as moral. They argue that the law is less likely to be able to call upon people's moral motivations to support the legal system when its values are viewed as divergent from those of the public. Hence, the law can engage moral values when and if the law is consistent with the moral values held by the public.

Of course, morality and legitimacy can be in conflict. A conflict between legitimacy and morality can occur with mundane and everyday practices, as when the government seems to criminalize drug use or certain sexual practices without the support of public morality (Darley, Tyler, and Bilz 2003), or it can involve dramatic and high-stakes conflicts, as when the government seeks to compel people to serve in wars they think are unjust, or to pay taxes to support policies they view as immoral. Unlike legitimacy, morality is not linked to the role of the authority and its independent roots in personal ethical values mean that while morality usually supports following laws (Tyler 2006a), the two internal forces do not always support one another.

Identity

Another arena within which instrumental and social motivations can be contrasted is the general relationship between people and organizations. Social psychology has long asked the question, What links people to groups, organizations, and communities? This question can be answered by reference to people's desire to create and maintain a favorable identity and a positive sense of self. Theories linked to identity argue that organizations serve the social function of providing people with an identity, which they draw at least in part from the organizations to which they belong. That argument can be made utilizing group-based social identity or emotional identification.

Social Identity

The argument that groups serve a role in defining and evaluating one's identity, and thereby in shaping a sense of self, is a key suggestion of models of social identification (Ellemers, De Gilder, and Haslam 2004; Haslam 2004; Hogg and Abrams 1988; Whetten and Godfrey 1998).

Drawing upon the work of social identity theorists (Ellemers, Spears, and Doosje 2002; Hogg and Abrams 1988; Hogg et al. 2004; Tajfel and Turner 1979), identity in group-based terms will be conceptualized through the use of organizational membership to shape identity and to define status and self. It is argued that one source of information about status is information about the organizations to which one belongs. People use this information to shape the degree to which they merge their identities and sense of self with the organization, making an identity-based investment in the group. It is argued that when people make such an identity-based investment their sense of self becomes linked to the future of the group and they become motivated to work on behalf of the group as a way of bolstering their own identity. There is a large literature on social identity within social psychology (Hogg and Abrams 1988) and a number of discussions of the influence of identity on conflict and cooperation within and between groups.

Social identity theory was originally developed to examine intergroup relations. Tyler and others extend this theoretical perspective and use it to explore the relationship between people and the groups to which they belong (Ellemers, Spears, and Doosje 2002; Tyler and Blader 2000; Tyler and Smith 1999). In this context types of identity-relevant judgments are distinguished: identification and status judgments. Identification is the most direct extension of social identity theory and involves the merger of one's sense of self with the group. To the degree that people think of themselves in terms of group membership, they are drawing their identity from the group. Status judgments determine the valence of the group, with people identifying more strongly when identification enhances their sense of self and feelings of self-esteem and self-worth.

What is identity (Tyler and Smith 1999)? The group engagement model distinguishes among three aspects of identity: identification, pride, and respect (Tyler and Blader 2000, 2001, 2002, 2009). One approach to identity is to define it as identification, or as the degree to which people merge their sense of self with the group (thinking of themselves and the group in similar terms) and defining themselves in terms of their group membership (identification with the group). The group engagement model hypothesizes that when people identify more strongly with a group they will be more willing to act cooperatively in that group—investing their time and energy in working to see the group succeed.

Status assessments reflect two different concepts—pride and respect. Pride reflects judgments about the status of the group, also indexed by measures of group prestige (Mael and Asforth 1992). It expresses people's views about the status of their group. People who belong to groups that they feel have high status feel good about themselves by virtue of their association with the group. These feelings stem primarily from noncomparative judgments of inclusion or exclusion in a high-status group rather than from comparisons of one's group to other groups (Tyler and Blader 2002).

Respect reflects judgments about one's status within the group. It expresses people's views about their status in the eyes of other group members. Respect is also referred to as social reputation (Emler and Hopkins 1990; Emler and Reicher 1995). While social identity theory was originally focused on the status of groups (i.e., on intergroup phenomena), it is also recognized that people are influenced by their judgments of their status within groups (Tyler and Smith 1999).

From the perspective of encouraging cooperation, we would like to have people merging their identities into the institutions to which they belong when we want them to act in terms of the interests of the group, and not in terms of their own self-interest (see De Cremer and Tyler 2005b; Tyler and Blader 2000). In fact, when a person draws her sense of self from a group, the idea of self-interest disappears. Acting in the interests of the group is acting in one's self-interest in an identity sense because one's identity is supported by the group. This argument is similar to the distinction between proself and prosocial motivation, in that prosocial motivation takes account of the needs of others, as well as one's own needs (Van Lange et al. 2007). From an identity perspective, people do so when they have merged their identity with others, so that self-interest and the interests of others are intertwined.

The social identity literature makes the further point that when people identify with a group it changes how they think about cooperation. In fact, recent research shows that cooperation in public good dilemmas is reinforced when people exhibit strong identification with the group, because their motives are transformed from the personal to the group level. As a consequence people think of the interests of the group as being their own interests (De Cremer and Tyler 2005b) and become intrinsically motivated to pursue the group's interest.

It is possible to directly test the influence of group identification on cooperation by looking at whether identification encourages loyalty to the group and leads to cooperation. Dominic Abrams, Kaori Ando, and Steve Hinkle (1998) demonstrate that employees who identify with their work institution are less likely to quit, while Tyler and Blader (2000) show that identification predicts both job performance and rule-following in work groups. These findings demonstrate that, in field settings, social motivations play an important role in shaping cooperative behavior. The findings also suggest that particular social motivations shape voluntary forms of cooperation—that is, extra-role behavior.[6]

Emotional Identification

A second identity-based literature is the literature on emotional identification. Since the pioneering work of Kelman on persuasion and attitude change (Kelman 1958, 1961), it has been recognized that people's motivations for altering their views in response to attitude change efforts can differ. One reason for being influenced by others is that emotional ties to others provide an important input into identity. To maintain those ties, people alter their attitudes, values, and behaviors. In Kelman's more recent statement of this model (2006), attachment is linked to meeting role expectations for self-maintenance reasons. Those reasons are linked to "self-defining" relationships, which the person is motivated to maintain by appropriately enacting social roles. In their work on authority Kelman and Hamilton elaborate on the idea of identification by arguing that "accepting influence from another through identification, then, is a way of establishing or maintaining the desired relationship to that other and the self-definition that is anchored in this relationship" (1989, 104).

The importance of emotional connections to others has been more generally recognized within the social psychological literature. In a classic paper, Roy Baumeister and Mark Leary argue that the need to belong—that is, to have attachments to others—is a fundamental human motivation. They posit that people have a "drive to form and maintain at least a minimum quantity of lasting, positive, and significant interpersonal relationships" (1995, 497).

This type of identity involves the development of bonds with others in the group, and with organizational values and traditions. It is linked to the degree to which people make an emotional investment in the group. When people become emotionally invested in the group, their emotional well-being becomes intertwined with its fate and they become socially motivated to act on behalf of the group . If the group falters, the emotional ties that are linked to employees' social needs can no longer be met.

While Kelman (1961) uses the idea of identification to understand attitude change, the roots of this idea can be found in the literature on childhood socialization. Developmental psychologists, interested in understanding why children take on their parent's values, argue that one reason for doing so is as a result of the emotional bond that exists between parents and children. Because children feel an emotional connection with their parents, it is argued, they are motivated to adopt the ideas of their parents as their own (see Hoffman 1977).

Charles O'Reilly and Jennifer Chatman (1986) draw upon Kelman's work to understand people's emotional identifications within work organizations. They argue that one dimension of commitment is linked to identification or affiliation—the desire to maintain satisfying relationships with others. Consistent with the argument made here, their work shows that identification is linked to prosocial behavior in work settings, and that that influence is distinct from the influence of compliance-based motivations.

Economists have also recognized the potential importance of identity (Akerlof and Kranton 2000, 2002). The key is the person's sense of self. In the case of education, for example, it can be argued that the primary factor motivating students is their identity, with students learning in order to enhance their self-image. The most extensive discussion of identity is found in George Akerlof's American Economics Association presidential address (2006), in which he talks about "missing motivation" in economic theory. In particular, Akerlof notes the importance of people's views about how they should behave—that is, views of appropriate norms of conduct. One of many examples he cites is the work of Truman Bewley (1999), which shows how wage changes do not track market conditions because of social norms about what is appropriate; managers could lower wages during periods when leaving and finding another job would be difficult for employees, but they feel it is inappropriate to do so. This perspective is consistent with the social identification argument that people are motivated by the desire to create and maintain a favorable view of themselves.

Procedural Justice

An additional social motivation can be drawn from the literature on justice (Tyler 2000b). There are two key forms of justice: distributive and procedural. *Distributive justice* refers to the fairness of outcomes, while *procedural justice* reflects the justice of the procedures through which outcomes are distributed and decisions made.[7] The justice literature suggests that people's procedural justice judgments are social in nature and are linked to their connections to others (Tyler 1994b, 2000b; Tyler, Degoey, and Smith 1996). Hence, the influence of procedural justice upon cooperation is an instance of the impact of social motivation.

The original goal of social justice research was to demonstrate the power of justice judgments to shape people's thoughts, feelings, and actions (Tyler 2000b; Tyler et al. 1997; Tyler and Smith 1998). Justice studies have, in fact, continually provided strong and consistent demonstrations of support for this basic justice hypothesis. Justice has an impact; it is substantial in magnitude; it is consistently found across a wide variety of group and organizational contexts; and it is distinct from judgments of self-interest or personal/group gain. This conclusion suggests that information about justice is central to people's evaluations of social situations (Tyler et al. 1997). There is, in other words, a great deal of evidence that people are motivated by their justice judgments.

Motive-based Trust

Finally, the literature on trust suggests that people are more willing to cooperate with others whom they view as being "trustworthy" because they infer that motivations for their actions are benevolent and show concern with the well-being of others (Kramer 1999; Kramer and Tyler 1996; Tyler and Huo 2002). One type of trust, that which is motive based, is linked to inferences about the character of the other. This form of trust is linked to relationships to others and is a social motive.[8]

Research in real-world organizations indicates that people are more willing to cooperate with those whom they trust (Kramer 1999; Kramer and Tyler 1996). Political scientists link trust in others to civic engagement (Putnam 1993); organizational researchers suggest that trust facilitates cooperation in work organizations (Hosmer 1995; Tyler and Degoey 1996); lawyers view trust as an antecedent of successful dispute resolution (Gilson and Mnookin 1994; Mitchell 1995); and experimental studies of cooperation indicate that people are more willing to cooperate when they trust others to also cooperate (Brann and Foddy 1987; De Cremer, Snyder, and Dewitte 2001; Yamagishi, Cook, and Watabe 1998).

Typical of the arguments made is Peter Blau's note that trust is "essential for stable social relationships" (1964, 99), the suggestion of Robert Golembiewski and Mark McConkie that "[t]here is no single variable which so thoroughly influences interpersonal and group behavior as does trust" (1975, 131), and the argument of J. Davis Lewis and Andrew Weigert (1985) that trust is "indispensable in social relationships" (1985, 968).[9]

Because of the emphasis in the management literature on creating conditions that facilitate productive interactions, trust has been a central concern within studies of work organizations (Kramer and Tyler 1996). In recent years the justice literature has evolved in its focus to a concern about the organizational conditions that promote cooperation, leading to increasing parallels between the literatures on justice and trust.

As is true in the prior discussion of the psychology of justice, a key issue that follows from the recognition that trust is important is the nature of the motivation underlying the influence of trust. Trust is important to the success of groups and organizations, but the trust that matters could potentially be either instrumental or social in nature.

Motive-based trust is not based on risk calculation. Instead, it involves social inferences beyond whether someone else will keep specific promises or commitments. Motive-based trust involves inferences about intentions behind actions, intentions that flow from a person's unobservable traits and character. It is a judgment about the character of another person. In this sense, motive-based trust involves the expectation of actions based upon ethical principles. If, for example, we view someone as honest, we expect her to act in ways that are consistent with that character trait. She is not expected to lie, even when lying is in her personal self-interest.

Motive-based trust is an estimate of the likely character and motives of others. It is based upon the assumption that knowing another's character and motives tells us whether she will act reasonably toward us in the future. Hence, our expectation is not that the person will engage in particular actions that she has agreed to perform. Instead, we expect that she will act based upon her character.

In the case of authorities, people tend to view those who occupy particular roles, such as judge or doctor, as trustworthy. These authorities act as agents of society, fulfilling a particular social role. Part of that role is a set of responsibilities and obligations mandating that the authorities act in the interests of those whom they represent. These responsibilities are created and reinforced through training into a specialized role, and via various accounting mechanisms (Meyerson, Weick, and Kramer 1996). One aspect of trust involves issues of technical competence. The other—the focus here—involves the expectation of moral responsibility—that authorities will act in the best interests of others.

The concept of a fiduciary relationship is central in all situations in which an authority has power over the lives or property of others. Key to such relationships is the expectation that the authority involved will act in the interests of those for whom she exercises authority. That person is trusted. Trust, in these cases, refers to a judgment about the intentions or motives of the fiduciary agent—that is, a reliance on the "goodwill" of that person (Baier 1986).

This focus on the intentions or motives of the authorities can be clearly distinguished from a focus on the "truth" or "correctness" of their decisions. Well-intentioned authorities can act in good faith and make mistakes. But such a failure to make a correct prediction or decision does not destroy motive-based trust, if we believe that authorities have good intentions. Philosophers similarly recognize the distinction between intention and result (Bok 1978), with intention viewed as reflecting a person's motivations. The law makes this distinction as well. The "business judgment rule" used by the courts to evaluate corporate authorities recognizes that "decisions made by a board in good faith, with due care, and with regard to the best interests of the corporation" should not be evaluated by courts based upon whether they lead to good or bad results (Mitchell 1995).

People also make the distinction between intention and result. For example, as Tom Tyler and Peter Degoey (1996) have found, "Some people interviewed indicated that police officers and judges are acting in a nonneutral, biased way, yet nonetheless evaluated those authorities to be fair. People seemed willing to forgive surface features of racism and sexism, for example, if they felt that the authorities involved are basically motivated to act in a benevolent manner. It was the trustworthiness of the intentions of the authorities that shaped reactions to the procedures they employed, not surface features of those procedures (e.g., neutrality)" (334).[10]

Summary

Five types of social motivation have been distinguished. These can be viewed as reflecting two clusters. The first cluster involves general dispositions—that is, broad orientations toward a group, organization, or community. Dispositions include attitudes, values, and identity. Second are group-based policies and practices. Such policies and practices include the procedural justice of group decision making and inferences about the trustworthiness of the motives and intentions of others.

What Leads a Motivation to Be a Social Motivation?

This volume will characterize the additional motivations described—attitudes, values, identity, procedural justice, and motive-based trust—as social motivations to distinguish them from instrumental motivations. As has been noted, instrumental motivations reflect people's desire to gain material resources and to avoid material losses. Social motivations, as discussed by psychologists, differ in that they flow from within the person.

There are four ways to distinguish between instrumental and social motivations. The first is by the content of the concerns that people express within each domain. Instrumental concerns focus on the potential for material gains and/or the possibility of material losses—gains as rewards, or losses as costs or punishments. In contrast, social motivations are linked to gains and losses of a nonmaterial nature. These are linked to issues such as personal identity and consistency with ethical/moral values.

Second, indicators of social motivations should be found to be empirically distinct from indicators of material gain or loss. For example, in the literature on social justice, it is found that people distinguish between receiving a favorable outcome and receiving fair treatment (Tyler et al. 1997). Hence, judgments about justice are found to be distinct from the favorability of one's outcomes. This distinction is clear in the literature on distributive justice, a literature in which the fairness of outcomes is distinguished from their desirability (Walster, Walster, and Berscheid 1978). It is even clearer in the literature on procedural justice, which focuses on the fairness of the procedures by which allocation decisions are made (Lind and Tyler 1988). If people simply viewed a favorable outcome as fair, for example, social motivations would not be distinct from material judgments. However, this is not the case.

Third, social motivations should have a distinct influence on cooperative behavior. Again, the justice literature finds that the degree to which people are willing to accept an outcome from an authority is linked, first, to the favorability of that outcome. In addition, however, people are more willing to accept an outcome that they evaluate as being fair and fairly arrived at. Hence, their fairness judgments exercise an independent influence upon their acceptance behavior that cannot be explained by outcome favorability.

Fourth, social motivations should produce a consistency of behavior across situations and over time. If, for example, someone feels an obligation to obey rules, her behavior should consistently reflect higher levels of cooperation across settings that vary in her reward and cost characteristics. Further, she should show the same behavior in the same situation across time. This does not mean that situational forces will not influence behavior, but it will be possible to see constancies in behavior that are linked to social motivations. Further, those constancies will not be linked to variations in instrumental factors.

The best way to understand the value of this larger motivational framework is to consider it within the context of a particular type of socially important behavior. In this discussion I will focus on cooperative behavior. Cooperation is valuable for groups, and securing cooperation has been the focus of social science research across a variety of fields, including both economics and psychology.

Some Qualifications

First, while this analysis distinguishes between motivations linked to material self-interest and other, more social, motivations, it is important to note that the thesis being argued is not that either social psychologists or economists have been unaware of the potential importance of social motivations. There are instances within each group of individuals who have acknowledged the importance of social motivations, and some have studied them. This work will be noted throughout the manuscript. This analysis is based upon the observation that the dominant way of talking about instrumental motivation has been to focus on material gains and losses.

Second, it is impossible to completely separate instrumental and social motivations. While this volume will develop this distinction across various literatures it will be constantly observed that indices of instrumental and social motivation within a given field of study are correlated. This indicates that these two aspects of motivation are connected within the minds of the respondents. On the other hand, it is equally clear from the information respondents provide that these two aspects of motivation are distinct. If they were not distinct, then regression analyses would not find independent influences of each when both are included within the same equation.

Beyond empirical demonstrations of their distinction, this volume will argue that instrumental and social motivations are theoretically distinct. This is the case because social motivations arise out of the desire to maintain conditions that lead to long-term social benefits. It is not argued that people are indifferent to the material benefits of social relationships; rather, it is being suggested that even in the short term people are not focused on material benefits—they are focused on social connections.

This conceptual argument is consistent with the psychological argument that motivations become functionally autonomous. That is, whatever the reason that people are initially motivated to engage in social relationships, those relationships become autonomous—become an end in themselves and are motivating for their own sake. People develop concerns about their identities that become

important in and of themselves. So, for example, theories of socialization sometimes argue that children take on their parent's values to preserve ties that have
a material basis. The motivation to uphold those values, however, then becomes
incorporated into the self and becomes distinct. Even when children no longer
need material resources from their parents, they continue to be motivated to behave in ways that are consistent with their values. So the motivations for cooperation become linked to social connections, not material resources (Argyle 1991).

Social Motivations and Cooperative Behavior

This analysis focuses on approaches based upon appeals to social motivations. If
people have social motivations that lead them to cooperate with authorities and
to act in ways that help the group, then authorities need not seek to compel such
behavior through promises of reward or threats of punishment. They can instead
rely upon people's willingness to engage in the behavior. Social motivations offer
the possibility of moving beyond the use of incentives and sanctions when seeking to motivate cooperative behavior.

The Plan for the Next Section

The next three chapters of this volume will review evidence from three distinct
arenas of social life. Chapter 3 examines cooperation among employees in work
settings. Chapter 4 considers cooperation with authorities involved in regulating behavior in community settings. Chapter 5 is concerned with participation
in the political process by working with political leaders and voting. Each of
these chapters contrasts the influence of instrumental and social motivations on
cooperative behavior with the goal of demonstrating the breadth and importance
of social motivations.

Empirical Findings

CHAPTER THREE

Cooperation with Managerial Authorities in Work Settings

This volume is based upon surveys conducted in three settings. The first is a panel study of a sample of American employees. Each employee completed a web-based questionnaire about their attitudes, values, and behaviors in the workplace.[1] The employees were drawn from a panel study of a representative sample of American employees. In the first wave of the study 4,430 employees completed a questionnaire concerning their workplace attitudes, values, and behaviors. In the second wave of the study 2,680 of these employees were reinterviewed about the same topics one year later.[2]

In addition, for some employees interviews were also conducted with their supervisors. These interviews asked supervisors to rate the behavior of their employees along similar dimensions to those already used by the employees to rate their own behavior. In the first wave 831 supervisors were interviewed. These interviews were used to provide an independent perspective on the behavior of employees.

This analysis focuses on one type of organizational setting—work organizations. Within that setting the analysis explores the motivations that lead employees in work settings to cooperate with their work organizations. Work was chosen as the focus of this study because work settings are typically viewed as settings in which people are motivated by incentives and sanctions.

The analysis does not consider any one single work organization. Instead, in this study a random sample of American employees are each asked questions about their own particular work organizations. These organizations vary widely, ranging from one-person businesses to multinational corporations.

The Study Design

The study draws respondents from a national panel of participants who complete questionnaires via the Internet in exchange for reimbursement. This panel is maintained by Knowledge Networks of Menlo Park, California. Each participant receives remuneration for participating in research projects chosen from a variety of potential projects. For this study a sample of participants in the ongoing panel were offered the opportunity to participate in a study, to be completed in two parts, that asked them questions about their work experiences.[3]

Approximately one year after they completed the first set of questionnaires, each of the respondents still within the national panel and still working at the same company was given the opportunity to complete the same questionnaire again. As before, the questionnaire was completed over two weeks. Of those originally involved, 2,366 employees completed answering the second-wave questions.

The demographics of the first wave employee sample indicated that the questionnaire respondents came from a variety of organizations. Twenty-four percent worked for small businesses, 20 percent for large companies in one location, 36 percent for large multicity American companies, and 20 percent in multinational companies. Of those in the sample, 59 percent were men, 84 percent were white, 32 percent had a college degree or postgraduate education, and 50 percent had a household income of over $50,000. The mean age was forty-three years.[4]

Cooperation in Work Settings

Following the theoretical framework outlined, four forms of cooperation were distinguished: in-role behavior (doing one's specified job),[5] extra-role behavior (engaging in behavior to help the group beyond what is required),[6] compliance behavior (adhering to rules),[7] and following rules voluntarily.[8] All of the forms of cooperation considered in this study were assessed using scales ranging from 1 to 7, with higher scores indicating higher levels of cooperation.

On average on a scale ranging from 1 to 7, with 7 reflecting high levels of cooperation, the score for required cooperation was 6.19, while the average for voluntary cooperation was 4.78. This distinction was greater with performance. The mean for in-role performance was 6.46, and for extra-role behavior 5.46. In the case of rule-following, the mean for required compliance was 5.91 and for voluntary deference 5.46. In general, these means showed that respondents indicated that they engaged in generally high levels of cooperation. As would be expected, voluntary forms of cooperation were less common than were required forms.

An examination of these forms of cooperation within the sample of employees considered here indicated that the four forms of cooperation were loosely connected. In other words, people were generally found to be cooperative, with those who engaged in one form of cooperation also engaging in others. The mean correlation between the four forms of cooperation was $r = 0.40$, $p < .001$. At the same time, the correlation among these forms of cooperation was relatively low, suggesting that there could well be distinct antecedents of each form of cooperation.

Summary

The primary focus of this volume is on employees' cooperation with their work organizations. Four forms of cooperation were identified, and scales reflecting each constructed. An empirical analysis suggests that these forms of cooperation are distinct, but correlated. A similar distinction among forms of cooperation is also made in interviews with the supervisors of a subset of workers. Again, scales reflecting these forms of cooperative behavior are created and found to be distinct, but related.

Instrumental Motivations

Five types of instructional motivations were considered:

Environmental contingencies. In this analysis instrumental motivation was assessed in two ways. First, respondents were asked about the strength of the connection between good/bad workplace behavior and incentives/ sanctions—that is, the likelihood that good performance would be rewarded and rule-breaking punished.[9] Second, they were asked about the magnitude of the incentives/sanctions linked to good/bad behavior.[10] Finally, the interaction between these two judgments was measured.[11]

Investment. The long-term possibilities for gain through the company,[12] and the favorability of company policies,[13] were measured.

Dependence. People were asked whether their orientation toward work was instrumental—that is, if they worked only for money[14]—and whether they needed their job for financial reasons.[15]

Distributive fairness. Distributive fairness was assessed at two levels: organizational and personal.[16]

Instrumental trust. Calculative trust—which is an estimate by the respondent of the likelihood that others will be trustworthy if they are trusted—was measured.[17]

Social Motivations

Five types of social motivations were considered:

Attitudes. Three aspects of attitudes were considered: attitudes toward the company,[18] attitudes toward one's job,[19] and work-related emotion/affect.[20]

Values. Feelings of obligation are measured in four ways: the legitimacy of workplace rules,[21] the degree to which the respondent felt obligated to de-

liver high-performance work,[22] the degree to which the respondent felt obligated to stay at his current work organization,[23] and the congruence of
company policies with the employee's moral values.[24]

Identity indicators. This analysis drew upon the conceptualization of Tom
Tyler (Tyler and Blader 2000; Tyler and Smith 1999) and operationalized
identity in terms of respect,[25] pride,[26] and identification.[27] In the case of
pride, the measurement looks at pride linked to the status of the group
(Tyler and Blader 2000).[28] In addition, emotional identification (as conceptualized in Kelman 1958, 1961) was measured.[29]

Procedural justice. Procedural justice was measured in four ways: the general
procedural justice of the organization,[30] the personal procedural justice experienced at the organization,[31] supervisor procedural justice of decision
making/interpersonal treatment,[32] and organizational level procedural justice of decision making/interpersonal treatment.[33]

Motive-based trust and cooperation. In this analysis three indices were used.
measuring motive-based trust,[34] trust in management,[35] and trust in one's
supervisor.[36]

Analysis

Consistent with the argument that instrumental and social motivations are distinct but not independent, the overall average correlation between instrumental and social motivations was $r = 0.40$, $p < .001$. Hence, the respondents in
this study who were instrumentally motivated were also socially motivated, and
vice versa.[37]

Factors Shaping Cooperation

Because instrumental and social motivations were linked together, it was important to consider the simultaneous independent contribution of each type of motivation to cooperation. In other words, we needed to use a procedure that would
remove whatever joint variance there was and identify the unique contribution
that instrumental and social motivations make to cooperation. The standardized
regression coefficients ("beta weights") in the regression analysis shown here
reflect the unique influence of the various factors in the equation once their
common variance has been removed. And the relative size of the beta weights
represents the relative distinct contribution of each type of motivation to explaining cooperation.

One approach to performing a regression analysis is to use structural equation modeling, a form of regression analysis that allows the indices of the five

TABLE 3.1

The Influence of Instrumental and Social Motivation on Cooperation

	First wave	*Second wave*
Overall cooperation		
First-wave factors		
Instrumental	0.04***	0.03
Social	0.62***	0.11***
Cooperation	—	0.59***
Adjusted R-squared	38%	43%
Required cooperation		
First-wave factors		
Instrumental	0.11***	0.00
Social	0.53***	0.13***
Cooperation	—	0.65***
Adjusted R-squared	29%	45%
Voluntary cooperation		
First-wave factors		
Instrumental	0.16***	−0.01
Social	0.75***	0.23***
Cooperation	—	0.69***
Adjusted R-squared	59%	53%
n	4,430	2,680

Note: ***$p < .001$.

instrumental and the five social clusters to load upon latent instrumental and social factors.[38] Those underlying or latent factors can then be used to predict cooperation. In the analyses shown here cooperation—the dependent variable— is also treated as an underlying or latent factor, reflecting the four indices of cooperation.[39] This analysis is first conducted on the first-wave respondents and then on the second-wave respondents. This consideration of the second-wave respondents is a panel analysis because all of those respondents also completed first-wave interviews. In this second analysis, respondent cooperation in the first wave is controlled upon when explaining cooperation in the second wave. This means that the analysis examines the factors that shape changes in level of co-operation from the first to the second wave of interviews. The results of these analyses are shown in table 3.1.

In the first-wave analysis the estimated influence of social motivations is beta = 0.62, $p < .001$ and for instrumental factors beta = 0.04, $p < .001$. Overall, 38 percent of the variance in cooperation is explained by both factors considered together. These findings suggest that, while both social and instrumental motivations significantly influence cooperation, we can more effectively account for cooperation by considering social motivations than by a focus on instrumental motivations.[40]

That view is reinforced by the panel analysis also shown in table 3.1, in this case in the second column.[41] When the dependent variable is a second-wave measure of cooperation and the analysis contains controls for first-wave cooperation, the results demonstrate that the best predictor of cooperation at the second wave is cooperation at at the first (beta = 0.59, $p < .001$). However, when first-wave instrumental and social motivation indices are included in the equation, it is social motivation that is the better predictor of second-wave cooperation (beta = 0.11, $p < .001$). No significant influence of instrumental motivations on second-wave cooperation is found (beta = 0.03, n.s.).

The equations presented in table 3.1 summarize a great deal of information. They present an overall finding about the relative impact of instrumental and social motivations on cooperation, which includes all forms of each motivation and all four types of cooperation. Hence, these figures provide an overall snapshot of the factors shaping cooperation and, in so doing, the findings suggest the importance of social motivations in shaping cooperative behavior in work settings. They also emphasize that social motivations are especially important with voluntary cooperation.

Usefulness Analysis

The regression analysis results strongly support the argument that social motivations shape cooperation. Another approach to conducting this analysis is to include all the indices from each motivational cluster within a regression equation at the same time, using structural equation modeling of the type already outlined, and to consider the degree of variance explained. This also allows the statistical program to weight each index in the manner that maximizes explanation of the dependent variables—that is, there can be unequal weighting between clusters.

Two numbers are of potential interest in such a regression analysis: the total adjusted square of the variance, which reflects the total proportion of the variance in a dependent variable explained by all the variables in an equation, and the unique contribution of each cluster. The unique contribution of a cluster reflects the degree of variance that the variables within one cluster explain beyond the variance explained by a prior cluster. In other words, all of the joint variance, which can be explained by variables in either cluster, is placed within the first cluster, and the additional variance beyond that explained by the second cluster

TABLE 3.2

Combined Analysis: Usefulness Approach (n = 4,430)

	Cooperation				
	Summary index of cooperation	*In-role*	*Compliance*	*Extra-role*	*Deference*
Instrumental motivations	0%	0%	1%	1%	0%
Social motivations	25%	8%	19%	18%	24%
Total adjusted R-squared	38%***	11***	28%***	25%***	38%***

Notes: ***$p < .001$; the summary index combines the four forms of cooperation.

is considered. This approach is conservative, since all joint variance is allowed to the cluster that is not the focus of concern.

The results of this analysis are shown in table 3.2. Consider, first, the case of the summary index of cooperation. Altogether, the variables considered in this analysis explain approximately 38 percent of the variance in the summary index of cooperation, as is indicated in table 3.2. Of that variance, 25 percent is uniquely explained by social motivations and 0 percent by instrumental motivations. In other words, we can best predict cooperation by knowing people's social motivations. Unlike the findings of the prior analysis, this approach suggests that instrumental variables do not contribute to explaining cooperation beyond what can be understood using social variables. However, both analyses agree that social motivations dominate the explanation of cooperation.

As has been noted, a key distinction made earlier is between required and voluntary cooperation. The importance of that distinction is first indicated in table 3.1, but is further illustrated by the findings shown in table 3.2. In the table 3.2 analysis, for required cooperation (in-role behavior, compliance), 13.5 percent of the variance is uniquely explained by social motivations, and 0.5 percent by instrumental motivations. For voluntary cooperation (extra-role behavior; deference), 21 percent of the variance is uniquely explained by social motivtions, and 0.5 percent by instrumental motivations. Hence, if the primary concern is with nderstanding voluntary cooperation, social motivations are especially important.

Factors Shaping Cooperation

A comparison of the different overall analyses allows us to consider which findings might be confidently accepted and which might be more heavily dependent upon the particular form of the analysis. Both of the analyses support the basic argument that there is a great deal to be gained from an expansion of the variables considered in a motivational analysis of cooperation. Across the areas examined, social motivations always make a contribution to our ability to understand cooperation, regardless of which form of cooperation is being considered. The magnitude of this contribution varies depending upon the approach to the analysis that is being used. Irrespective of which form of analysis is used, however, social motivations explain many times as much variance in cooperation, as do instrumental motivations.

A key element of this study is that it is conducted in a setting—a work organization—that allows the analysis to include strong measures of all the aspects of the model outlined. First, in a work setting both aspects of cooperation—that is, regulation and productivity—are important issues; further, both required and voluntary forms of these two aspects of cooperation occur with frequency. Second, all of the various types of instrumental and social motivations of relevance are potentially important to employees. Hence, work settings are the ideal arena in which to consider issues of cooperation and to examine the role of instrumental and social issues in shaping cooperation. This is true both methodologically and theoretically.

Implications

The core concern of this volume is with understanding how to motivate cooperation in organizations. All types of organizations—legal, political, community-based, or work-centered—benefit when the people within them coperate more fully. The organizational design issue is how to encourage such cooperation.

This analysis compares the potential importance of two broad classes of motivation: instrumental and social. It begins by noting that these two classes of motivation are not completely distinct. Nonetheless, across several areas of social theory and research the instrumental-social distinction is made, and indices of these two conceptual categories are found to be distinct. The goal of this analysis is to explore the potential importance of the indices of each conceptual cluster as antecedents of cooperation.

The results reported first demonstrate that both instrumental and social indices shape cooperation. This suggests that those in positions of authority within organizations might potentially shape the behavior of the members of their organization by encouraging either type of motivation.

It is important to emphasize that these findings are consistent with prior research in arguing that there is some evidence that instrumental motivations shape cooperation. Significant influences of instrumental judgments are found. Hence, one important way to motivate employees is by shaping their material self-interest. However, as with prior research (see, e.g., Tyler 2006a) instrumental motivations are weaker than social motivations.

The results reported further suggest that the two types of motivation do not have an equally powerful influence on cooperation. They consistently suggest that social motivations are a more powerful factor shaping cooperation in organizations. Hence, efforts at motivation might be most profitably directed at understanding how to encourage social motivations.

Of course, the relative influence of social and instrumental variables is not always equally balanced. Social motivations are especially dominant when the issue involved is voluntary/discretionary behavior rather than required/mandatory behavior.

These arguments receive support with two distinct types of cooperation: performance and rule-following. While these are distinct forms of cooperation, which each pose particular implementation issues for organizations, these results suggest that the psychology underlying these two forms of cooperation is strikingly similar.

Generality of the Findings

To provide results that generalized broadly across organizations this study drew upon a random sample of American employees and, through them, a broad range of work settings. As has already been outlined, those work settings range from small companies to large multinational corporations. Hence, it is reasonable to argue that the findings have broad generality across types of work organizations for a diverse sample of employees.

However, it also makes sense to look within the sample at some potentially important differences among the employees. Two issues were considered: the relationship of the employees to their work organizations, and the demographic characteristics of the employees. Two elements of the employee-organization relationship were addressed: the nature of the work organization and the length of time that the employees had worked at their organizations. In addition, five aspects of employees were examined: gender, ethnicity, age, education, and income.

Regression analysis including interaction terms to reflect the size of the organization and length of employment were conducted to examine whether these characteristics influenced the role of instrumental and social motivations in shaping cooperation. The results of this analysis suggest that there was no influence of organizational size on the weight placed upon either instrumental (beta = 0.01, n.s.) or social (beta = 0.07, n.s.) motivations. On the other hand, those employees who had worked at an organization longer were found to be less strongly

influenced by instrumental issues (beta = −.32, $p < .05$), but were not significantly more strongly influenced by social motivations (beta = 0.22, n.s.).

A similar analysis of employee characteristics indicates that none of the five
demographic characteristics considered—age, race, gender, education, or income—interacted with the weight placed upon either instrumental or social motivations. This is not to say that these factors did not matter. The study found that
women (beta = 0.24, $p < .001$) and older employees (beta = 0.20, $p < .01$) were
more likely to cooperate. However, there was no evidence that any demographic
variables shaped the degree to which cooperation was shaped by either instrumental or social motivations.

These findings are consistent with the argument made in earlier studies of
procedural justice in communities that demographic characteristics have no influence in shaping either the weight placed upon issues of procedural justice or
the manner in which fair procedures were defined (Lind, Huo, and Tyler 1994;
Tyler 1994, 2000a). The findings suggest that demographic variables generally
had little impact upon the strength of the relationship between social motivations
and cooperation. In other words, people are people, and their relationship to
their work organization is not found to differ based upon their gender, race, and
the like. People do differ in their motivations in work settings, but demographic
characteristics do not predict these differences.

Does Organizational Context Matter?

Two additional samples of employees were used to test the argument that organizational context matters by repeating the basic analysis already conducted
upon samples of employees of different types. One was a sample of corporate
banking employees. This sample was chosen because this is a group of people
who are highly compensated and work in an environment in which compensation is central to the definition of their jobs and their relationship to their work
organizations. The second sample is that of agents of social control—police officers, federal agents, and soldiers in the army. This sample was selected because
these are people who work in military or quasi-military environments in which
command-and-control mechanisms are the dominant form of organization. By
contrasting these two samples to each other and to the broader sample already
outlined, the influence of context will be addressed.

Corporate Employees

The analysis already outlined does not suggest that employees who have higher
incomes are more influenced by instrumental considerations than are those with

lower incomes. Nonetheless, it is often argued that people making higher incomes will have their performance more heavily shaped by instrumental judgments. To test this argument, a separate sample of corporate bankers was analyzed. (For details about this study see Tyler and Blader 2005.) The study is based upon questionnaires completed by employees in a corporate banking division of a major multinational corporation.

Five hundred forty (540) employees of a single division within a national financial services organization responded to a survey that included the measures assessing workplace judgments and behaviors (a total of 1,350 employees, representing the entire division, received the survey, and thus there was a 40 percent response rate). Employees received the questionnaires via interoffice mail, and were asked to complete them while at work and to return them directly to the investigators using enclosed business-reply envelopes. They were assured confidentiality by both the investigators and the organization's management. Supervisor surveys were also distributed to the immediate supervisors of all 1,350 employees in the division. Four hundred and fifteen (415) of these surveys were returned (for a 31 percent response rate).

Of the 540 respondents, 44 percent were men, and 50 percent had pursued some postgraduate education. The mean tenure with the firm was thirteen years and the mean age was forty-two years. The sample was somewhat heterogeneous with respect to race, with 74 percent white, 11 percent Latino, 5 percent African American, 6 percent Asian, and 4 percent other. The demographics of the respondent sample closely resembled that of the overall sample, which contained 41 percent men, having an average tenure of 13 years, an average age of 43 years, and a fairly similar distribution with respect to race (63 percent white, 17 percent Latino, 11 percent African American, and 8 percent Asian). The average salary of the overall sample was \$84,000.[42] The type of job ranged from clerical to managerial, with the bulk of the employees involved in directly providing private banking services to customers.

The questionnaire completed by the corporate banking employees paralleled that used in this study. The five social motivations—attitudes, values, identity, procedural justice, and motive-based trust—were each assessed, as were instrumental motivations.[43] And the four forms of cooperation—in-role behavior, compliance, extra-role behavior, and deference—were measured.

Summary indices reflecting instrumental and social motivations were created, and regression analysis used to examine their influence on cooperative behavior. (The type of analysis conducted is that already shown in table 3.1.) The results are shown in table 3.3. As before, instrumental and social motivations were found to be correlated ($r = 0.68$). And, as in the sample already examined, social motivations had a distinct influence on all four dependent variables.

TABLE 3.3

Factors Shaping Cooperation among Corporate Bankers (*n* = 540)

	In-role	*Compliance*	*Extra-role*	*Deference*
Beta weights				
Instrumental	0.12*	–0.04	0.01	0.09
Social	0.16**	0.25***	0.32***	0.24***
Adjusted R-squared	6%***	5%***	10%***	9%***

Notes: $*p < .05$; $**p < .01$; $***p < .001$.

The findings replicate those of the broader study of employees already presented in showing that social motivations were important and, in particular, were more important when voluntary behavior was involved. And as a result, more variance in voluntary behavior was explained. Approximately 9–10 percent of the variance in voluntary behavior and 5–6 percent of the variance in mandatory behavior was explained by instrumental and social behavior combined, with the biggest social motivational effects found with discretionary behavior. This is particularly true of extra-role behavior, which was especially strongly shaped by social motivations.

Agents of Social Control

The goal in obtaining this data was to gather information from employees working in environments characterized by high levels of command and control. Such environments are typical of the military and of quasi-military groups like the police. Hence, these groups were the target, and samples were obtained from police officers, federal agents, and soldiers. This sample examines the role of social motivations in an organizational environment in which instrumental constraints are dominant and highly salient. (A more detailed discussion of the sample is available in Tyler, Callahan, and Frost 2007.)

The total sample size was 419. Two groups were approached: law enforcement agents (e.g., city police officers and federal law enforcement agents; *n* = 209) and soldiers in a combat setting (*n* = 210). Within each group questionnaires were made available and anonymous participation was invited. It was not possible to establish the size of the populations, so the response rate was unclear. To obtain the law enforcement information, questionnaires were distributed within two agencies—a large federal law enforcement agency and one of the largest U.S. city police departments. With the cooperation of supervisors, who encouraged participation, voluntary participation was solicited. A "snowball sampling" technique was used, with officers encouraged to identify others possibly interested in completing a questionnaire. In addition, those local respondents who requested it received $10 compensation. A total of 209 questionnaires were returned. Because participation was informally solicited, a response rate cannot be computed.

The sample of 209 law enforcement agents was 75 percent male, the mean age was thirty-nine, and the sample was 70 percent white. Of those in the sample, 29 percent had some college education, while 59 percent were college graduates or had some postgraduate education. The sample comprised 57 percent federal agents and 43 percent local police officers. The group included 98 percent with experience as active field officers.

To obtain the military sample, with the approval and cooperation of field commanders in several units stationed in Iraq, soldiers were given the opportunity to anonymously complete questionnaires about their units and about the army. Again, a "snowball technique" was used, with those commanders willing to participate asked to invite participation by those in their units. (For further details, see Callahan 2006.)

The sample of 210 soldiers was 98 percent male. the mean age was thirty, and the sample was also 66 percent white. Of those in the sample 69 percent had some college, while 11 percent were college graduates or had some postgraduate education. The sample was 4 percent officers, and 96 percent enlisted soldiers. All of those interviewed were in an active field operation (Iraq).

The questionnaire parallels that used in the multicompany employee study that has already been outlined. Again, the five social motivations—attitudes, values, identity, procedural justice, and motive-based trust—were measured and a combined index created. Similarly, instrumental questions were combined into a single index. The correlation between the two indices was $r = 0.64$. As with the sample of corporate bankers already outlined, these two indices were used in regression equations whose dependent variable was cooperation. The four forms of cooperation that are the focus of this volume were also assessed, and formed the dependent variable for the analysis shown.

The results of the regression equations are shown in table 3.4. They suggest that among the social control agents considered, social motivations were again central to cooperation.[44] In this sample social motivations were generally important, but the distinction between required and voluntary behavior was not as clear: 24 percent of the variance in required cooperation and 27 percent of the variance in voluntary cooperation were explained. Further, social motivations were not more important for one type of cooperation than for another. Instead, social motivations were generally important with all four forms of cooperation. As in the other samples, instrumental motivations were primarily important with required actions, particularly compliance.

TABLE 3.4

Factors Shaping Cooperation among Agents of Social Control (*n* = 419)

	In-role	*Compliance*	*Extra-role*	*Deference*
Beta weights				
Instrumental	0.04	0.22***	0.10	0.02
Social	0.48***	0.31***	0.39***	0.57***
Adjusted R-squared	25%***	23%***	20%***	33%***

Notes: ***$p < .01$.

Comparing Samples

The correlation between the instrumental and relational indices in the multi-company study was, on average, $r = 0.40$. So both of the new samples considered indicate a higher degree of connection ($r = 0.68$ for corporate bankers; $r = 0.64$ for agents of social control). Nonetheless, in each analysis distinct and significant influences of social motivation were found once the influence of instrumental variables had been taken into account. Hence, social motivations always explain significant variance in cooperation beyond that explained by instrumental motivations.

When the results are compared, they indicate that there was an influence of context. In the multicompany study social motivations generally dominated, and they played an especially strong role in shaping voluntary behavior. Among both of the additional samples this general pattern was maintained. However, among corporate bankers instrumental factors were more important with in-role behavior, while among agents of social control instrumental factors were more important with compliance. This is consistent with the argument that the banking environment focuses on incentives for doing one's job, while the command-and-control structure of military organizations focuses on the sanctions associated with failure to comply with rules.

Summary

The question that frames this analysis is, What motivates cooperation on the part of the people within groups, organizations, and communities? And the findings provide a clear and compelling answer—social motivations. These motivations—attitudes, values, identity, procedural justice, and motive-based trust—consistently shape all four types of cooperative behavior. And they have an especially strong influence upon voluntary behavior. Hence, those interested in designing organizations need to focus their attention upon understanding how to encourage and sustain social motivations.

Of course, it is important to note that the analysis presented thus far is focused upon work organizations. Several types of work organization are distinguished, and the results are similar across them. The findings do not support the argument that the influence of social motivations is limited by social context. It is clear that there are variations linked to social context, but they do not alter the basic argument made in the volume—that social motivations are a key to cooperation.

The argument presented draws upon a broad range of both instrumental and social motivations. It is based upon a more complex conceptualization of the idea of cooperation than is my earlier work (see Tyler 2006a; Tyler and Huo 2002), which focused upon the legal arena, within which the traditional concern has been with compliance with the law. That compliance model is expanded here in several ways. The present study focuses upon voluntary cooperation rather than upon compliance. One form of such cooperation is voluntary deference. However, more recent writing in the area of law emphasizes that it is also desirable for people to proactively work with legal authorities rather than simply deferring to their decisions and rules. Hence, that early framework is expanded here by being more broadly concerned about voluntary cooperation and by recognizing that both rule-following and performance are important. In the legal arena this means that we would ideally like people to both follow the law and willingly help the police by working with them within the community. This broader framework is used in the legal arena in the data reported in chapter 4. Doing so allows for a test of the power of social motivations outside of work settings.

CHAPTER FOUR

Cooperation with Legal Authorities in Local Communities

In chapter 3, I examined the factors that motivate employees to cooperate with the organizations for which they work. That analysis distinguishes between two forms of cooperation—rule-following and performance. In this chapter I will extend that analysis to a second arena, that of cooperation with legal authorities—that is, the police, the courts, and the law.

My purpose in testing my ideas in this new arena is to examine the breadth of the influence of social motivations in social settings. To do so I am choosing an arena that is quite distinct from work organizations. Here I focus on communities and on people's behavior in the communities in which they live. That behavior involves compliance with the law, but also cooperation with the police to deal with the community problems of crime and social disorder. People can help the police by reporting crime and criminals and/or by working with others to help manage problems in their community.[1]

In the past, as has been noted, cooperation with legal authorities has been conceptualized as involving compliance. Compliance is important because a core function of social regulatory authorities like the police and the courts is to bring the behavior of members of the public into line with the law. This is true both in personal encounters between members of the public and legal authorities, in which police officers or judges make decisions about what is appropriate conduct that people need to accept and follow, and in the case of people's everyday compliance with the law.

The ability to shape people's behavior is key to the effectiveness of legal authorities since, if the law does not shape the behavior of most people most of the time, the legal system is not effectively fulfilling its social regulatory function. The need for legal authorities to be able to secure compliance has been widely noted by legal scholars and social scientists (Fuller 1969). This is the case because the effective exercise of legal authority requires compliance from "the bulk of [the citizens] most of the time" (Easton 1975, 185). Decisions by police officers or judges mean very little if people generally ignore them, and laws lack importance if they do not affect public behavior (Tyler 2006a, 2006b).

Such compliance by members of the public can never be taken for granted. As Stephen Mastrofski, Jeffrey Snipes, and Anne Supina suggest, "Although deference to legal authorities is the norm, disobedience occurs with sufficient frequency that skill in handling the rebellious, the disgruntled, and the hard to manage—or those potentially so—has become the street officer's performance litmus test" (1996, 272). Similarly, Lawrence Sherman (1993) highlights the problem of defiance by the public, and the need to minimize resistance to the directives of the police.

The studies by Mastrofski and colleagues in which social scientists observed police behavior provide some evidence about the frequency of such problems. The researchers observed police encounters with the public in Richmond, Virginia, and found an overall noncompliance rate of 22 percent: 19 percent of the time when the police told a person to leave another person alone; 33 percent of the time when the police told a person to cease some form of disorder; and 18 percent of the time when the police told a person to cease illegal behavior (Mastrofski, Snipes, and Supina 1996, 281). A replication of this study in Indianapolis and St. Petersburg found an overall noncompliance rate of 20 percent: 14 percent of the time when the police told people to leave another person alone; 25 percent of the time when the police told a person to cease some form of disorder; and 21 percent of the time when the police told a person to cease illegal behavior (McCluskey, Mastrofski, and Parks 1999, 400).

Further, the studies outlined look just at immediate compliance—that is, whether people did as instructed—and not at whether people willingly accepted the decisions made by the authorities, buying into their resolution to a problem or understanding why the restrictions of their behavior are appropriate and reasonable. As the researchers note, "citizens who acquiesce at the scene can renege" (Mastrofski et al. 1996, 283). People may renege in their future behavior if they have complied in the face of coercive power. If they do so, this requires further police intervention at future times.

Recognizing the importance of gaining widespread compliance with the law, most discussions of social regulation focus on why people obey or disobey the law both in response to specific decisions and in their everyday lives. Addressing this question is the key to developing effective policing strategies, since to be able to regulate the behavior of the public, legal authorities need to accurately understand the factors that motivate people's law-related behavior.

The form of cooperation that we would like to motivate on the part of the residents of communities has changed over the years. Early social order–based discussions of the type of public cooperation that were viewed as desirable focused upon compliance with legal rules and the decisions of legal authorities. Such compliance continues to be important (Tyler 2006a). Recent discussions have expanded that compliance frame to include the recognition of the value of voluntary compliance—that is, deference (Sunshine and Tyler 2003; Tyler and Huo 2002). However, increasingly it has become clear that we want more from community residents than mere compliance with the law.

To be effective in lowering crime and creating secure communities, the police must be able to elicit cooperation from community residents. Security cannot be produced by either the police or community residents acting alone—it requires cooperation. Such cooperation potentially involves, on the part of the public, both obeying the law (Tyler 2006a) and working with the police or with others in the community to help combat crime in the community (Sampson, Raudenbush, and Earls 1997). We need the active cooperation of members of the community to effectively manage community problems. The police, for example, need community cooperation in the form of reporting crime and criminals, as well as in joining collective efforts to combat crime via community patrols or neighborhood watch programs (Sampson et al. 1997).

In this chapter I will focus directly upon two forms of public cooperation that actively aid the police. Both reflect a type of discretionary—that is, voluntary—action in which individuals can choose whether or not to engage. The first is the willingness to cooperate with the police by providing information relevant to dealing with crime; this includes information about the location of criminals, the occurrence of crime, and other information that aids police officers in doing their jobs. The second type of cooperation involves working with the police by attending community meetings, participating in neighborhood watches, and engaging in other types of joint activities to deal with crime and disorder in the community.

It has always been recognized that the police and courts benefit when those in the communities they regulate cooperate with them in joint efforts to enforce the law and to fight crime and criminal behavior. Recent research emphasizes this point and even raises questions about whether legal authorities can effectively manage the problems of community crime control without public cooperation (Sampson and Bartusch 1998). As Mark Moore notes, "The loss of popular legitimacy for the criminal justice system produces disastrous consequences for the system's performance. If citizens do not trust the system, they will not use it" (1997, 17).

Instrumental Motivations for Cooperation

Just as was true in the case of work settings, one important tradition is the social control or instrumental perspective, which argues that people's actions are governed by their self-interest, either in the form of sanctions or incentives (Nagin 1998). The sanction risk involves the belief that rule-breakers are punished (Bayley 1998; Nagin 1998). The incentive involved is linked to police performance; the police can encourage cooperative behavior by giving cooperation greater potential for personal benefit for community residents in demonstrating, for example, that the police are effective in fighting crime (Kelling and Coles 1996) and/or that rule-breakers are punished (Bayley 1998; Nagin 1998).

Discussions of public trust and confidence in the police often assume that the key to public feelings about the police, the courts, and the legal system is the public's evaluation of the outcomes that the public receives from these legal authorities. In the case of the police, their ability or inability to engage in effective crime control is frequently seen as driving the valence of public evaluations. Shared beliefs that the community can be effective in fighting crime have, for example, been shown to motivate community residents to work with each other to fight crime and disorder in their communities (Sampson et al. 1997).

Unfortunately, from the instrumental perspective, it is often not in the short-term self-interest of individuals to cooperate with law enforcement agencies. People often see little immediate personal utility in supporting police efforts to control crime by reporting crimes and criminals or by helping in community efforts to fight crime. Hence, strategies appealing to self-interest are often an inadequate basis for managing crime and security. Empirical research supports this argument by finding only weak correlations between risk and compliance (MacCoun 1993), as well as little connection between police performance and public evaluations of and cooperation with the police (National Research Council 2004; Skogan and Meares 2004).

An additional type of instrumental motivation is distributive justice. Another type of instrumental model links public behavior and policy support to issues of police fairness in the distribution of their services and protection across the community. Here the issue is whether the police fairly distribute police services, providing "equal protection to all." Austin Sarat (1977) argues that the demand for equal treatment is a core theme running through public evaluations of the police and the courts. He suggests that the "perception of unequal treatment is the single most important source of popular dissatisfaction with the American legal system. According to available survey evidence, Americans believe that the ideal of equal protection, which epitomizes what they find most valuable in their legal system, is betrayed by police, lawyers, judges, and other legal officials" (Sarat 1977, 434). This argument roots evaluations of the police, and public reactions to them, in views about how the police distribute public resources and services. For example, a common view in poor and minority communities is that the police patrol those areas less aggressively and respond to calls for help less quickly than they do in rich and white neighborhoods. In the case of the police there are two issues: first, whether the police have provided the person being interviewed with fair outcomes, and second, whether they distribute the outcomes they provide fairly across different social and economic groups—that is, whether they discriminate against particular groups or communities.

The notion that people's behavior with respect to the law is shaped by calculations of expected gains and losses is a core premise of rational choice theory, which is derived from neoclassical economics (Blumstein, Cohen, and Nagin 1978; Nagin 1998). It is assumed that most people will calculate expected utilities by multiplying the probability of an outcome (e.g., getting caught for armed robbery or drunk driving) by its valence (very, very bad). If the laws are well calibrated, people will arrive at the desired conclusion that they should follow the law. Thus, rational self-interest is the motivational engine of the deterrence/social control model. To regulate behavior, this model suggests that decision makers should adjust criminal sanctions to the needed level so that the expected losses associated with lawbreaking will minimize the likelihood that people will indeed break laws.

Such models focus on the ability of legal authorities and institutions to shape people's behavior by threatening to deliver or by actually delivering negative sanctions for rule-breaking. To implement such deterrence strategies, police officers carry guns and clubs and can threaten citizens with physical injury and incapacitation, in addition to financial penalties. Their goal is to establish their authority and "[t]he uniform, badge, truncheon, and arms all may play a role in asserting authority" in the effort to "gain control of the situation" (Reiss 1971, 46). The police seek to control the individual's behavior "by manipulating an individual's calculus regarding whether 'crime pays' in the particular instance" (Meares 2000, 396). Judges similarly shape people's acceptance of their decisions by threatening fines or even jail time for failure to comply.

While the focus of this analysis is on cooperation, this deterrence approach is still important. It matters because of the suggestion that people focus on whether they see evidence that those who break the law are punished. Hence, deterrence is a key sign of instrumental effectiveness and is linked to performance in combating crime. Thus, people view the ability of the police to manage community problems, something that an instrumental model argues should be related to the motivation to cooperate, as being linked to whether they can credibly shape the behavior of potential rule violators.

There are many bases for a critique of an instrumental model of social order maintenance. The key one that will be advanced here is that it is a costly and minimally effective system of social control (Tyler 2007). This argument flows cleanly from the discussion of instrumental mechanisms in the introduction to this volume. There instrumental mechanisms were found to be effective, but marginally so. Their influence was inconsistently discernable, and when found it was weak. Further, as outlined, that influence is resource intensive—that is, costly to create and maintain.

The high cost of the system stems from the need to create and maintain a credible threat of punishment and, relatedly, compelling evidence of performance effectiveness. People will only change their behavior when they feel that there is a reasonable risk of being caught and punished for wrongdoing, both when they are personally considering rule-breaking and when they are evaluating whether they believe that the authorities are effectively managing the problem of crime and social order in their community. People will try to hide their illegal behavior, so a system of surveillance is needed to identify wrongdoing, and that system has to both work and be seen to work.

The problems of surveillance are central to the effectiveness of performance in deterrence models, since research suggests that it is the probability of punishment, not its severity, that shapes rule-related behavior. As a consequence, a system for detecting wrongdoing must be created and maintained. It is not realistic to substitute draconian punishments for a more costly system that creates credible risks of being detected while engaging in wrongdoing. For this reason, as Tracey Meares notes, the effectiveness of "instrumental means of producing compliance always depend[s] on resource limits" (2000, 401). The relevant questions are how much in terms of financial and other benefits and burdens authorities are willing to expend in order to control crime, and how much power to intrude into citizens' lives people are willing to allow the authorities to have.

Research does support the notion that variations in the perceived certainty of punishment do affect people's compliance with the law, at least to some degree. People's behavior is often, though not always, shaped by their estimate of the likelihood that if they disobey the law they will be caught and punished (see Nagin and Paternoster 1991; Paternoster 1987, 1989; Paternoster and Iovanni 1986; Paternoster, Saltzman, Waldo, Chiricos 1983). At the same time, however, perceptions of the likelihood of being caught and punished seem to have a relatively minor influence on people's behavior, as has already been outlined (MacCoun 1993; Robinson and Darley 1995, 1997; Ross 1982). Consequently, social control strategies based exclusively on a deterrence model of human behavior have had at best limited success (see also Tyler 1997, 1998). Raymond Paternoster notes that "perceived certainty [of punishment] plays virtually no role in explaining deviant/criminal conduct" (1987, 191). Hence, deterrence is a very high cost strategy that yields identifiable, but weak, results.[2]

Of course, performance-based instrumental models are not always an equally effective or ineffective strategy. One of the key problems with sanctioning systems is that they require near constant surveillance of individual behavior. For obvious reasons, people are strongly motivated to hide their behavior from authorities to avoid punishment; authorities must therefore develop surveillance systems for detecting rule-breaking behavior. Deterrence is more effective when surveillance is easy, because the structure of the situation makes it easy. For example, wage earners' incomes are easy for the government to monitor, because businesses withhold percentages from each paycheck and send the withheld amount to the government in the form of tax payments. This makes tax violations among this group relatively easy to prosecute. In other cases, however, surveillance can be quite difficult. The police, for example, have tremendous difficulty monitoring public behavior in order to identify people who are using illegal drugs, just as tax authorities have trouble monitoring the incomes of street vendors, waiters, and people who run small businesses.

The deterrence model probably also works best in the case of crimes that are committed for instrumental reasons. For example, car theft, burglary, and instrumentally motivated crimes of this type are at least to some extent motivated by calculations about the costs and benefits expected from lawbreaking behavior. Thus, deterrence approaches work best in affecting the occurrence of instrumentally motivated crimes—that is, with crimes that are motivated by rational calculations about gain and loss. So, for example, it is known that making one's home resistant to burglary by putting in locks is very effective since instrumentally motivated thieves quickly move to the next home. Similarly, locking one's car is very effective in lowering the likelihood that it will be stolen. These instrumental actions are significantly less effective in controlling criminal behavior that is motivated by factors other than economic gain. For example, when rape or murder occur in the context of a specific relationship, the wrongdoer is unlikely to simply move to other victims when he encounters difficulties.

There are many other crimes that are motivated not by instrumental concerns but by temporary emotional states (Katz 1988). For example, crimes such as rape, assault, and many murders occur on the "spur of the moment" and in the "heat of passion." In such cases, the assumption that rational calculations of costs and benefits enter into the perpetrator's "decision" about whether or not to commit such crimes is naive in the extreme. In part, this is because of intrapersonal empathy gaps: the person who is in a "hot state" cannot access or identify with how he will think or feel later upon returning to a "cold state." Thus, crimes of passion as well as crimes committed under states of intoxication are relatively unaffected by deterrence strategies, regardless of the actual or even perceived likelihood of being caught and punished for wrongdoing.

Deterrence works reasonably well in at least some cases, such as murder, because society has devoted considerable resources to preventing murder and enforcing penalties for it. The objective risk of being caught and punished for murder is relatively high: approximately 45 percent (Robinson and Darley 1997). The likelihood of being caught for committing a murder is high enough for deterrence to be effective in lowering the murder rate. Even in this case, however, criminals are not as sensitive to the magnitude of the penalty as they are to the estimated probability of being apprehended. As a result, capital punishment does not serve to deter murder more effectively than does life imprisonment (Ellsworth and Mauro 1998).[3]

Social Motivations

Issues regarding the limits of instrumental motivations are clear (Tyler 2007). The question for legal authorities is whether there are other motivations that might be tapped to supplement efforts to engage public cooperation. In this case, the other motivations that we are concerned with are social motivations. This study considers the five types of social motivation outlined in the prior discussion of work motivation: attitudes, values, identity, procedural justice, and motive-based trust.

Attitudes involve people's feelings toward legal authorities. In the case of legal authorities these items reflect generally favorable or unfavorable feelings toward the law and legal authorities.

Values included legitimacy and moral value congruence. Legitimacy reflects feelings of obligation toward the law and toward legal authorities. Moral value congruence is the degree to which people believe that the law reflects moral values and the police act morally.

Identity was assessed by degree of identification with the police. It reflects the respondents' views about whether they share values, background, and concerns with police officers in their neighborhood. They were also asked whether they felt that the police respected them and their values and lifestyle.

Procedural justice reflected judgments about the appropriateness of police behavior. It included evaluations of the fairness of decision making (neutrality, transparency, factuality, allowing opportunities for input) and of interpersonal treatment (treatment with respect and dignity, respect for rights).

Finally, motive-based trust was based upon evaluations of the motives of the police. It reflected the extent to which police officers were judged to genuinely care about the public and take account of their needs and concerns.

Prior Studies

Tom Tyler (2006a) has examined the role of instrumental and social motivations in shaping compliance with the law in the everyday life of Chicagoans. That study provided preliminary evidence that social motivations independently shape compliance, but focused only on a narrow set of such motivations (i.e., values). However, the study does not examine the factors shaping voluntary cooperation with legal authorities in the form of actively helping legal authorities to combat crime. Similarly, the findings of Tom Tyler and Yuen Huo (2002), a study of personal experiences with the police and courts, suggest that social motivations are important in shaping voluntary decision acceptance when dealing with the police and the courts. However, this study also does not examine the antecedents of active cooperation.

A Study of New Yorkers

This is a panel study in which New Yorkers were interviewed over the telephone at two points in time.[4] (For details, see Sunshine and Tyler 2003, study 2; and Tyler and Fagan 2008.) The first-wave sample consisted of 1,653 interviews with residents of New York City, and was drawn from a stratified random sample of telephone numbers in the city, with an overrepresentation of nonwhite residents designed to produce a high proportion of Latino and African American respondents. Approximately one year following the first interview, attempts were made to recontact and reinterview all of the respondents interviewed. A subset of 830 of those originally interviewed was successfully reinterviewed. A comparison of those reinterviewed to the original sample indicates no significant differences in ethnicity, gender, age, income, or education.

The sample frame was based upon lists of eligible telephone numbers, and did not include cell phones; it was weighted by census tract to produce an ethnically diverse sample of New Yorkers. If an answering machine was reached, respondents were called again. The interviews were conducted in English or in Spanish. The ethnicity of the respondent and the interviewer was not matched. When a home was reached, the individual with the most recent birthday was interviewed. The response rate for the the first-wave survey was 64 percent of eligible respondents.

In the second-wave survey efforts were made to contact all first-wave respondents, and 53 percent were identified and reinterviewed ($n = 879$). Although efforts were made to trace and reinterview those respondents who had moved, only those respondents still living within the same neighborhood were included in this analysis ($n = 830$).

As it was designed to be, the first-wave sample ($n = 1,653$) was 34 percent white, 25 percent Latino, 28 percent African American, and 13 percent other nonwhite. And this diversity was maintained among those who were reinterviewed during the second time of the study ($n = 879$). In the second-wave sample 39 percent were white, 22 percent Latino, 28 percent African American, and 11 percent other nonwhite. In addition, the original sample was 46 percent male (44 percent in the second wave); 40 percent were age thirty-four or under (33 percent in the second wave); 65 percent had some college or postgraduate education (66 percent in the second wave); and 34 percent made under $30,000 per year (32 percent in the second wave). As planned, the original sample was diverse, and that diversity was maintained among the panel respondents.

Respondents answered a series of questions presented over the telephone with fixed response alternatives. Questions examined a variety of issues, including instrumental judgments about police performance, sanctioning risk, and distributive fairness as well as social judgments about the legitimacy of the police, identification with the police, and police procedural fairness and trustworthiness. Respondents were also asked about their voluntary cooperation with the police. The variables were assessed using the same questions in the first and second waves.

Cooperation

Cooperation involved voluntary efforts to help the police. It was assessed by asking respondents, if the situation arose, how likely they would be to call the police to report a crime, help the police to find someone suspected of a crime, report dangerous or suspicious activity, volunteer time to help the police, patrol the streets as part of an organized group, or volunteer to attend community meetings to discuss crime. The response scale was: (4) very likely, (3) somewhat likely, (2) not too likely, and (1) not likely at all.

Instrumental Motivations

Four instrumental motivations were assessed: the likelihood that rule-breakers are caught and punished (sanction risk),[5] the ability of the police to fight crime (performance),[6] group-based distributive justice,[7] and personal distributive justice.[8]

Social Motivations

Five social motivations were measured: attitudes toward the law,[9] values (i.e., the legitimacy of the police and law,[10] the congruence of law with moral values[11]), identification with the police,[12] the procedural justice of the behavior of the police (overall,[13] the quality of decision making,[14] and the quality of treatment[15]), and motive-based trust.[16]

Demographics

Ethnicity, age, gender, education and income were measured and included in the analysis.

Analysis

Instrumental and social judgments were found to be related ($r = 0.23$). Those members of the community who believed that the police were instrumentally effective also had social motivations for cooperating with them. Hence, instrumental and social motivations were linked. However, the linkage is weaker in this context, since the correlation in the general previous study of employees was $r = 0.40$.

Structural equation modeling was used to examine the influence of instrumental and social factors in shaping cooperation. That analysis used the same approach that was used in the prior study of employees, including separate analyses for the first-wave sample and for the panel sample. Because of the community context, demographic variables were included in this analysis. Prior research indicates that there are large differences in cooperation with the police that are linked to demographic factors—in particular, race. As a consequence, this analysis was expanded to include demographic influences.

The results for the first-wave cross-sectional analysis suggest that both factors play an important role in shaping cooperation. There were strong influences of social motivations (beta = 0.40, $p < .001$), demographics (beta = 0.12, $p < .001$), and instrumental motivations (beta = 0.12, $p < .001$). Notably, as was true in the prior analysis, when controls were placed upon prior cooperation through the use of panel analysis, only social motivations remained important (beta = 0.08, $p < .01$). The panel results suggest that social motivation remains important with a more sensitive panel design, while the influence of instrumental variables disappears.

These findings support the argument that social motivations are important in settings beyond work organizations. As was true in the prior study of employees, people's willingness to cooperate with the police was shaped by both their instrumental judgments of police effectiveness and by their social motivations toward the police. But, as before, social motivations predominated, especially when a panel analysis was conducted. That panel analysis controlled for cooperation

TABLE 4.1

Motivation in a Community Setting

	Voluntary cooperation with the police	
	First wave	*Second wave*
First-wave factors		
Demographics	0.12***	0.06
Instrumental motivations	0.12***	0.03
Social motivations	0.40***	0.08*
Cooperation	—	0.54***
Adjusted explained variance	19%	58%
	1,653	830

Notes: $*p < .05$; $**p < .01$; $***p < .001$.

during the first-wave interviews in an analysis focused upon cooperation during the second-wave interviews, one year later.

It is also important to note that the relative influence of social motivations is weaker in this case than was true in the management setting studied. This is consistent with the argument that there may be social-context effects, and that the balance of instrumental and social motivations may vary depending upon situational factors. In this case, ties to one's community and to the police were weaker than ties to one's work organization.

While it is tempting to conclude that social context is the key factor distinguishing this community-based study from the prior study of work organizations, it is also important to recognize the broader scope of the employee study. That study interviewed employees from a sample of workplaces that varied widely in size, location, nature of work tasks, and the like. Hence, it captured a wide variance in both instrumental and social motivations. This study focused upon one city's police department. While there is certainly variation across neighborhoods, and the results show that there is variation across individuals, the range of these variations is restricted by the common setting. If, for example, this study interviewed a random sample of Americans about their local police departments, there would be much greater variation in both the effectiveness of the police and in social judgments about them. Hence, it is also possible that the findings of this study are restricted by these limitations.

Tyler and Huo (2002) also explored the basis of reactions to decisions by legal authorities. They did so in two communities—Los Angeles and Oakland, California—with different histories of police-community relations. Further, they also focused on white and minority group members. Their results suggest that context had little to do with reactions to the police. Rather, people's reactions were primarily a response to issues of trust and procedural justice (i.e., social motivations).

Cooperation in the Regulation of a Scarce Resource

Communities cooperate to manage many problems besides crime. One example is the management of scarce natural resources (Tyler and Degoey, 1995). In this case I will examine a study conducted in the context of a naturally occurring resource allocation problem—a water shortage. This drought occurred in northern California and the respondents were residents of one affected community—San Francisco. For the study, a random sample of 636 of the adults living in San Francisco were interviewed by telephone.[17]

The problem of cooperation in the consumption of limited resources is an example of the type of cooperation of concern in this volume. While it is possible to restrict water use by coercion and fines, it is difficult to do so. We cannot imagine the police, for example, patrolling neighborhoods to look for people watering their lawns, filling their pools, and so on. However, another approach is to motivate voluntary cooperation with rules restricting water use via social motivations. In this case, water use rules are created by a public commission, and residents are urged to voluntarily follow them.

The focus of concern is voluntary conservation. Respondents were asked how willing they would be to conserve water if asked to do so by the water commission.[18] They were also asked how important they felt it was for government to intervene and create required mechanisms for motivating compliance with rules.[19]

In this study, two types of instrumental motivation were measured: feeling the impact of the water shortage and viewing government policies as favorable. Those who experience the shortage as more of a problem,[20] or view policies as less favorable,[21] would be expected to be less motivated to voluntarily conserve. Three social motivations were measured: the procedural justice of the water commission,[22] trust in the motivations of its members,[23] and the legitimacy of that commission.[24]

The results of a regression analysis of the type already outlined are shown in table 4.2. They support the suggestion that social motivations have a distinct influence on voluntary cooperation (beta = 0.19, $p < .001$). In addition, instrumental motivations shape cooperation (beta = 0.19, $p < .001$). Together these variables explain 9 percent of the variance in voluntary conservation behavior. The analysis also suggests that social motivations are strongly linked to accepting government rules. If respondents view government as procedurally just and

TABLE 4.2

Cooperating with Authorities to Limit Resource Consumption

	Voluntary cooperation	*Support for government regulation*
Beta weights		
Instrumental motivations	0.19***	0.25***
Social motivations	0.19***	0.12*
Adjusted R-squared	9%***	9%***

Notes: *p < .05;   ***p < .001.

trustworthy, they are more willing to support government imposed rules (beta = 0.12, *p* < .05). Similarly, people support rules when the problem is having a greater impact upon them and is thus more relevant in instrumental terms (beta = 0.25, *p* < .001).

These findings suggest that the arguments made in the context of community efforts to fight crime are broader in scope. People will cooperate voluntarily with authorities seeking to restrict their use of common resources based upon social motivations. Interestingly, social motivations are also key to being willing to accept imposed government regulation. The extension of the findings to the arena of imposed regulations also illustrates the point made in the prior section—that context matters. Instrumental issues were found to be relatively more important in the context of imposed government regulation.

Policy Implications

The distinction between instrumentally based estimates and social motivations as antecedents of cooperative behavior highlights the possibility of two types of legal culture. The first is a culture that builds public cooperation on the basis of people's judgments that the police, the courts, and the legal system can effectively manage problems of crime and social disorder. Such an instrumentally based society depends upon the ability of legal authorities to create and maintain a credible threat of punishment for wrongdoing, as well as more generally demonstrating that they can control crime.

The important role played by social motivations in shaping people's law-related behavior indicates the possibility of creating a society in which citizens have social motivations that lead to cooperation. Such a society is based upon the willing cooperation of citizens, a cooperation flowing from supportive attitudes and values, identifying with the police, and viewing police policies and practices as both fair and as suggesting that the authorities are trustworthy.

Socially motivated cooperation develops from people's own feelings about what is appropriate social behavior, and is not linked simply to the risks of apprehension and punishment or to evidence of police competence. The results reported make clear that such a society is possible in the sense that social motivations shape cooperation. If people's social motivations are engaged they are more voluntarily cooperative with legal authorities.

CHAPTER FIVE

Cooperation with Political Authorities

The prior discussion of public interactions with the police is an example of the general category of governmental concerns when dealing with local communities and individuals within them. That study was directed at people's connections to their local communities and to the actions of the police within those communities.

A broader concern is with political authorities. It involves the question of how public views and public satisfaction/dissatisfaction should be studied. I would argue that any government program or policy should be viewed through the framework of how it influences or shapes the relationship that members of the public have with the government. This is equally true of local authorities with whom community residents have personal contact, and national-level political and legal authorities.

The government depends heavily on such voluntary cooperation from citizens (Tyler 2002). We want citizens to cooperate with government in many ways, including to willingly obey the law (Tyler 2006a), to help the police to fight crime and terrorism (Sunshine and Tyler 2003), to be willing to assume duties such as fighting in wars (Levi 1997) and paying taxes (Scholz and Lubell 1998; Scholz and Pinney 1995), and to generally be engaged in their communities and in the political process (Putnam 1993). All of these behaviors are shaped by public views about the government and of its policies and actions. I will argue that these views are social motivations and that government policies and actions need to be viewed through a lens of how they shape the social connections between people and their government. Because it supports such cooperative behavior on the part of citizens, I will argue that social motivations help political systems to be more effective and viable.

For example, the effectiveness of legal authorities, law, and government depends upon the widespread belief among citizens that these are legitimate and entitled to be obeyed. The classic argument of political and social theorists has been that for authorities to perform effectively those in power must convince everyone else that they "deserve" to rule and make decisions that influence the quality of everyone's lives. It is the belief that some decision made or rule created by these authorities is "valid" in the sense that it is entitled to be obeyed by virtue of who made the decision or how it was made that is central to the idea of legitimacy. While some argue that it is impossible to rule using only power, and others suggest that it is possible but more difficult, it is widely agreed that authorities benefit from having legitimacy, and find governance easier and more effective when a feeling that they are entitled to rule is widespread within the population.

Given the importance of this value, we need to understand how public views about legitimacy—that is, public "trust and confidence"—are created and maintained (Levi and Stoker 2000). If we understand the conditions under which supportive public values, such as legitimacy, play an important role in shaping public actions, we can understand how to build a civic society in which people take the personal responsibility and obligation to be good citizens onto themselves (Tyler and Darley 2000).

One factor that influences legitimacy is public reaction to the organizational issues—the justice of the procedures used to wield political authority and trust in political leaders—leading the impact of governmental policies and practices to shape public views about government. Hence, these social factors need to be a key concern in the long-term effort to create and maintain public support for political authorities and institutions, and for the government more generally. Studies consistently find that a key antecedent of assessments of the legitimacy of government is the judgment about the fairness of the procedures the government uses to exercise governmental authority, and of the trustworthiness of government authorities and institutions (Tyler and Mitchell 1994). And in the political context the judgment of the fairness of the procedures used to empower authority are also found to be distinct and separately important (Gonzalez and Tyler 2008).

Although both outcomes and procedural justice/trust in authorities are found to shape people's satisfaction with their outcomes when they are dealing with legal authorities (Casper, Tyler, and Fisher 1998), it is the procedural justice of government actions/trustworthiness of government authorities that generalizes to shape views about law and government (Tyler, Casper, and Fisher 1989). Hence, when it makes policies, the government needs to not only be sensitive to the objective quality of those policies but to how their creation and implementation is viewed by the public.

Underlying our policy analysis is the view that government depends upon the goodwill and voluntary acceptance of most of the members of the community most of the time. In the terms already outlined, the public needs to be positively disposed toward government and hence more willing to voluntarily cooperate with government authorities and institutions. This means that to be effective, government authorities must be sensitive to the appearance of fairness as well as to its reality; they need to create and implement public policies with an awareness of how the public views those policies. Based upon empirical research it is clear that the public is very ethical in its evaluations of authorities, judging them against criteria of fairness and trustworthiness. In particular, the public is very sensitive to its assessment of whether the authorities are exercising their authority in ways that are fair. Such procedural justice judgments shape the legitimacy of the authorities in the eyes of citizens and influence whether people cooperate with authorities.

The goal of this examination of political authority is to expand the consideration of the motivations underlying cooperation in several ways. Most obviously, the scope of the study is enlarged by the type of cooperation being examined. Here the focus is on two types of voluntary cooperation in the political arena.

The first type is participation in the political process by attending political meetings, raising political issues, contacting political authorities, and becoming involved in the political process through attending rallies and demonstrations. The second type is voting in elections.

Second, this research moves beyond that already discussed because it considers societies in which both instrumental and social factors vary more extremely than is true within the United States. In the case of Africa, for example, people are focused upon basic instrumental necessities such as having food or water. There are also dramatic variations in the justice of government procedures, the trustworthiness of political authorities, and the legitimacy of government. Hence, the range of the variables under consideration is larger than has been true in the previous analyses.

Social Motivations in Political Settings

In discussing social motivations in managerial and community settings, I have used the results of panel data sets. In examining the role of social motivations in political settings, I rely upon secondary analysis of two previously collected cross-sectional data sets that are based upon interviews with samples of people living in Africa. The first, Afrobarometer Round 1, contains 21,531 interviews with people from twelve African countries. The interviews were conducted in 1999–2001.[1] The second, Afrobarometer Round 3, includes 25,397 interviews with people from eighteen African countries that were conducted in 2005.[2] The Round 2 interviews were not considered in this analysis because they did not include relevant questions.

My focus in analyzing both surveys is upon the antecedents of two types of participation: political participation and voting behavior. Instrumental motivations are those linked to government performance in meeting basic economic and social needs. Social motivations include attitudes toward government, values, identity, procedural justice, and trust in authorities.

Each analysis includes several types of control. First, dummy variables were included to account for the country in which the interview occurred. Second, country-level objective indices of economic performance and quality of governance were included.[3] Finally, respondent demographic characteristics—age, gender, and education—were included. These controls were added during the first stage of a two-stage regression analysis. Instrumental and social motivations were added during the second stage.[4]

Round 1

Respondents were asked about their participation in their community, using items that included both attending community meetings and raising political issues as well as their recent voting behavior.[5] Both indices reflect voluntary behavior. The participation index ranged from never (0) to often (3). The mean level of participation was 0.84. Among those registered to vote, in countries that had elections, 5 percent indicated that they decided not to vote; 15 percent did not vote, for whatever reason; and 80 percent voted.

Instrumental motivations include, first, the level of social welfare, which is the frequency with which people get basic services such as food and water,[6] and government economic performance in dealing with social problems.[7] Social motivations included attitudes toward government,[8] legitimacy,[9] identification with society,[10] procedural justice,[11] and trust in specific government institutions.[12] These two overall indices were moderately intercorrelated ($r = 0.19, p < .001$).

Round 3

Respondents were asked about their participation in their community, including attending community meetings, raising political issues, and contacting political authorities,[13] as well as their recent voting behavior. Both indices reflect voluntary behavior. In the case of participation, the index ranged from never (0) to often (3). The mean level of participation was 0.46. In the case of voting, 5 percent of those interviewed decided not to register; 2 percent registered, but then decided not to vote; 3 percent registered and intended to vote but for some reason were unable to do so; and 90 percent registered and voted.

Instrumental motivations include the level of social welfare,[14] government economic performance,[15] and the degree of enforcement of the law.[16] Social motivations included attitudes toward government,[17] legitimacy,[18] procedural jus-

TABLE 5.1

Antecedents of Cooperation

	Round 1 (n = 21,531)		*Round 3 (n = 25,397)*	
	Participation in the community	*Voting behavior*	*Participation in the community*	*Voting behavior*
Beta weights				
Social	0.08***	0.12***	0.08***	0.12***
Instrumental	0.04***	0.03***	0.01	–0.01
Adjusted R-squared	12%***	17%***	20%***	5%***

Notes: The equation includes controls for country; two country-level objective indices; age, gender, and education; **$p < .01$; ***$p < .001$.

tice,[19] and trust in specific government institutions.[20] The correlation between social and economic indices was 0.38 ($p < .001$).

The results of the regression analysis are shown in table 5.1.[21] In both of the surveys, people's attitudes, values, identity, and judgments about procedural justice and trust influenced the two cooperative behaviors considered—political participation and voting. Further, that influence was found to be distinct from the effects of instrumental judgments about instrumental issues such as social welfare and the quality of government performance. In Round 1 the influence of social motivations upon participation decisions was twice as strong as that of instrumental motivations, while in Round 3 only social motivations influenced decisions about participation. In Round 1 social motivations were four times as influential in decisions about whether to vote as were instrumental motivations, while in Round 3 only social motivations influenced the decision about whether to vote.

The findings suggest that people are more likely to participate in the political process of their community by attending meetings, raising issues, and contacting government and other authorities when they have favorable social motivations—that is, favorable attitudes, supportive values, a positive identity, a view that the procedures of government are fair, and a trust in political authorities. There is also some evidence that better economic/social conditions (i.e., favorable instrumental conditions) promote cooperation.

An alternative approach to examining the influence of social motivations upon cooperation is to consider the respondents' judgments without including objective information about their social/political environment. This approach was

TABLE 5.2

Antecedents of Cooperation among African Respondents

	Round 1	*Round 3*
Beta weights		
Social motivations	0.31***	0.53***
Instrumental motivations	–0.07*	–0.021***
Adjusted R-squared	6%***	19%***

Notes: *$p < .05$; ***$p < .001$.

used with a structural equation model in which economic and social motivations were treated as indicators of latent factors and were used to predict a latent factor of cooperation. The results are shown in table 5.2.[22]

The results support the suggestion that social motivations have a reliable and distinct influence upon cooperation. And because these results examine that influence when considered alone, they also provide an estimate of the magnitude of that influence. In Round 1, it is 6 percent of the variance in cooperation; in Round 3, 19 percent. This increase reflects the better measurement of both types of motivation in the later round of the Afrobarometer. If we completely exclude instrumental indices from the analysis and simply consider the ability of social motivations to explain cooperation, the amount of variance in cooperation explained for Round 1 is 6 percent, and for Round 3, 18 percent. In other words, the social motivations are the primary factors shaping the overall equations shown in table 5.2, since the amount of variance explained remains essentially the same irrespective of whether instrumental judgments are considered.

These findings reinforce those in table 5.1, which shows that instrumental and social motivations influence cooperation above and beyond the objective nature of people's economic and political environment. Of the two, social motivations show the strongest distinct influence. Further, that effect is consistently positive, with greater procedural justice and trust, stronger favorable attitudes and identity, and more supportive values leading people to engage in more voluntary cooperation. The analysis in table 5.2 similarly supports the argument that social motivations have a distinct positive influence and suggests that their influence can be strong. This strength is most clearly suggested in the Round 3 data, where both social and instrumental motivations are better measured.

As noted at the beginning of this chapter, one motivation for using an African data set is the centrality of instrumental issues to people's lives. For example, in

TABLE 5.3

The Influence of Social Motivations under Varying Economic Situations

	Social welfare		*Economic conditions*		*Laws enforced*	
	Low	*High*	*Poor*	*Good*	*Seldom*	*Often*
Beta weights						
Social motivation	0.80***	0.52***	0.54***	0.48***	0.41***	0.42***
Instrumental motivation	–0.36***	–0.16***	–0.27***	–0.16***	–0.20***	–0.02
Adjusted R-squared	32%	19%	21%	16%	11%	17%

Note: ***$p < .001$.

Round 3, 38 percent indicated going without food several times or more, while 37 percent indicated a similar frequency of going without water, 42 percent without medical care, 66 percent without a cash income, and 30 percent without cooking fuel. Hence, instrumentally based social welfare issues are central to people's lives, and this setting is a key one in which to consider the influence of social motivations. Are people whose lives are focused on issues such as obtaining basic resources still affected by social motivations in deciding whether to be involved in the political process?

To examine the influence of instrumental circumstances on social motivations, respondents were divided at the median on the three instrumental indices: social welfare (frequency of receiving basic services), economic conditions (government performance in dealing with economic problems), and whether or not the laws were enforced against the wealthy and connected.

The structural equation-based regression shown in table 5.2 was then run within the subgroups created. The results are shown in table 5.3. The findings are consistent across the three instrumental variables. First, having a more difficult instrumental situation led people to be more likely to participate in the political process for instrumental reasons. This is reflected in the negative coefficients shown in table 5.3, which consistently indicate that negative circumstances lead to more political behavior. In addition, however, those who have stronger social motivations were consistently found to be more politically cooperative, irrespective of their instrumental circumstances. In fact, to the extent that there is variation, social motivations were more strongly linked to political cooperation under more negative instrumental circumstances. There was no evidence that social motivations became irrelevant under more unfavorable social and economic circumstances, but instrumental issues do become more important.

Discussion

These findings suggest that when we consider an environment where both instrumental and social motivations vary more widely than they did in the American samples already considered, we continue to find strong evidence of the effects of social motivation upon voluntary cooperation. Further, we find these effects upon cooperation to be of a new type—interactions with political authorities and institutions. Here the focus is upon political cooperation, both by generally participating in the political process and by voting. Hence, these findings support the prior suggestion that social motivations shape cooperation.

I have already noted that cooperation with authorities is especially key during times of scarcity and crisis, when collective resources are stressed and greater sacrifices are required from members for a society to be able to prevail. These findings reinforce the view that in such settings social motivations are a key antecedent of the willingness of the public to cooperate in the political process under difficult circumstances. Margaret Levi (1997) gives one example of this connection by showing a link between trust in government and the willingness to serve in the military during wartime, and the findings herein support that suggestion and extend it to the link between social motivations (of which trust is one) and general political cooperation.

Combined with our prior findings these results suggest that, irrespective of whether our focus is on groups, institutions, or society in general, social motivation is an important antecedent of effectiveness because it leads to high levels of engagement and motivation among group members. People who feel connected to groups do what is needed to help them succeed when they feel a link to group authorities and institutions.

The argument that supportive attitudes and values—such as trust and confidence in political authorities and institutions—facilitate group effectiveness parallels the findings reported here based upon studies of managerial and legal authority. All of the types of institutions discussed rely heavily upon the loyalty of their members and, as a result, benefit enormously from members' willingness to "go the extra mile" to help them. Employees who support management are more invested in their jobs and bring to the workplace more creativity and a greater willingness to put in whatever effort is needed to get the job done. The result is that such companies are more likely to prevail in competitive business environments. The degree to which firms have desirable attitudes, such as trust, among their employees shapes the quality and quality of the work performed. Through their influence upon work performed employee attitudes shape the profitability of organizations and, consequently, their likelihood of long-term survival. Similarly, political scientists argue that if citizens support government and are willing to act on its behalf, the government is more stable and effective.

As I have noted, previous authors have argued for the importance of legitimacy to effective governance. These findings support the argument that social motivations play a distinct role in shaping voluntary political behaviors. These findings support that argument, but make the broader point that social motivations, which include legitimacy, have a distinct influence on voluntary cooperation. That point reinforces the argument of the prior chapters which showed a similar effect in managerial and community settings.

The large literature on the value of social capital for communities that has developed in recent years argues that it is important for people to have the types of associations with others that build trust and encourage active political participation (Putnam 2000). Within work organizations researchers have shown the importance of voluntary extra-role behaviors to the effectiveness of work organizations (Tyler and Blader 2000). And legal authorities have emphasized the centrality of public cooperation to efforts to maintain social order. Hence, the importance of being able to engage people's internal motivations has become more widely recognized.

Policy Implications

The data examined herein explore the influence of social motivations, including trust and procedural justice, upon participation in the political process in Africa. They suggest that social motivations shape cooperative behavior in this environment, one characterized by high levels of instrumental need and wide variations in procedural justice, trustworthiness, institutional legitimacy, identification with society, and supportive attitudes toward government. Hence, these findings suggest the breadth of the findings already outlined and their potential applicability to a wide variety of social contexts.

Implications

The Psychology of Cooperation

T he key concern addressed in this volume is how to most effectively motivate cooperative behavior in groups. The analyses in the prior chapters
suggest that social motivations are generally important in any effort to
motivate cooperation within groups, organizations, communities, or societies.
And this is especially the case when voluntary cooperation is at stake. While
the prior chapters address this point directly, they do not consider a subsequent
question arising from the importance of social motivations. That question is how
to best understand the interrelation among social motivations. This issue is addressed by Tom Tyler and Steven Blader (2000, 2003) in the context of the group
engagement model. Here I want to address this question by distinguishing between those aspects of social motivation that are directly linked to group structure—group-based policies and practices—and those social motivations that are
dispositional in character. This distinction is important because it is those social motivations that are linked to group-based policies and practices that shape
dispositions and influence cooperative behaviors. They need to be the focus of
efforts to motivate desired behavior. Procedural justice and trust are elements of
groups that are linked to their policies and practices and therefore can be shaped
by changes in how groups function. They are, therefore, the natural focus of efforts at institutional design.

Procedural Justice

The argument underlying the procedural justice literature is that people defer to
decisions because those decisions are made through fair processes. This procedural justice effect is found to be distinct from the influence of concerns about
either outcome favorability or outcome fairness. As such, procedural justice provides a way for acceptable decisions to be made in situations in which people
cannot be given what they want or feel they deserve. Similarly, the literature on
trust argues that people will defer to authorities that they infer are trustworthy
(Tyler and Huo 2002).[1]

John Thibaut and Laurens Walker (1975) conducted the original procedural
justice research, and their hope was that people would be willing to accept out-

comes because those outcomes are fairly decided upon—that is, because of the justice of the decision-making procedures used to achieve them. Thibaut and Walker performed the first systematic set of experiments designed to show the impact of procedural justice. Their studies demonstrate that people's assessments of the fairness of third-party decision-making procedures independently shape their satisfaction with their outcomes. This finding has been widely confirmed in subsequent laboratory studies of procedural justice (Lind and Tyler 1988; Tyler et al. 1997).

The original hope of Thibaut and Walker was that the willingness of all the parties to a dispute to accept decisions that they viewed as fairly arrived at would provide a mechanism through which social conflicts could be resolved. Subsequent studies find that when third-party decisions are fairly made, people are more willing to voluntarily accept them (Kitzman and Emery 1993; Lind et al. 1993; MacCoun et al. 1988; Wissler 1995). What is striking about these studies is that procedural justice effects are found in studies of real disputes, in real settings. They confirm the earlier experimental findings of Thibaut and Walker. The results of procedural justice research are optimistic about the ability of social authorities to bridge differences in interests and values and to make decisions that the parties to a dispute will accept. Their arguments point to a particular perspective on institutional design and provide evidence to support that perspective.

Procedural justice judgments are found to have an especially important role in shaping adherence to agreements over time. For example, Dean Pruitt and colleagues have studied the factors that lead those involved in disputes to adhere to mediation agreements that end disputes (Pruitt et al. 1993). They find that procedural fairness judgments about the initial mediation session are a central determinant of whether people are adhering to the mediation agreement six months later.

A second study also suggests that procedural justice encourages long-term obedience to the law. Raymond Paternoster and colleagues examined the long-term behavior of people who dealt with the police because the police were called to their home on a domestic violence call (Paternoster et al. 1997). In such cases the problem was typically that a man was abusing his spouse/significant other. When they were at the person's home the police could threaten the man, and even arrest and take him into custody. The researchers explored the impact of various police actions upon the man's likelihood of committing future abuse. Their study found that a strong predictor of future rule-breaking was whether the man involved experienced his treatment by the police as fair. If he did, he was less likely to break the law in the future.

Beyond the fairness of the manner in which authorities make particular decisions, studies generally find that when a climate or culture of procedural justice characterizes an institution, compliance with rules is more widespread and more easily obtained. Consider the case of prisons, institutions that people often think of as highly coercive. Even in prisons authorities seek and benefit from cooperation by prisoners, and studies of prisons suggest that the fair administration of prison rules facilitates such cooperation (Sparks, Bottoms, and Hay 1996).

The argument that legitimacy is rooted in the fair exercise of authority is not a new one, or one that only applies to policing. Philip Selznick's classic examination of industrial settings makes a similar point about workplace rules, commenting that "There is a demand that the rules be legitimate, not only in emanating from established authority, but also in the manner of their formulation, in the way they are applied, and in their fidelity to agreed-upon institutional purposes. The idea spreads that the obligation to obey has some relation to the quality of the rules and the integrity of their administration" (1969, 29). This argument has received widespread support in studies of employee behavior in workplaces (see, e.g., Tyler and Blader 2000).

Similarly, discussions of national level legal authority—in particular, the U.S. Supreme Court—emphasize that its legitimacy is linked to public views about the fairness of its decision making procedures. Walter Murphy and Joseph Tanenhaus (1968) have noted that the Court has retained a substantial reservoir of public support even when it makes unpopular decisions. They attribute this continued support for the legitimacy of the Court's role as an interpreter of the U.S. Constitution to the public belief that the Court's decisions are principled applications of legal rules and not political in character. This point has been emphasized by members of the Court itself, when arguing that it must present an image of "principled" decision making to retain public support (Tyler and Mitchell 1994).

Motive-based Trust

This analysis treats motive-based trust as developing in parallel with procedural justice. Of the two constructs, it is motive-based trust that is the less clearly defined. Procedural justice refers to definable procedural features. On the other hand, trust is an inference about something unobserved—the intentions, motives, and character of an authority. However, as Fritz Heider recognized in his classic work on interpersonal perception (1959), it is this unobservable set of motives and intentions that people infer from the behaviors that they observe in others. And studies in groups consistently find that people place considerable weight upon their inferences about other's character and motives (Tyler and Degoey 1996), using such judgments to evaluate and respond to people's actions.

Hence, the same action can be responded to very differently depending upon inferences about the motives that underlie it. In this analysis, trust and procedural justice are treated as two aspects of group-based policies and practices.

Testing the Model

Is a focus on procedural justice and motive-based trust a good way to shape dispositions and motivate voluntary cooperation? In other words, if we distinguish between policies and practices (procedural justice, trust), dispositions (attitudes, values, identification), and cooperative behaviors, is there evidence that policies and practices shape cooperation by influencing dispositions?

This argument can be tested using causal modeling and the panel datasets that have already been outlined: one on employees in work settings, the other on residents in communities. First, consider the panel study of employees. We can create latent variables to reflect three constructs: social motivations (procedural justice, motive-based trust), instrumental motivations, and dispositions (attitudes, values, identity). Using those latent constructs, the influence of group-based policies and practices upon attitudes and cooperative behaviors can be examined.

Figure 6.1 examines the influence of group-based policies and practices upon dispositions and on voluntary rule-following within the sample of employees. Figure 6.2 presents a similar analysis using extra-role behavior as the dependent variable. In each analysis the dispositions and behaviors in the model are those measured during the second-wave interviews, while social motivations and instrumental judgments are measured during the first-wave interviews. As a consequence, the causal flow is from group-based policies and practices to dispositions and behaviors. And because the design is a panel design it is possible to control for the influence of cooperation as reported during the first interview.

In both cases the panel analyses results support the argument that a focus upon social motivations is a good way to understand how to shape dispositions and influence cooperative behavior in work settings. In both social motivations are the primary factor shaping dispositions, with a secondary influence of instrumental motivations. Hence, loyalty to groups is strongly related to evaluating those groups as having fair procedures and trustworthy authorities. And people are more strongly loyal to those groups that deliver desired resources.

The results also indicate that dispositions shape voluntary cooperation. In both models there are no direct paths from either social or instrumental aspects of group-based policies and practices. Rather, both paths flow through disposi-

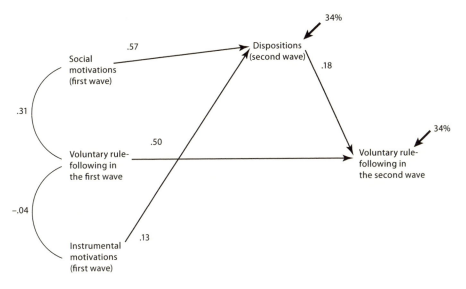

FIGURE 6.1. Employee voluntary rule-following (CFI = 0.81).

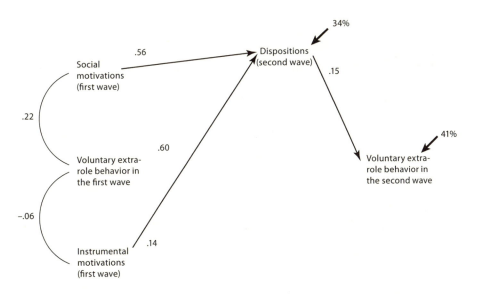

FIGURE 6.2. Employee extra-role behavior (CFI = 0.80).

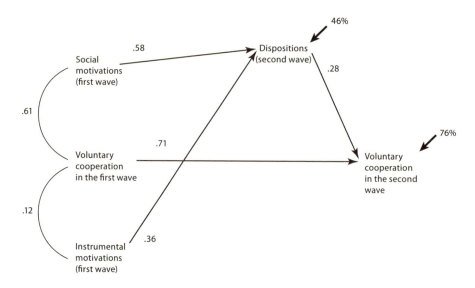

FIGURE 6.3. Voluntary cooperation with the police (CFI = 0.83).

tions. Hence, developing favorable dispositions toward the group is the key to promoting voluntary behavior. Although two distinct types of voluntary behavior are considered—voluntary rule-following and extra-role behavior—what is most striking about the analyses is their similarity. There are no differences linked to what type of voluntary cooperation is at issue.

Figure 6.3 shows a similar analysis of cooperation in the case of the residents of New York whose panel interviews were considered in chapter 4 and focus on their willingness to cooperate with the police. In this case, the issue is the willingness to engage in actions that help the police to manage social order in one's community either by reporting crime and criminals or by joining collective efforts to police the community. This could be motivated by instrumental judgments, such as the effectiveness of the performance of the police, or by social motivations, including identification with the police, judgments about their legitimacy and morality, and the favorability of attitudes toward them. Again, voluntary cooperation flows from favorable dispositions that are shaped primarily by procedural justice and motive-based trust, but also by instrumental evaluations. In this case, the balance between social motivations and instrumental motivations is more even, with instrumental motivations having a greater role in shaping dispositions. However, as before, the influence of both social and instrumental motivations flows through dispositions.

The Influence of Social Motivations on Dispositions

These analyses indicate that policies and practices shape dispositions, and through them influence voluntary cooperation. The link to dispositions is important because it shows the effect of policies and practices on people's general orientation toward their group. In other words, the particular actions taken by authorities and the policies they adopt have a broad and long-lasting impact upon people because they lead to a general disposition toward the group. This general orientation then shapes whatever forms of cooperative behavior are relevant in any given context and at any particular moment.

Further, while the figures in this chapter show an overall effect of policies and practices upon dispositions a separate analysis of each disposition indicates that in both of the studies procedural justice and motive-based trust have a distinct influence upon each of the four dispositions: identification with the police, attitudes toward the police, legitimacy, and moral value congruence.

Process-based Design

The analyses outlined provide a theoretical framework for understanding the psychology underlying cooperation. Process-based design is a strategy for managing within groups, organizations, communities, and societies that is based upon the arguments of this psychological model. Such an approach can be applied to work organizations through process-based management, to law with process-based regulation, and in politics via process-based governance.

In unpacking the social motivations described in the model it is important to make a distinction between group-based policies and practices that lead authorities to be viewed as procedurally just and trustworthy, dispositional factors (attitudes, values), identity, and cooperative behaviors. The reason for making this distinction is to allow a focus on strategies for building social motivation and securing high levels of voluntary cooperation.

The goal here is to articulate and support empirically a model for exercising authority in groups, organizations, and communities that I believe provides authorities with useful insights about how to create and sustain motivation. This model is process-based. Process-based design applies the ideas of the social psychology of procedural justice (Lind and Tyler 1988; Tyler 2001; Tyler et al. 1997; Tyler and Lind 1992; Tyler and Smith 1998) and motive-based trust (Tyler and Huo 2002) to issues central to all types of groups. This volume presents a particular perspective on the psychology of justice and on its implications for the dynamics of groups, organizations, and communities.

As I will demonstrate, research in widely disparate types of groups suggests that common principles underlie motivation across diverse settings. My suggestion is that these common principles inform the exercise of authority irrespective of whether a person is managing a group, an organization, or a community, and irrespective of whether one is wielding legal, political, managerial, or some other form of authority. Of course, context matters, and there are distinct issues within any particular type of group. However, my goal in this volume is to stress what is common across these diverse types of social settings.

I will contrast the process-based approach to group design to the instrumentally based command-and-control model of authority. This model concentrates collective resources in authorities, who then use those resources to shape the behavior of group members via strategies involving the use of incentives and sanctions. Studies suggest that such approaches are able to shape cooperative behavior. However, as I have already outlined in some detail, they are often costly and inefficient, and I argue that process-based approaches are a valuable addition to the strategies that authorities can use to motivate behavior in groups.

It is difficult to attempt management in a process-based manner because it goes against our intuitions about "human nature." As noted earlier, the "the myth of self-interest" has been coined in recognition of the widespread belief in our society that people are motivated by the desire for personal gain. People, themselves, describe their motivations, as well as the motivations of others, as being to gain all that they can for themselves. Further, people think about such gains in terms of material gains—that is, as money, possessions, power. So we "know" that people really care about outcomes, and it is difficult not to manage based upon the belief that people's thoughts, feelings, and behaviors are shaped by their reactions to the favorability and fairness of the resources they gain or lose when dealing with others.

We tend to assume that people are motivated by the level and favorability of the resources they receive in groups. So we expect that people will work harder if paid more, will follow the rules if they think they would be caught and punished for breaking them, and will leave a group when given the opportunity to move to a group with greater resources and opportunities.

This view of human motivation flows easily into a widespread model of authority—the command-and-control model—that argues that authorities manage by providing incentives for desired behaviors and threatening or delivering sanctions for undesirable behavior. By deploying their resources, authorities can shape the gains and loses experienced by those within their groups and thereby shape their behavior.

The process-based and command-and-control models differ in several ways. First, they differ in their view about how to exercise authority in groups. Instrumental approaches lend themselves to a command-and-control approach to the exercise of authority. Resources and power are concentrated in authorities, who then deploy those resources in systems of incentives and sanctions. Second, they differ in their view about the goal of authorities. Instrumental approaches focus on the aim of creating and maintaining structures within which people's behavior is instrumentally motivated to move in line with group goals. The maintenance of desired behavior requires the continued presence of systems for delivering incentives and for the surveillance of behavior and the delivery of sanctions.

The process-based approach to design focuses on the concerns of those people within a group. It builds systems of authority and management in an effort to understand and connect with the concerns of the individuals within the group. Because this model builds itself on the premise that people's own internal judgments are motivating, it seeks to activate those internal motivations. Once activated, these motivations are separate from instrumental aspects of the person's relationship to the group. Hence, the process-based model is based on the idea of gaining commitment from group members by focusing on their perspective about what a just group climate is. This climate includes, but is not necessarily limited to, group procedures for decision making. It also involves how people are treated by authorities during decision making, something typically found to be influential in shaping trust. This leads to supportive attitudes and values and a merging of self and group in the formation of identity (Tyler and Blader 2000).

These two sets of motivations—instrumental and process-based—are not completely independent of one another. And it is not necessary that they be independent for process-based approaches to be an effective strategy. What is important is that process-based motivations be distinct from instrumental motivations, something tested in the studies examined in this volume. Of course, instrumental motivations also support identity and can potentially join with social motivations in building identity and encouraging cooperation.[2]

As intuitively plausible as the outcome-based view of human nature and motivation is, research does not support it as an exclusive focus. Process-based management builds on that research by focusing on other issues that people are actually found to care about, including processes and the motivations of authorities.

One simple reason to focus on procedures is that, as has been shown, people's cooperation within organizations is strongly shaped by their judgments about processes. Although people could potentially make decisions about whether to accept decisions, whether to work hard, and/or whether to stay or leave based upon either outcomes or processes, research consistently finds that people are actually the most strongly influenced by their process-based judgments and their assessments of the trustworthiness of authorities. Process-based approaches build directly on this finding by leading to the exercise of authority in ways that shape these judgments. By so doing, those engaged in the process-based exercise of authority are managing by giving people what they want when they deal with authorities and organizations. People want to experience fair processes, and they want to feel that the authorities and institutions with whom they are dealing are worthy of their trust. By focusing on exercising authority in ways that connect with these human desires, authorities can more effectively gain desirable behavior from those within their groups.

While social and instrumental motivations can act in conjunction, as noted, it is also important to remember that instrumental motivations can undermine social motivations. Further, even when they act in concert, there are reasons to prefer social motivations. In particular, even when they are effective, instrumental motivations require large amounts of collective resources to deliver incentives and/or maintain credible sanctioning risks. Social motivations do not require the use of such collective resources and can, therefore, free up resources for other group tasks.

A further gain associated with process-based approaches is that they build up supportive attitudes and values among group members. Such attitudes and values are desirable because when people have these internal motivations, they are personally motivated to engage in desirable behaviors and do so without the need for incentives or surveillance. Their behavior becomes self-motivated in the sense that their actions are governed by their own values and are not linked to external resources. Hence, an additional reason for focusing on the process-based issues of procedural justice and trust is that these judgments about experience have a strong influence on people's internal motivations—that is, their attitudes and values. People can potentially be motivated by either extrinsic or internal motivations, but the advantages of self-motivation are clear.

Tom Tyler (2009) presents this argument in the context of law and legal authority, arguing for a self-regulatory approach to social order. The point here is similar. However, regulation has traditionally dealt with only one aspect of cooperation: stopping undesirable behavior. The broader argument here is that self-motivation leads both to self-regulation and also to the desire to do what helps groups.

Elements of Procedural Justice

An understanding of the elements of procedural fairness that form the basis for process-based management strategies can best be based on the four-component model of procedural justice, which was developed in work settings (Blader and Tyler 2003b). This model identifies four procedural components, or evaluations, each of which contributes to overall procedural justice judgments. Those components are defined by (1) two distinct aspects of organizational processes, and (2) two sources of information about procedures. Each of these four components influences employee definitions of procedural justice.

One of the aspects of organizational processes considered in the model refers to the organization's decision-making procedures. Specifically, the model considers employees' evaluations of the *quality of decision making* in their organization. Consideration of these evaluations links to the elements of legal procedures and emphasizes issues of decision maker neutrality, the objectivity and factuality of decision making, and the consistency of rule application (Lind and Tyler 1988; Tyler and Lind 1992).

There is a distinct, but potentially equally important, issue involving *the quality of people's treatment by organizational authorities*. Quality of interpersonal treatment constitutes the second aspect of organizational processes. Quality of treatment involves treatment with politeness and dignity, concern for people's rights, and other aspects of procedures that are not directly linked to the decisions being made through the procedure.

Each of these two aspects of procedures (quality of decision making, quality of treatment) can potentially be linked to two sources of procedure. One source of information involves *the rules of the organization*. The formal rules and structures of the organization, as well as statements of organizational values, communicate information about organizational procedures. For example, organizations vary in terms of whether they have formal grievance procedures that allow people to voice complaints. They also differ in their statements of corporate values ("corporate vision statements"). One common formal organizational statement that concerns relationships among employees is to "treat each other with respect, dignity, and common courtesy" and "express disagreements openly and respectfully." These are both statements about the type of procedures that the corporation views as reflecting its values.

The other source of information is *an employee's experience with his supervisor or supervisors*. While they are constrained by formal institutions and procedures, organizational authorities typically have considerable discretion concerning the manner in which they implement decision-making procedures and how they make decisions regarding issues that have no formal procedures associated with them. Further, they have a great deal of flexibility about how they treat those with whom they deal. The same decision-making procedure can be implemented in a way that emphasizes the dignity of those involved, or employees can be treated rudely or dismissively. A similar situation is found with the law. There are formal laws and rules constraining the conduct of police officers and judges. However, those authorities typically have considerable latitude in the manner in which they exercise their authority within the framework of those rules.

TABLE 6.1

Components of Procedural Justice: Employees

Beta weights	*Procedural justice*	
Organizational-level decision making	.44***	.29***
Organizational-level treatment	.26***	.22***
Work-group-level decision making	.09***	.06***
Work-group-level treatment	.33***	.29***
Instrumental judgments	—	.45***
Adjusted R.-squared	38%	42%

Note: ***$p < .001$.

The four-component model argues that each of the four elements defined by these two dimensions has an important role in the definition of the fairness of procedures. While the four-component model provides a guideline for the types of evaluations that compose overall evaluations of an organization's procedural justice, the essential argument advanced here is that the nature of those evaluations is noninstrumental and nonmaterial. Neither of the aspects of organizational processes emphasized in this model of the antecedents of procedural justice (quality of decision making, quality of treatment) is directly linked to evaluations of the favorability or fairness of the outcomes people receive.

The four-component model highlights a set of procedural criteria that are distinct from judgments about the favorability or fairness of employee's outcomes. This is, of course, typical of procedures in any type of organization. We can, for example, distinguish the adversary trial procedure from the verdict of the trial, and can contrast that procedure to other ways of making decisions, such as the inquisitorial trial procedure.

Is the four-component model supported by the findings of the studies outlined? To test the model the four components were measured in the study of employees, and a structural equation model–based regression analysis was used to test the influence of each component on overall judgments of procedural justice and motive-based trust. This test was conducted with and without controls on instrumental judgments. The instrumental judgments were treated as indicators of a single observable indicator of instrumental elements of the job.

The results of the analysis are shown in table 6.1. They support the suggestion of the four-component model in finding that the four elements each contribute to overall procedural justice, irrespective of whether instrumental judgments are included in the equation. The four-component model is a good framework

TABLE 6.2

Components of Procedural Justice: Community

Beta weights	Procedural justice	
Community-level decision making	0.19***	0.18***
Community-level treatment	0.42***	0.41***
Instrumental judgments	—	0.07**
Adjusted R.-squared	34%	28%

Note: **$p < .01$; ***$p < .001$.

within which to understand the organizational policies and practices that are central to justice.

A similar analysis was conducted using the community-based sample and similar results are shown in table 6.2.[3] In this case, overall indices of decision making and interpersonal treatment were used, since there is no parallel distinction between work group and organization; hence, the judgments are community level assessments. Again, both decision making and interpersonal treatment were important for procedural justice, irrespective of whether instrumental judgments were controlled for.

Trust

I have presented a four-component model that is shown to have wide applicability. It focuses upon two key components: quality of decision making and quality of interpersonal treatment. These two elements are found to have distinct influence, an influence that occurs both at the general organizational level and in subgroups, such as work groups in organizations. How does this analysis relate to issues of trust? In contrast to the literature on procedural justice, the literature on trust has not developed a detailed model of the antecedents of trust. As a consequence, this analysis will consider the influence of the same aspects of policy and practices that have been shown to shape procedural justice.

Why Are Authorities Trusted?

The analysis in this volume follows that of Tom Tyler and Yuen Huo (2002) and treats trust as a distinct aspect of authorities, not something that is part of procedural justice. But the two are intertwined. Trust is sometimes seen as an an-

TABLE 6.3

Components of Trust: Employees

Beta weights	Motive-based trust	
Organizational-level decision making	0.40***	0.28***
Organizational-level treatment	0.45***	0.43***
Work-group-level decision making	0.22***	0.21***
Work-group-level treatment	0.40***	0.37***
Instrumental judgments	—	0.39***
Adjusted R-squared	57%	60%

Note: ***$p < .001$.

TABLE 6.4

Components of Trust: Community

Beta weights	Motive-based trust	
Community-level decision making	0.14***	0.14***
Community level treatment	0.76***	0.76***
Instrumental judgments	—	0.02***
Adjusted R-squared	77%	77%

Note: ***$p < .001$.

tecedent of procedural justice, and sometimes treated as occurring in parallel to procedural justice. When we do treat trust as an antecedent of procedural justice we typically find that it is the most important issue shaping procedural justice judgments in the context of personal experiences with an authority. When we treat trust and procedural justice as independent we find that both contribute strongly to decision acceptance.

Treating trust as distinct from procedural justice allows the issue of what promotes trust to be directly addressed. One element revealed as important in these analyses is the quality of decision making. If people are allowed to present their concerns to a neutral authority, they are more likely to trust it. Further, when people feel treated with dignity and respect they are more trusting. Authorities can facilitate these beliefs by justifying their decisions in ways that make clear that they have considered the arguments raised and either can or cannot accept those arguments. It is also important for authorities to make clear that they are sincerely interested in the well-being of the parties involved—for example, through acknowledging the needs of those involved, the difficulties they may be operating under, and/or their efforts to act in good faith.

Although the framework for understanding policies and practices used to consider trust was developed in the context of procedural justice, it also helps us to understand motive-based trust. Hence, the elements of fair decision making and just interpersonal treatment that shape overall assessments about the fairness of group procedures also shape trust in group authorities. These two judgments are clearly intertwined, and regardless of whether we treat them as distinct and parallel influences or consider trust as an element of procedural justice, the broader implication is the same. Policies and practices of the type outlined shape dispositions and influence cooperation.

Implications

The underlying theme of this volume is that there are similarities across groups irrespective of whether they are groups involved in management, regulation, or governance. At the same time it is equally important to consider the particular concerns associated with each arena and explore the issues those distinct concerns raise for the general model.

Application to For-profit Work Organizations: Process-based Management

The central implication of these findings is that policies and practices shaping procedural justice and trust are the key to voluntary cooperation. This is true of both the motivation to follow rules, which shapes corporate regulation, and the motivation to work on behalf of one's company, which influences effort to do one's job, as well as willingness to engage in voluntary, extra-role behaviors, designed to enhance company productivity and success. The value of such positive actions has already been outlined and supported by Tom Tyler and Steven Blader (2000), who review literature that emphasizes the link of extra-role behavior, in particular, to organizational success.

The management arena is especially useful for a comparison of instrumental and social motivations because it provides opportunities for both rewarding desirable behavior and punishing undesirable behavior. And prior efforts to estimate the impact of instrumental variables on attitudes and behaviors in work environments find stronger instrumental influences than do studies that consider only the role of sanctions in regulatory settings (see Podsakoff et al. 2006). Therefore it is particularly important that the data from work settings—in particular, the general study of workers—suggests that social motivations play a central role in motivating voluntary cooperation.

The central implication of the general study of workers is that work environments should be structured with a focus on procedural justice and trust, since these factors shape dispositions and, through them, motivate positive efforts to both do one's job and engage in voluntary extra-role behaviors motivated by the desire to help one's organization. This finding is strong in empirical terms and consistent across both methods of analysis and diverse workplace contexts. It supports the argument made elsewhere that organizational structures need to focus upon how to best motivate employees, which is a key to organizational success (Pfeffer 1994). This analysis supports the results of an earlier study by Tyler and Blader (2000) by suggesting that the best way to achieve this objective is to focus upon social motivations—in particular, upon creating an environment characterized by procedural justice and trust in authorities, two aspects of organizational design that are easy to develop and sustain.

Of course, organizational design should not only focus upon procedural justice and trust. The results of the analyses of employees suggests that extra-role behavior is also responsive to instrumental judgments (see chapter 6). This accords with the widespread suggestion that incentives can influence productivity (see Guzzo, Jette, and Katzell 1985), and especially in-role performance (Locke and Latham 1991). However, the results of this study suggest that when incentives and/or sanctions do influence cooperative behavior in work settings, their role is secondary and strongest when in-role and not extra-role behavior is being examined. Given the centrality of voluntary behaviors to workplace success this supports the value of a focus on social motivations.

Managing Corporate Misconduct

While the general link between self-regulation and productivity has already been illustrated by Tyler and Blader (2000), a goal of this volume is to indicate how this shift in perspective is important to organizational design. I will use two recently important issues to address this question: corporate governance and managing agents of social control.

An example of how the shift in focus advocated in this volume is relevant to current issues in corporate structure and governance is provided by the efforts being made in companies today to ensure that employees do not engage in unethical conduct (Tyler, Dienhart, and Thomas 2007). Ethics and compliance programs in work organizations began in the 1980s in the defense industry. That industry's scandals of the 1980s, and the 1991 Federal Sentencing Guidelines for Organizations, are credited with the rapid spread of ethics and compliance offices in organizations. As the number of ethics officers grew, the development of national organizations such as the Ethics and Compliance Officers Association and the Ethics Resource Center followed (Schminke 1998; Trevino and Nelson 2007). These early programs were focused on compliance and took a command-and-control approach. They consisted of rules, and stipulated penalties for employees when they violated those rules. In other words, they were instrumentally focused.

By the 1990s, ethics and compliance programs began to shift to a "values" or "integrity" focus. Lynn Sharp Paine (1994) has contrasted command-and-control compliance programs with market-oriented values-based programs. A compliance approach rests on rules enforced by external force—usually from the company itself, but with threats of civil and criminal punishment lurking in the background. Unfortunately, when employees are not monitored, the fear of being caught and punished diminishes and compliance declines.

The values approach, Paine argues, rests on employees governing their own behavior by voluntarily choosing such behavior in the same manner as one chooses the most appealing product in the marketplace—that is, with employees being internally motivated to engage in ethical behavior in work settings. Paine argues that the goal is to have employees engage with and adopt the values of the organization as their own. When this occurs, employees are more likely to comply with rules even when they are not monitored. Such employees come to be good stewards of the company's values, helping to instill them in new employees and actively discouraging those who seek to violate them. Ethics and compliance programs based on values view the organization's policies as principles to which an employee is encouraged to willingly adhere—an approach consistent with the social motivation model.

In 1999, Linda Trevino and colleagues undertook an organizational study on the relative merits of these two approaches. The study (Trevino et al. 1999) was the first large-scale attempt to measure and compare the effectiveness of compliance-based and values-based business conduct programs, and supports Paine's contention that a values approach is more effective than a compliance approach. The researchers surveyed 10,000 employees in six industries. Compared to compliance-based programs, values-based programs had fewer reports of unethical conduct, higher levels of ethical awareness, more employees seeking advice about ethical issues, and a higher likelihood of employees reporting violations. Employee commitment, in particular, was found to be much higher in a values-based program than in a compliance-based program.

Trevino and colleagues also looked at ethical culture as a factor separate from formal programs, and here the results were especially eye-opening. Culture had more influence on employee behavior than did either ethics or compliance programs, regardless of their focus. The top five features of cultures in which employees most frequently followed the rules were, in order of strength: supervisory leadership, fair treatment, rewarding ethical behavior (tied with fair treatment), executive leadership, and punishing unethical behavior. In other words, if we ask what the most important things are that supervisors and executives can do to create an ethical culture, these data suggest that among the key factors would be treating employees fairly, rewarding ethical behavior, and punishing unethical behavior.

Overall, Trevino and her coauthors found that a values approach increased compliance better than a command-and-control approach. In other words, like the findings in this volume, it supported a social motivational approach to cooperation rather than an instrumental approach. Self-regulation emerged as a key to the management of misconduct.

The research by Tyler and Blader (2000) further supports the importance of culture, finding that estimates of the likelihood of being caught and punished for wrongdoing has a less powerful influence on rule related behavior than did two key values. The first value was the belief that authorities were legitimate and ought to be obeyed. The second value was the belief that company policies were moral. These two values are the values considered in this analysis within the larger framework of social motivations.

The Trevino and colleagues and Tyler and Blader studies make two important points. First, they show that engaging the internal values of employees strongly influences compliance behavior in the workplace. External threats of punishment have a weaker influence. Second, they suggest that the organizational culture can engage employee values to promote ethical and compliance behavior. These findings are united in supporting the role of institutional design and suggesting that it is the values of the culture within groups that need to be effectively created and maintained.

The influence of culture on employee behavior established by Trevino and colleagues (1999) is an important finding. However, it has been difficult to operationalize these insights about "culture" due to the nebulous nature of the term itself. In particular, those seeking to use these findings have not known which elements of culture were most important in shaping employee behavior.

In this analysis, I use empirical research to identify and argue for the importance of those aspects of organizations ("cultural elements") that are linked to procedural justice and motive-based trust. Procedural justice/motive-based trust are important because they shape the extent to which it is possible to build a values-based organizational culture. And, I argue, procedurally just cultures not only promote compliance but increase the probability that employees will become committed to their organizations' values and go beyond their job descriptions to help the organization succeed. In particular, employees will voluntarily follow rules. Psychological research findings in a number of organizational settings support the conclusions reported here and suggest that the fairness of organizational procedures is especially important (Cohen-Charash and Spector 2001; Colquitt et al. 2001).

This research has several practical implications for ethics and compliance programs. First, it suggests that the main target of such programs should be organizational culture, since culture is the major influence of employee behavior. This means focusing on building employee attitudes and values toward, and identification with, the organization. To do so, the focus should be on ensuring that decisions in organizations are made in procedurally fair ways so as to communicate the trustworthiness of managerial authorities.

One of the organizational and policy implications of this argument is worth noting now. The importance of procedural fairness/motive-based trust to an ethical culture has implications for companies that want to meet the organizational culture standard in the revised Federal Sentencing Guidelines for Organizations. The guidelines state that organizations should "promote an organizational culture that encourages ethical conduct and a commitment to compliance with the law." Creating and maintaining such a culture requires that employees regard the rules and procedures of the organization as fundamentally fair and view managerial authorities as trustworthy.

The literature in this area, including the studies outlined in this volume, argue for three propositions. The first is that employees are more likely to follow rules if they view management as legitimate and managerial policies as moral and if they identify with the company. The second is that procedural justice and motive-based trust are powerful factors in shaping employees' judgments that their management is legitimate, that their management policies are moral, and that they as employees can identify with the company. The third is that employees who believe that their workplace is procedurally fair and their managers trustworthy are more likely to go beyond their job descriptions to help their organizations. It is this final point that moves beyond regulation. Policies and practices that lead to rule-following also lead to voluntary helping, suggesting that while focusing upon ethical issues companies can also engage in policies and practices that improve their productivity and capacity to succeed in competitive business environments.

The core elements of procedural justice and motive-based trust have already been outlined. Prior studies of procedural justice in work settings identify two key dimensions of employee procedural fairness judgments: fairness of decision making and fairness of interpersonal treatment. These two types of fairness can be evaluated at the organizational and work group levels. This results in four procedural factors: decision-making fairness at the organizational level, interpersonal fairness at the organizational level, decision-making fairness at the work group level, and interpersonal fairness at the work group level.

Studies suggest that employees are influenced by all four of these aspects of procedural justice. At the organizational level employees evaluate the procedural fairness of their overall organization, its policies and procedures, and the actions of the CEO and board. Separately, they assess the fairness of the procedures used by their work group supervisor and coworkers. At each level both aspects of procedure—decision making and interpersonal fairness—independently and collectively contribute to overall procedural justice evaluations.

The most obvious aspect of procedures is that they are mechanisms for making decisions. When thinking about those mechanisms, employees evaluate fairness along several dimensions. First, do they have opportunities for input before decisions are made? Second, are decisions made following understandable and transparent rules? Third, are decision-making bodies acting neutrally, basing their decisions upon objective information and appropriate criteria, rather than acting out of personal prejudices and biases? Fourth, are the rules applied consistently across people and over time?

Quality of interpersonal treatment is found to be equally important. It involves the manner in which people are treated during the decision-making process. First, are people's rights as employees respected? For example, do managers follow the rules specified in organizational manuals or employment contracts? Second, is their right as a person to be treated politely and with dignity acknowledged, and does such treatment occur? Third, do managers consider employee input when making decisions, and are the decision makers concerned about employee needs and concerns when they make decisions? Finally, do the decision makers account for their actions by giving honest explanations about what they have decided and why they made their decisions?

As I have noted, research shows that each of these four aspects of the policies and practices of an organization plays a distinct role in shaping employee judgments about whether their workplace is fair (Blader and Tyler 2003a, 2003b). My argument is supported by empirical analyses in which the influence of the four elements is considered and the results indicate that each element is independently important, with employees considering organizational level issues of decision making and interpersonal quality of treatment as well as work group/supervisor level judgments of the same two issues.

Ethics and compliance officers can improve the ethical culture of their organizations by focusing on two levels: the work group and the organizational level. On each level they can target two issues: the quality of decision making and the quality of interpersonal treatment.

Efforts to improve the quality of decision making could potentially involve managers discussing issues of importance with employees before making a decision; making efforts to more clearly articulate the procedures being used for pay and promotion decisions, as well as the criteria involved; and highlighting the consistency in decision making across people to minimize the belief that some people receive favorable treatment or that others are subject to prejudice or other biases.

The quality of interpersonal treatment is improved when the focus is upon respecting employees and their rights, both as employees and as people. People in all organizations value their good standing in the group, and treatment with courtesy and dignity affirms that they are valued and respected.

Also, employees want to trust management and to believe that those who make decisions care about their needs, concerns, and well-being. While studies often find that employees are cynical about their managers, they consistently show that employees who are asked about what they want in a workplace indicate that they want to work for people that they trust (Tyler and Blader 2005). Managers can communicate that they are trustworthy by listening to their employees and, when implementing decisions, accounting for their actions by explaining how they have considered the employees—that is, by acting using fair procedures.

Getting employee input does not mean that managers must do what employees suggest; regardless of the ultimate outcome, employees tend to accept management decisions when they feel that their perspective has been considered during the decision-making process, even if their preferred course of action is not taken. Nor do employees need voice for all decisions and procedures. I am by no means advocating management's abdication of the responsibility to make decisions. I do, however, suggest that transparency in the process of decision making will result in higher levels of employee buy-in and satisfaction.

Ethics and compliance officers often complain that they are cast in the position of naysayers—telling others in their companies that they cannot engage in profitable activities because those activities violate ethical precepts or codes of behavior. Because their work is framed in command-and-control terms they are agents of regulation, seeking to identify wrongdoing and wrongdoers who will be subject to sanctioning.

I believe that there is room for an expanded role for ethics and compliance officers in for-profit companies that brings them into alignment with the general management goal of increasing productivity and building company worth. This is true because, beyond motivating rule adherence, the strategies I have outlined have the additional benefit of more broadly engaging employees in their work organizations, leading them to be willing to engage in voluntary activities on behalf of their companies. Hence, there is a win-win solution in which the strategies advocated for motivating desirable rule adherence also motivate generally valuable workplace behaviors that are linked to company profitability. As has been clear from the research outlined in this volume, the same psychological model that motivates voluntary rule adherence also motivates efforts to work hard to help one's organization succeed.

Consider the case of the corporate bankers mentioned in chapter 3. Their multinational organization benefits when these bankers are more willing to act voluntarily on behalf of their firm, doing things at work that help the company but for which they will not necessarily receive credit or compensation. What motivates corporate bankers to voluntarily help their banks? When influence of the three workplace factors already outlined—procedural fairness, distributive fairness, and outcome favorability—was compared empirically it was found that voluntary behavior to help the organization was linked to the procedural fairness of the workplace.

This finding suggests that ethics and compliance officers need not be at odds with other managers in their organization about the importance of reaching business objectives. The strategies proposed as mechanisms for motivating employees to adhere to rules and follow policies also advance the more general goals of management. They simultaneously help increase company value by leading to a more engaged workforce that is more willing to do what is needed to help the company succeed, as well as to help prevent losses by virtue of greater compliance. Hence, ethics and business success can go hand in hand.

In discussing compliance, I have distinguished between complying out of fear of punishment and voluntarily accepting rules based upon personal values. Social motivation–based models rely upon free and willing choice among employees—that is, the desire to follow rules because doing so is viewed as appropriate, as the "right thing to do."

Voluntary acceptance is a desirable form of employee behavior because it frees companies to use their resources for productive purposes rather than having to enact costly surveillance and oversight mechanisms. While some surveillance is important, and the threat of sanctions is an essential component of regulation, companies can minimize the need for this costly set of regulatory mechanisms by emphasizing values-based self-regulation. Similarly, companies can benefit when employees engage in voluntary extra-role behaviors motivated by the desire to help their organization be successful (Smith, Organ, and Near 1983).

Unfortunately, the passage of the Sarbanes-Oxley Act in 2002 has legislated a return to the command-and-control approach in the United States. It encourages companies to focus on the creation of penalties and the development of monitoring systems to enforce them, with compliance and ethics groups acting in the role of corporate policeman. From the perspective advocated here this is a retrogressive step that, ironically, is likely to reduce compliance. On the other hand, as noted, the Federal Sentencing Guidelines encourage companies to develop an ethical workplace culture, although they do not specify what that means.

The findings outlined have important implications for companies who want to meet the culture requirements of the 2004 revision of the Federal Sentencing Guidelines for Organizations. The specific language used by the guidelines dictates that organizations should "promote an organizational culture that encourages ethical conduct and a commitment to compliance with the law." In conjunction with earlier studies, the data presented here show that a procedurally just culture and one with trusted authorities will promote ethical conduct and a commitment to comply with the law more than the command-and-control approach. To be more specific, the data indicates that creating a procedurally just culture is the best way of encouraging a *commitment* to comply with the law. It simultaneously leads to self-regulation, and at the same time leads to self-motivation to help the company in which employees are psychologically committed through shared values, a common identity, and favorable commitments.

Just as companies must use due diligence when hiring, auditing, or performing other activities that present risks to the organization, this work suggests that companies should use due diligence regarding the procedural fairness of the enterprise and their work groups. They must make a good faith effort to create the organizational policies and practices that lead to supportive attitudes and values among their employees. It is here that ethics and compliance officers can play a broader role in their organizations beyond being ethical gatekeepers. The values-based approach is literally good for business because the same procedural features that are key to voluntary acceptance of the rules are also the antecedents of voluntary extra-role behavior. Such voluntary behavior on behalf of work organizations is desirable on its own terms and has benefits that go beyond the arena of ethics and regulation. Thus, an effective ethics and compliance organization is one that makes the business case for ethical behavior in a positive sense rather than solely as a preventative or loss-avoidance measure. Ethics officers are well advised to translate, to the greatest extent possible, the tangible monetary benefits to be gained by an energized, empowered workforce when promoting the benefits of ethics and self-regulation.

This study also has policy implications for developing state and national regulations to influence the behavior of organizations. While it is always dangerous to transfer practices at one level of analysis to another, there are striking similarities to what is seen inside organizations and developments in government regulation of business. As we have seen, command-and-control programs in organizations do not effectively engage employee values. The limitations of the command-and-control approach used by government to regulate business have been understood since the 1980s. It was during this time that government began instituting environmental regulations that relied on market mechanisms (Anderson and Leal 2001). In Europe there is a movement toward "soft law" or "cooperative regulation." Cooperative regulation stipulates goals that organizations should attain, but leaves room for the participation of those regulated to make sure that goals are attained in the most efficient and fair way (Collier 2007; Senden 2005). If this local autonomy leads to opportunities for participation in decision making, the experience of procedural justice and trust in management leads to the favorable dispositions discussed.

Unfortunately, the recent U.S. response to business scandals such as those at Enron and WorldCom has been a major step in what I argue, based on the data outlined, is the wrong direction. In passing the Sarbanes-Oxley Act in 2002, the U.S. Congress moved many of the best practices in which the most progressive companies voluntarily engaged into the realm of mandated activity. Thus, ironically, the legislative response to a handful of ethical failures—admittedly spectacular and devastating—was to impose upon *all* companies a set of the very sorts of rigid command-and-control-based compliance requirements that are demonstrably outmoded. Beyond the enormous social costs and financial burdens incurred by the heightened level of vigilance required by Sarbanes-Oxley, my data suggest that such an approach is actually harmful to the goal of creating cultures in which rule-following is voluntarily, even enthusiastically, embraced. For this reason, the stifling restrictions of Sarbanes-Oxley, hastily passed in the heated aftermath of the spate of corporate disasters that befell the United States in the span of just a few months, should, in retrospect, be reevaluated in light of data of the type outlined in this volume.

I am not so naive as to suggest that the practices I advocate will guarantee that another Enron or WorldCom will never happen. Scoundrels and cheats will exist in any human system, and where they ascend to the top of the corporate ladder, as they did in these scandals, they will likely violate the rules to the greatest extent they can. I do argue, however, that a culture of voluntary rule-following will minimize their opportunities to do so in several important ways. First, in a culture in which transparent procedures are voluntarily embraced, the self-policing mechanisms that will thrive in the organization will be more likely to expose wrongdoing in its infancy—that is, employees will be motivated by their loyalty to the company to take the risks associated with bringing misconduct to light because they do not want it to damage their work organization. Second, a culture in which rule-following is the expected norm and cynicism is low will be a far less comfortable environment for those who would prefer to break the rules. And finally, in a culture in which rule-following is the accepted norm, scoundrels and cheats will be far less likely to ascend to the positions of power in which they can do significant damage.

My goal is to articulate a broader role for the ethics and compliance officer than the traditional one of managing compliance with organizational rules via monitoring and sanctioning. I argue that a values-based approach in which organizations seek to motivate employees to develop and act on ethical values is a more effective approach to managing rule adherence. This argument is supported by the empirical research already presented in chapter 3, which points to the importance of values as an antecedent of deference to rules. I argue that the organizational features most strongly associated with both the development of supportive values and deference to rules are procedural justice and motive-based trust.

The key role that procedural justice plays in shaping adherence to rules provides an opportunity for an expanded role for the ethics and compliance officer, since the same aspects of organizational procedures that promote the development of ethical values also lead employees to be productive and to engage in voluntary behavior on behalf of the organization. Finally, empirical research points to key factors shaping employee judgments about the fairness of the procedures within work organizations.

Application to Social Control Agents

A second arena in which there are potentially important policy implications of the social motivational model and of a focus on procedural justice and trust involves models for managing social control agents (Tyler, Callahan, and Frost 2007). Recent evidence of prisoner mistreatment in Iraq and of human rights violations such as the burning of prisoners' bodies in Afghanistan reflect a new manifestation of recurrent problems of inappropriate conduct by agents of social control—in this case, soldiers (Hartle 1989; Wakin 1979; Wasserstrom 1970). These examples point attention to the long-term question of how societies can effectively regulate the behavior of their agents of social control (Huntington 1957; Kelman and Hamilton 1989; Shapiro 1988). Rules, laws, and policies exist to prohibit inappropriate conduct by those engaged in the maintenance of order, and those identified as engaging in such conduct can be charged, tried, and punished for it. However, a preferable strategy would be to create a framework within which such conduct was minimized or did not occur at all.

The issue of regulating agents of social control is not unique to the military. Research on policing similarly documents a wide variety of ways in which law enforcement officers sometimes abuse their power by engaging in unlawful activities (Brown 1981; Goldstein 1977; National Research Council 2004; Skolnick and Fyfe 1993). Abuses of authority occur in street stops and arrests, in detentions, in interrogations, in searches and seizures, and in cases of the use of excessive nonlethal and lethal force. These practices, whether they involve soldiers or law enforcement agents, can reflect cases of the failure to effectively implement adherence to organizational rules and regulations. These failures illustrate why civilian and upper management control is needed to regulate the conduct of those involved in order maintenance.

An important reason for the persistence of problems in preventing misconduct among those responsible for order maintenance is the nature of the situation in which social control agents work—that is, the nature of the tasks they perform and the institutional structure and the dynamics that surround those engaged in these tasks (Tyler 2006a, 2006b; Tyler and Blader 2000).

As societies' primary formal instruments of social control, those responsible for order maintenance are given a great deal of power. They have the right to use coercion, even lethal force, for social control purposes. For example, in contrast to the elaborate legal procedures required before the state can impose the death penalty, law enforcement officers and members of the armed forces are authorized to make split-second life and death decisions. On a more mundane level, the police decide whether people are stopped and questioned, whether they are arrested, and whether they receive help with problems and in emergency situations, while the armed forces exercise widespread control over the everyday lives of civil populations during times of strife. Of course, in both groups such discretion is not total. Behavior is guided and influenced by law and public policy.

Society creates order maintenance agents to exercise social control by bringing the behavior of the people over whom they exercise authority into line with legal rules and regulations (Tyler 2003; Tyler and Huo 2002). And the effectiveness of the actions of those authorities shapes the degree to which societies can effectively maintain social order. But how does society ensure that the behavior of order maintenance agents themselves is consistent with the rules and laws societies creates to govern their actions? The issue of regulating those in charge of order maintenance is a long-standing challenge to societies, and is central to the relationship between societies and their various types of "armed forces." In other words, the state claims a monopoly on the use of coercive force against its citizens, and, as a result, effective governance requires the state to have ways to regulate its agents of coercion by facilitating their adherence to rules, laws, and policies governing their actions.

The problems of regulating those involved in order maintenance are rooted in a central contradiction in the organizational structures of the military and law enforcement. Those structures are heavily dominated by command-and-control approaches to the management of subordinates, with an emphasis upon receiving and following directives from superiors. Such authority structures depend heavily for their success upon the effective deployment of systems of surveillance and on supervision by authorities. Authority structures of this type are, of course, not unique to order maintenance and are also found in other types of highly structured hierarchical work environments such as factories (Tyler and Blader 2000). They are pervasive in agencies of order maintenance.

Given their great power over others, it seems reasonable that those involved in order maintenance should work within a framework of close supervision and tight control. However, this is often not the case. The organizational problem is

that while order maintenance organizations are typically organized in a hierarchical fashion, the tasks that those within them engage in often require them to
exercise considerable unsupervised discretion. Because conditions vary widely
across situations and individuals, and because success is viewed as being linked
to the use of intuition and good judgment within a broad latitude for action,
a great deal of discretion is given to decide whether to investigate suspicious
activities, to determine how to manage contacts with civilians, and to decide
when to intimidate or use force against others—all based upon interpretations
of the exigencies of the situation and understandings of the rules, policies, and
laws that govern their actions (Hawkins 1992). Such a situation is not unique to
the police or soldiers; other authorities—for example, forest rangers (Kaufman
1960)—also work under conditions of autonomy.

Police work, like the work of many legal authorities (Hawkins 1992), inher-
ently involves the exercise of large amounts of discretion based on the "reading" of situations. This widespread exercise of discretionary authority is basic to
policing activities (Gottfredson and Gottfredson 1988). Laws are often ambigu-
ous and require interpretation concerning how enforcement should take place
(Calavita 1998; Edelman 1990; Grattet and Jenness 2005; Hawkins 2002). Far
from being a problem, the recommendation of most policing experts is that im-
proving police performance requires *increasing* police discretion: "Decentral-
izing, reducing hierarchy, granting officers more independence, and trusting in
their professionalism, are the organizational reforms of choice today, not tight-
ening up the management screws to further constrain officer discretion" (Skogan
and Meares 2004, 68). This increased discretion should be coupled with the
development of aids to better decision making and to better selection and training of officers. In sum, everything about policing makes the regulation of both
local and federal law enforcement agents difficult: these agents have power, they
are given discretion in the use of that power, and it is difficult to consistently
monitor their actions.

And, of course, the need for discretion is not unique to the police. These same
dynamics generally describe the situation of the members of the armed forces.
While many aspects of military life are highly regimented (Demchek 1991),
performance in field settings such as combat involves the exercise of initiative
(Choen and Thompson 2001; Schmitt and Klein 1998). In fact, it is the emphasis
on individual initiative in democratic culture that is credited with the superior
military effectiveness of democracies during wars (Reiter and Stam 1998, 2002).
Greater willingness to exercise initiative is one of two key combat advantages of
democracies, the other being better leadership (Reitman and Stam 2002, chap.
3). Effectiveness in highly fluid and rapidly changing scenarios such as those
found in combat requires the ability to improvise and adapt, rapidly making

decisions appropriate to unique and often dangerous situations. And, as with the police, the ability to exercise initiative, when properly exercised, is a key to military effectiveness (Lind 1985).

Hence, the structure of institutions of order maintenance involves an organizational contradiction. It involves the ability to perform tasks requiring the ability to act independently and to make discretionary tactical decisions about desirable behavior under conditions of uncertainty and novelty, but decisions about the appropriateness of actions must be taken by agents of social control who are typically trained and managed in highly regimented and structured ways that on an everyday basis involve acting under high levels of supervision and control. Problems arise when law enforcement agents or soldiers lack close supervision and, in that situation, exercise their discretion poorly. Since the power differentials between agents of social control and the civilians with whom they deal are enormous, and the agents carry with them the means of deploying deadly force, the consequences for civilians are often quite dire.

The issue raised by problems of the abuse of power by agents of social control is how society can encourage higher levels of rule adherence under such complex organizational conditions. Discussions of policing recognize the centrality of this concern, noting that "controlling police behavior is a management problem . . . [but] to date, however, little research has examined the effectiveness of managerial strategies to secure officer compliance with department policies" (Skogan and Meares 2004, 78). One example of prior such efforts to control police behavior is found in the area of the shooting of civilians by the police, where management strategies are important (Geller and Scott 1992, chap. 5).

This concern about how to create an effective set of regulations that will deter misconduct has again been heightened by recent public events showing both the propensity for misconduct in conflict settings and the tremendous damage to the image of agents of social control (and ultimately to the mission of order maintenance) that such misconduct can cause. In the case of the army, for example, a particular advantage of democratic armies is that they are more likely to engage in ethical conduct. This has battlefield advantages, since the enemy is more likely to surrender, believing that it will receive humane treatment (Reiter and Stam 2002). Similarly, recent research on law enforcement emphasizes the value to the police of receiving active cooperation from the public. If they can draw upon community cooperation, they are more effective in fighting crime (National Research Council 2004; Sampson, Raudenbush, and Earls 1997).

The findings outlined in this volume, including those specifically drawn from samples of police officers and members of the armed forces, support the arguments outlined and point to approaches that can be taken to deal with the organizational difficulties delineated. In particular, it is possible to allow the use of greater discretion among agents of social control if a social motivational model is put in place, a model that focuses on self-regulation. We want authorities involved in activities that require flexibility and freedom to act in response to changing conditions to be able to do so, but we want that action not to result in harm to others. Hence, we want to encourage positive and useful action while simultaneously gaining the safety that flows from having the behavior of authorities constrained by close regulation. The key to so doing is to create an organizational framework within which those who are free to act are motivated to conform their behavior to organizational rules, norms, and purposes.

The distinction between the command-and-control approach and the self-regulatory approach has deep roots within the organizational and psychological literatures that were outlined in the opening chapters. The command-and-control approach is linked to extrinsic motivational models of human behavior in which people behave primarily in response to external contingencies in their environment. It is especially relevant to a quasi-military or military organizational structure. The self-regulatory approach, on the other hand, is linked to intrinsic motivational models of human behavior that emphasize individuals' innate preferences and desires as the fundamental drivers of behavior. These innate preferences are conceptualized as operating independent of contingencies in the environment for the performance or nonperformance of particular behaviors. As such, this latter model might initially seem ill-suited to the organizational settings in which agents of social control operate.

The results from the studies of law enforcement agents and the soldiers presented earlier in this volume confirm our central prediction that the self-regulatory approach represents a viable approach to fostering rule adherence among agents of social control who are involved in order maintenance activities. The social value judgments made regarding their organizations, embodied in their perceptions of the legitimacy of organizational authorities and the perceived congruence of their personal values with those of the organization, shaped rule and policy adherence. This was true for the voluntary rule-following behavior examined in this volume. These findings confirm that the self-regulatory strategy is a viable approach to attaining rule adherence even within the quasi-military and military contexts considered.

These results support the argument that social value judgments shape behavior and, in particular, rule-following behavior. Those judgments are a major motivation leading to adherence with organizational policies and rules. These results suggest that one promising way to bring the behavior of law enforcement agents and members of the military into line with codes of conduct is to tap into their social values—their motivation to defer to legitimate rules and authorities and to engage in actions congruent with their own moral values. To gain acceptance for rules and policies, organizations should activate employee values. These values are central to the self-regulatory strategy for motivating voluntary compliance.

Of course, the activation of values is not the only way to influence rule-related behavior. As is the practice in many organizations, organizational efforts to monitor and sanction/reward behavior may likewise motivate the following of organizational policies, consistent with the command-and-control approach. However, in the data analyzed here, the utility of that approach overall is weaker than that of a self-regulatory approach. Although there were significant influences of the command-and-control approach in some instances, these influences were typically secondary in magnitude to the influence of the variables in the self-regulatory approach. Hence, we suggest that the self-regulatory approach is more than just *another* approach to regulation—it is a *more effective* approach.

These findings suggest that both law enforcement and military organizations have a great deal to gain by going beyond instrumental strategies of social control and focusing attention on the activation of values that are consistent with a self-regulatory strategy. Overall, the results presented here indicate the viability of such a strategy and, furthermore, the potential superiority of that strategy over the more traditional command-and-control approach. This alternative strategy leads to cooperation much more efficiently and effectively, since those in the organization become self-regulatory and take the responsibility of following rules onto themselves. Further, they do so without reference to the likelihood of being punished for wrongdoing or rewarded for acting appropriately.

The use of self-regulatory approaches is also important because it addresses the organizational issues outlined. If it is important for those involved in order maintenance to be able to act with discretion, then the solution to the problem of rule adherence must work within a discretionary environment. Because values are an aspect of self-regulation, they work in such an environment. If agents are following rules based upon their internal values, their behavior should continue to be consistent with the rules when they are not being controlled by direct surveillance from their superiors.

As might be expected, those involved in training order maintenance agents to some degree already recognize the potential importance of value-based approaches. For example, the U.S. Army leadership training manual makes values a core part of leadership training and includes values such as respect and integrity. That manual illustrates integrity by pointing approvingly to an incident in which a soldier in Vietnam protected civilians from his own comrades by threat of force (U.S. Army 1999, 2–10). On the other hand, another field manual emphasizes the need to prevent misconduct but does not discuss the role of values with either soldiers or officers. Rather, it focuses upon the importance of high unit cohesion and building competence, courage, candor, and commitment among leaders (U.S. Army 1994, chap. 4). This alternative focus highlights the potential value to organizations of an emphasis upon the "sense of mission."

The argument advanced here is for a broader view on the part of those responsible for creating the organizational conditions that lead to rule-following in group settings. This approach looks at the influence of both instrumental and value-based motivations in shaping rule-following behavior. The results presented suggest that the consideration of both models together better explains such behavior than is possible via either model taken alone.

The view presented here includes not only the motivations traditionally studied—motivations that are linked to sanctions and incentives—but also social motivations for following group rules. These social motivations are linked to concerns about acting in fair ways in work settings. The case for this broader model rests on the finding that in a variety of work settings people are found to be motivated in their rule-following by their social values concerning legitimacy and morality, by their commitment to their organization, and by their identification with their group. These findings suggest that we would be better able to understand rule-following behavior in work organizations, as well as in other settings, if we adopted a broader model of human motivation that added an account of social motivations to our models of behavior.

While this discussion focuses upon two settings in which the management of rule-following is the key issue of concern, the larger issue is one of cooperation. And in both settings cooperation in the form of working on behalf of the group is found to be responsive to the same policies and practices that shape rule-following. Hence, policies and practices that are procedurally just and lead to trust in authorities lead people to both do their jobs well and engage in extra-role or voluntary actions to help their group (Tyler and Blader 2000).

Dealing with the Law: Process-based Regulation

The traditional objective of the law and of the actions of legal authorities is to gain public compliance with the law. This includes compliance in the context of the particular decisions made by legal authorities such as judges and police officers, and compliance with the law in everyday life. In both cases, a key societal objective is to be able to bring people's behavior into line with the law (Tyler 2006b). And, in both cases, public compliance cannot be taken for granted.

The problems involved in obtaining compliance with the law in everyday life are illustrated through compliance issues involving a wide variety of behaviors, ranging from traffic laws (Tyler 2006b) to drug laws (MacCoun 1993), illegal immigration (Cornelius and Salehyan 2007), and the payment of taxes (Braithwaite 2003; Scholz 1998; Scholz and Lubell 1998; Scholz and Pinney 1995). In each case, while most people comply with the law most of the time, legal authorities are confronted with sufficient noncompliance to be challenging to the resources normally devoted to social control. And in situations such as the illegal down-loading of music and the illegal copying of movies, levels of noncompliance are so high as to make effective regulation very difficult.

Similar problems arise with the decisions of legal authorities. Studies of per-sonal encounters with the police demonstrate that people often resist and even defy legal and judicial orders (Mastrofski, Snipes, and Supina 1996; Sherman 1993; Terrill 2001), and compliance can never be assumed. On the contrary, that ability to manage encounters with members of the public without provoking conflict and resistance is considered to be a core competency issue for police of-ficers. As Stephen Mastrofski, Jeffrey Snipes, and Anne Supina note, "Although deference to legal authorities is the norm, disobedience occurs with sufficient frequency that skill in handling the rebellious, the disgruntled, and the hard to manage—or those potentially so—has become the street officer's performance litmus test" (1996, 272). Based upon observational data, these authors estimate that the general noncompliance rate is around 22 percent.

Problems with noncompliance with the decisions of judges are also long stand-ing and are one major motivation for the alternative dispute resolution move-ment, which seeks nonadjudicative forums to traditional courtrooms partly in an effort to find a way to increase the willingness of involved parties to accept the decisions made by third-party authorities by replacing judges with mediators (Tyler 1989). Within all types of adjudicative settings judges have struggled to find ways to make decisions that are acceptable to the parties who bring the cases into court. An illustration of the type of cases that are particularly likely to raise acceptance issues are decisions about child custody and child support (Bryan 2006). With such cases it is important to make decisions that will be willingly followed by both parents and that will, to the degree possible, create positive postseparation dynamics in which both parents take responsibility for supporting their children financial and emotionally (Bryan 2006; Dillon and Emery 1996; Emery, Matthews, and Kitzman 1994; Kitzmann and Emery 1993). Hence, fam-ily law cases have been a particular focus of efforts to find ways to create accept-able decisions involving child custody and child support.

Irrespective of the type of case involved, the traditional means of obtaining compliance is via social control—that is, by seeking to deter rule-breaking by threatening to punish wrongdoing. It is argued that the fear of possible future punishment leads to compliance with the law. Risk calculations are potentially shaped by both the anticipated likelihood of punishment and by judgments about its severity. Of the two, research consistently suggests that it is the likelihood of punishment that is particularly important in shaping behavior, so that issue will be my primary focus here. Such deterrence approaches to compliance are currently the dominant model of motivation within the American criminal justice system (Blumstein, Cohen, and Nagin 1978; Cullen et al. 2002; MacKenzie 2002; May 2005; Nagin 1998; Petersilia 2003).

In the context of regulation I argue for the value of a self-regulatory approach based upon several arguments, each of which has been addressed and supported empirically in this volume. The first is that we need to change our goals regarding the behavior we want from the members of our society. The second is that this change in behavioral objectives leads to a change in the tactics that we should employ to obtain our goals.

There are tremendous benefits to shifting our focus toward voluntary acceptance of decisions and, beyond that, toward cooperation with legal authorities. And I will suggest that such a shift in behavioral focus requires a shift in motivational strategy away from deterrence and toward the creation and activation of values—that is, toward a self-regulatory approach to generating law-abiding behavior. The first aspect of such a model is the argument that people are motivated by their values.

The first argument of the self-regulatory approach is that the type of behavior we want from the members of society has changed (Tyler 2007, 2008, 2009). The roots of the compliance model lie in a focus upon rule-following backed up by risk assessments. Hence, people's focus is upon the environment—that is, upon the potential risks of punishment that they face. This means that their behavior will be limited in scope. First, they are unlikely to follow the law when they are in situations in which the likelihood of being caught and punished for wrongdoing is small; nor will they accept decisions when they see ways to evade them. Compliance requires the continual presence of a credible threat of punishment.

Further, although people do comply due to the presence of legal authority,[1] they often revert to their prior behavior once that authority is absent (McCluskey 2003). For example, people often cease to adhere to judicial orders once they are out of the courtroom, just as they resume illegal behavior once the police leave the scene. If citizens fail to fully agree with legal restrictions, further police intervention will eventually be required and the police will sometimes have to revisit the same problem multiple times. Hence, the legal system is also concerned with its ability to gain long-term, not just immediate, compliance. This is especially true when long-term relationships are important, as in the previously mentioned studies on family courts, in which the goal is for parents to be sharing financial and emotional child-rearing responsibilities long after the court case is over.

Because there is often insufficient risk to motivate compliance, and because of the need for continued rule-following over time, the legal system benefits when people voluntarily defer to regulations to some degree and follow them even when they do not anticipate being caught and punished if they don't. In addition, in the context of personal experiences with police officers or judges, the legal system is more effective if people voluntarily accept the decisions made by legal authorities. Absent such acceptance, legal authorities must engage in a continuing effort to create a credible threat of punishment to assure long-term rule-following/decision acceptance. Hence, it is important to move beyond a concern with compliance toward a focus upon voluntary acceptance and continued deference over time.

The shift from compliance to cooperation also requires us to expand the scope of our instrumental model, a model that can potentially involve both costs and benefits. While the legal system is based upon highlighting the cost of rule-breaking, law and legal authorities also offer potential benefits. Tom Tyler and Yuen Huo (2002) have found that the primary manner in which people have contact with the police and courts is by going to them for help. Hence, legal authorities can create benefits by their performance. They can resolve disputes and solve problems.

While compliance focuses upon motivating rule-following by emphasizing costs, a similar model argues for motivating cooperation by emphasizing the potential gains of cooperation. In this case, the gains are associated with the ability of legal authorities to effectively manage problems and resolve conflicts. In the case of the police, in particular, people may cooperate with them when they see them as effectively managing crime and community disorder. For example, the "broken windows model" argues that the police need to sanction minor crimes to prevent social disorder, so the ability of the police to suppress such behavior, as well as to deal with crime more generally, communicates an air of competence and thereby motivates people to cooperate with them. In addition, effective punishment of wrongdoing not only shapes individuals' behavior (i.e., deterrence) but communicates a message about competence that potentially has an impact on the larger community. Such a model focuses upon the gains of cooperation rather than the risks of rule-breaking. In the case of the justice system, performance issues involve the ability of the courts to resolve disputes in a timely and affordable manner, as well as to be authoritative and produce decisions that will be complied with. Like the deterrence model, the performance model links people's behavior to personal gain/loss calculations rather than to values.

Changing our behavioral focus from compliance to voluntary acceptance and cooperation leads to a change in the type of motivation that we need to create among community residents. The old focus has been upon creating and main-

taining a credible risk of being punished for rule-breaking behavior and/or demonstrating competence by controlling crime. The new focus needs to be upon the
internal motivation forces that lead people to undertake voluntary actions without calculating the risks of punishment for wrongdoing or the potential personal
gains for cooperation. People need to have an alternative basis for their actions.

The influence of social motivations upon voluntary cooperation has already
been addressed, and it has been shown that social motivations provide a key
input into voluntary cooperation. Several propositions are supported. One is that
people are more likely to obey a law due to social motivations. This argument
generates two empirically testable propositions. The first is that social motivations are distinct from fear of sanctioning or the benefits of performance and that
their influence is greater in magnitude than is that of the fear of sanctioning or
the benefits of performance. The second is that social motivations are particularly useful because they motivate voluntary deference and cooperation. Both
of these propositions receive support in this volume.

The most important aspect of the literature on process-based regulation is the
extensive body of work demonstrating that procedural justice and motive-based
trust shape attitudes, values, identification, and voluntary cooperation. It is very
clear that reactions to law and legal authorities are linked to judgments about
how authorities exercise their authority—that is, to procedural justice (Lind and
Tyler 1988; Tyler and Lind 1992). More specifically, values are rooted in the procedural justice of the actions of legal authorities. And the procedures by which
legal authority is exercised are typically under the control of legal authorities.

Accepting the Decisions of Legal Authorities

Does procedural justice lead people to voluntarily accept the decisions made by
legal authorities? Studies across a wide range of issues suggest that they do. This
includes the criminal justice arenas I outline below as well as administrative
hearings such as tax audits (Lawsky 2008), informal criminal procedures such
as plea bargaining (Beloff 2007; O'Hear 2007), and a variety of types of other
procedures in legal, managerial and community settings (Tyler 2006a).

Tyler and Huo (2002) interviewed 1,656 residents of Los Angeles and Oakland, California, each with a recent personal experience with the police and the
courts. They asked respondents to make a set of evaluations of their experience,
including the favorability of the outcome, the fairness of the outcome, the fairness of the procedures, and their willingness to accept the decisions made by the
legal authorities involved.

An examination of the role of outcome favorability, outcome fairness, and
procedural fairness in shaping voluntary acceptance indicates that the primary

factor shaping decision acceptance after a personal experience with the police or a judge is the fairness of the decision-making process. In this study, which explained 69 percent of variance in voluntary decision acceptance, the beta weight for procedural justice was 0.69; for distributive justice, 0.12; and for outcome favorability, 0.09 (see also Engel 2005; Gau and Brunson 2009; Reisig and Chandek 2001; Wiley and Hudik 1974; Wortley, Hagan, and Macmillan 1997).

This pattern of results is found to be true both for white and minority respondents. While minority group members are more likely to report having negative experiences with legal authorities and more frequently feel that they have been disrespected or treated unfairly (Weitzer and Tuch 2006), whites and minorities are similar in that both groups react primarily to whether or not they receive fair treatment rather than to the favorability or fairness of their outcomes.

It is possible to further distinguish such voluntary acceptance from simple compliance ("I did what I was told to do"), and when we do so, the centrality of procedural justice to voluntary deference becomes clear. Compliance is almost equally shaped by procedural justice (beta = 0.13) and the favorability of the outcome (beta = 0.08), while voluntary decision acceptance, as already noted, is almost totally the result of procedural justice.

A similar study of compliance with police orders also found that citizens focus on "how they are treated, in terms of respect" and concludes that "normative features of authority behavior matter. We find they are extremely powerful . . . in explaining obedience to police requests for self- control" (McCluskey 2003, 166, 172). And other studies reinforce the finding that procedural justice is an important concern to the members of minority groups. (For a study of personal experience see Shute, Hood, and Seemungal 2005; for a study of general judgments see Tyler 2001).

It is also important to directly address the issue of whether, at least for the police officers on the streets, it is important to firmly project authority—that is, to control people and situations by making unequivocal commands backed up by nonnegotiable displays of incontestable force. Lawrence Sherman (1993) raises this question in his framework of possible responses to police directives by noting that two possible responses are compliance and defiance both in terms of immediate resistance and long-term criminal behavior. Is there evidence addressing this concern in the context of immediate resistance? John McCluskey (2003) uses evidence collected in observer-based studies of police and citizen encounters in Indiana and Florida to explore the role of police coercion in motivating citizen compliance.

According to a force-based model the police should be able to increase citizen compliance by projecting authority. McCluskey tests this argument using observer ratings of police behavior. He focuses upon police requests for citizen self-control and findings that for initial requests by the police for compliance, "[s]urprisingly the coercive power that police bring to bear on a citizen in the form of commanding, handcuffing, arresting and so on, has a minimal impact on citizen's compliance decision" (2003, 100). At later points in the interaction Mc-Cluskey finds that "the higher the level of coercive power displayed by police, the less likely targets are to comply. . . . For every one unit increase in the index of coercion citizens are about twice as likely to rebel against the self-control request" (108). This leads him to conclude, "Though coercion may be a central component of the police role, it appears to serve little to enhance compliance when first asked or when requests are repeated by the police" (173).[2] As a consequence, William Terrill argues, "The best officers are those who use less, not more force (2001, 232; see also Belvedere, Worrall, and Tibbetts 2005; Bouffard and Piquero 2008).

In contrast to the general ineffectiveness of coercion, McCluskey finds that when the police use procedures that are fair, compliance increases substantially. He identifies three distinct aspects of procedural justice—ethicality, information seeking, and decision making—and shows that each independently contributes to the general increase in initial compliance that results from procedural justice. McCluskey describes people as "seekers of justice" (2003, 173).

Experience-based procedural justice also shapes legitimacy. Tom Tyler and Jeffrey Fagan (2008) used panel data to examine the influence of personal experience on legitimacy, controlling for prior differences among respondents both in terms of their demographic characteristics and their antecedent views about the legitimacy of the police. Their findings reaffirm the centrality of procedural justice in personal experiences to people's subsequent evaluations of legitimacy. These results indicate that views about legitimacy change significantly in response to personal experience and that such changes are distinct from the influence of outcome-based judgments.

Tyler and Fagan (2008) further demonstrate that both fair and unfair experiences significantly change views about legitimacy, although in different directions. Thus, the police can gain legitimacy by being fair and lose it by being unfair. This argument was disputed by Wesley Skogan (2006), but has recently received independent confirmation in a study of personal experiences with the police conducted in London, that concludes that "positive contacts do contain the potential to improve aspects of trust and confidence" (Bradford, Jackson, and Stanko 2009, 21).

The ability of procedural justice to facilitate decision acceptance in response to personal experiences with legal authorities shows that procedural justice can play an important role in facilitating the exercise of legal authority in criminal, civil, and administrative hearings (Braithwaite and Makkai 1994; Frazer 2006;

Martinson et al. 2006; McNeil 2008; Tyler 2006b; Winter and May 2001). This role is especially central to interactions in which trust in the authorities is low (Murphy 2004), legal authorities impose themselves upon community residents (Hinds and Murphy, 2007; Murphy 2005), or people question the legitimacy of the law (Murphy, Tyler, and Curtis 2009).

Because procedural justice is central to the exercise of legal authority, judges and court administrators have argued that court systems need to be designed so as to create an experience of procedural justice for the people who come before judges and other legal authorities. The argument is that people who believe that they have received procedural justice are more likely to be willing to accept the decisions of legal authorities and to abide by those decisions over time (Burke and Leben 2008; Greacen 2008; Leben 2000; McNeil 2009; Tyler 2006d).

The courts in several states have been making proactive efforts to design court procedures, and in some cases the entire state court system, with an eye to best policies and practices for creating procedures that are experienced by those who deal with the courts as litigants or jurors or in other roles evaluate its procedures as fair (Benesh 2006; Gibson 2008). As noted, this includes treating people with dignity and respect, showing concern for people's rights and cultural backgrounds, using procedures that are judged to be unbiased and neutral, and giving everyone the opportunity to be heard (Denton 2008). There are several factors motivating courts to take such actions: the dramatic increase in self-represented litigants, increasing cultural diversity, and lower levels of trust and confidence in the courts.

One example of a statewide effort is the ongoing procedural fairness initiative in California. The Administrative Office of the Courts has been engaged in an ambitious multiyear effort that has involved redesigning courts to include features anticipated to increase perceived fairness among members of the public, such as help desks, improved translation services, informational pamphlets, and online resources such as informational videos and mechanisms for obtaining information and assistance. A parallel effort provides written and web-based resources for court personnel seeking to build such court systems (see Burke and Lefever 2007).

The Climate of Procedural Justice and Legitimacy

Jason Sunshine and Tom Tyler (2003) have explored the influence of general evaluations of the procedural justice of the police upon people's judgments about the legitimacy of the police. Their findings indicate that procedural justice is a key antecedent of legitimacy. If the police are evaluated as exercising their authority fairly, they are viewed as more legitimate (see also see Fischer, et al. 2008; Murphy, Hinds and Fleming 2008; Reisig, Bratton, and Gertz 2007). When authorities are viewed as procedurally unjust, their legitimacy is undermined, leading to support for disobedience and resistance (Fischer et al. 2008).

What is striking in these studies is the degree to which performance issues are not central to public evaluations. Tom Tyler (2001) analyzed several surveys of public views of the courts and found that issues such as delay and cost, while often mentioned in critiques of the courts by journalists and public figures, were a minor influence on public trust and confidence in the courts, a finding replicated in a study of the California courts (Rottman 2005).

In a analysis of the California data (Tyler and Rottman 2009) procedural justice was found to be the primary factor shaping confidence in the courts among those with personal experiences with the courts (beta = 0.36, $p < .001$). Performance issues (i.e., delay, cost, etc.) had no influence upon confidence among those who had been to court (beta = 0.15, n.s.). Among those without personal experience with the courts procedural justice was again the key issue (beta = 0.51, $p < .001$), and performance had a significant but lower influence (beta = 0.09, $p < .001$). Among attorneys, procedural justice also mattered (beta = 0.37, $p < .001$), as did issues of performance (beta = 0.21, $p < .001$). Similarly, Sunshine and Tyler (2003) found that judgments of police performance in fighting crime and estimates of the risk of being caught and punished for wrongdoing (which is an index of whether the police can present a credible threat to wrongdoers) had minor influences upon legitimacy. Legitimacy was primarily an issue of procedural justice, although performance had some influence.

The Organizational Climate

What about the ability of organizational authorities to shape legitimacy by the type of organizational climate they create? Here the boundary between regulation and management is blurred. The issue involves the regulation of employees within work groups, irrespective of whether those authorities are judges, police officers, or everyday workers. The members of two organizations are considered here: corporate employees and law enforcement agents. As has been noted, an examination of the role of procedural justice in shaping legitimacy within each group suggests that the influence of the procedures through which legal authority is exercised on views about the overall legitimacy of legal authorities is strong in both groups.

The findings regarding agents of social control are especially important and relevant to this discussion. Any effort to create a climate in which the people who deal with the law and legal authorities experience procedural justice leads to a focus on how policing organizations or courts can create an organizational framework that motivates their members to want to follow policies of fairness. These findings suggest that "street-level" legal authorities act fairly when they themselves experience justice in their own work organizations. This finding is supported by other studies of the police. Joseph DeAngelis and Aaron Kupchik have conducted an independent study of police officers and found that "the best predictor of officers' willingness to accept the decisions made by command staff appears to be perceptions of procedural justice" (2009, 277).

As I have noted, procedural justice can be divided into two components: the quality of decision making and the quality of interpersonal treatment. And it can be considered either in terms of those authorities with whom people have personal contact, or as an overall institutional issue. An examination of the data on personal encounters with particular legal authorities (Tyler and Huo 2002) suggests that both elements matter. However, the results suggest that, in personal experiences, quality of interpersonal treatment is a central issue. In other words, when people are dealing with authorities they are strongly influenced by issues such as politeness and respect for rights. This conclusion is reinforced by the panel findings of Tyler and Fagan (2008), which show interpersonal treatment as the key aspect of personal experience that influences legitimacy. These findings are intertwined with issue of trust, since trust and interpersonal treatment are strongly linked. When authorities are polite and respectful, their motives are trusted (Tyler and Wakslak 2004).

Of course, many people have little personal contact with the police or the courts. Nonetheless, they do have views about how the authorities generally exercise their authority. And those judgments shape their overall views about the legitimacy of the law. Using results from one of the studies of New Yorkers outlined (Tyler and Fagan 2008), we can consider how such general judgments about procedural justice shape views about legitimacy—in this case, the legitimacy of the police. The results of a regression equation indicate that both quality of decision making and quality of treatment were important in shaping the social motivation of legitimacy.

Tom Tyler and David Rottman (2009) have analyzed the results of a statewide survey of trust and confidence in the California courts and found that the quality of decision making (beta = 0.11, $p < .001$); the quality of treatment (beta = 0.42, $p < .001$); outcome fairness (beta 0.21, $p < .001$); and performance issues (beta = 0.09, $p < .001$) all shaped overall confidence in the courts. They also analyzed the views of attorneys and found that their confidence was influenced by quality of decision making (beta = 0.10, $p < .01$); the quality of treatment (beta = 0.30, $p < .001$); fairness of decisions (beta = 0.37, $p < .001$); and performance issues (beta = 0.20, $p < .001$).

Finally, the analysis of respondents within organizational settings examines these two issues at both the interpersonal (work group) and organizational levels. The results are strikingly similar across two distinct organizations, and in each case suggest that the fairness of treatment that people experience within the organization and the quality of decision making they experience from their immediate superiors both shape overall organizational legitimacy.

Whom Should We Study?

The studies outlined herein are concerned with general populations. In that respect, they do not address the small group of lifelong criminals that are the focus of much past criminological research. I want to acknowledge this concern and make a general argument about strategies of regulation drawn from the writing of Ian Ayres and John Braithwaite (1992).

Their argument is that the key issue in regulation is which strategy of regulation is presented first. If deterrence is the general strategy presented, then all of the members of society frame their interactions with the legal system in instrumental terms. It is better to frame the general strategy as one of engaging values. This strategy engages the values of the large group within the general population that has values that can serve as a basis for law-related behavior and maximizes the role of their values in shaping their behavior. Some members of society lack values, or lack the requisite trust and confidence in the law to act based upon engaged values. This smaller group may need to be the target of deterrence-based regulation. However, because the largest group of people within society is behaving based upon their values, the resources needed to deal with the smaller group are minimized. It is a value-based strategy that is most likely to broadly engage public values in the service or rule-following behavior.

And, of course, while implementing such a strategy, with rule breakers it makes sense to focus upon rehabilitation—that is, upon reconnecting people who have broken social rules with their values and their ties to society and its rules and authorities (Tyler 2006c). This is a core goal of restorative justice, which is an alternative to traditional adjudication and argues that it is important to reconnect offenders to their values as an approach to lowering the rate of recidivism. It is encouraging that recent research suggests that people can be affected by rehabilitation, even as adults (Lipsey and Cullen 2007), while studies of traditional punishment suggest that it is delegitimating (Franke, Bierie, and MacKenzie 2009).

We should also ask whether "hard-core" criminals are sensitive to issues of procedural justice, as well as whether they engage in value-based behaviors. Tyler and Huo (2002) focused upon the respondents within their general population sample that were young minority males. They then explored the basis of the reactions to personal experiences with legal authorities among the members of this group. Their results indicated that this group was as focused upon issues of procedural justice in making acceptance decisions as was the general minority population and, beyond that, people in general.

Tom Tyler, Jonathan Casper, and Bonnie Fisher (Casper, Tyler and Fisher 1988; Tyler, Casper and Fisher 1989) have analyzed the results of a panel study of defendants arrested for felonies—defendants who were generally young, from a minority, and male. They found that the evaluations of the procedural justice of the case disposition process made by these defendants had a strong influence upon their satisfaction with their experiences and was the primary factor shaping their generalization from their personal experience to their overall views about the legitimacy of the law and the legal system.

Other studies similarly suggest that procedural justice plays an important role in shaping the attitudes and behaviors of "criminals." This includes research showing that the procedural justice of prisons is related to inmate behavior (Bottoms 1999; Gray 2007; Sparks, Bottoms, and Hay 1996), that the justice of criminal procedures influences recidivism (Tyler 2009), that procedural justice shapes the reactions of domestic violence suspects (Paternoster et al. 1997), and that issues of quality of treatment by peers and authorities are central to the actions of the members of juveniles and the members of gangs (Bourgois 1996; Crawford 2009; Emler and Reicher 1995; Hinds 2007, 2009).

Summary

The results outlined herein support the two key empirical propositions I have advanced in this volume. First, social motivations shape voluntary rule-following. In the arena of regulation, legitimacy and moral value congruence are two particularly important social motivations, as is identification with the police (Tyler and Fagan 2008). In particular, values lead to voluntary behavior, including both voluntary decision acceptance and cooperation with legal authorities. Second, procedural justice and trust shape values. If authority is exercised fairly, the law and legal authorities are viewed as legitimate and entitled to be obeyed, their policies are viewed as moral, and they are more strongly identified with.

These findings suggest that there are mechanisms for building value-based regulation linked to social motivations, and maintaining social order relying more strongly on voluntary cooperation. This has clear societal advantages, since widespread voluntary cooperation with the law and legal authorities allows those authorities to concentrate their resources most effectively on pursuing the long-term goals of society. The authorities do not need to provide incentives or sanctions to all citizens to get them to support every rule or policy they enact, and the resources needed for order maintenance can be deployed in other ways.

The findings also support the arguments of the process-based regulation model by showing that procedural justice is a key antecedent of dispositions such as legitimacy and of voluntary rule-following behavior. This aspect of the self-regulatory approach is important because it suggests both that legal authorities have a mechanism for shaping attitudes and values and hence influencing voluntary rule-following behavior and provides clear suggestions about what that framework involves. It is possible to both craft policies and build training programs based upon the ideas of procedural justice and motive-based trust.

My focus in this discussion is on the United States, although it is clear that similar issues are central to regulation throughout the world (Tyler, Braga, et al. 2007). Recent studies suggest that different dynamics may shape the exercise of authority in societies in which legitimacy is low or the conception of the relationship between people and authorities does not involve the same set of articulated rights and duties that is characteristic of societies like the United States. For example, Justice Tankebe (2008) has found that while procedural justice shapes trust in the police, effectiveness is the key antecedent of political trust among people in Ghana. Michael Reisig and Gorazd Mesko (2009) have similarly found that procedural justice in a Slovene prison shaped both self-reported and institutionally recorded rule violation. However, the study did not find that procedural justice shaped legitimacy, nor that legitimacy led to rule-following.

One possible reason for variations in the effectiveness of this model is variations in values such as the legitimacy of law and legal authorities. Kristina Murphy, Tom Tyler, and Amy Curtis (2009) have examined the effectiveness of procedural justice mechanisms when people did not view the law as legitimate. Using survey data collected in three regulatory contexts—taxes, social security, and general law enforcement—they found that the acceptance of rules is more strongly linked to issues of procedural justice when people question the legitimacy of the law. Hence, there may be circumstances under which procedural justice directly influences behavior without legitimacy playing a mediating role.

The Exercise of Political Authority: Process-based Governance

The literature on political authority makes clear that legitimacy is a key resource for political authorities. Legitimacy enables authorities to take actions that are supported based upon their position as authorities, not upon agreement with the prior views of the authorities. There is substantial evidence that legitimacy encourages a wide variety of forms of public cooperation in many, but clearly not all, social settings. In particular, those who support authorities and institutions defer to their decisions and to the policies and rules they create (Elsbach 2001; Tyler 2001; Tyler and Huo 2002). Hence, the central empirical premise of legitimacy is well supported, and those who view system stability as a valuable attribute can and do benefit when they are able to create and maintain this supportive value.

The classic research of Kurt Lewin nicely frames one perspective on the advantages and disadvantages of democracy. His studies show that democratic leadership builds voluntary cooperation. In groups that are democratically managed, people act in socially desirable ways irrespective of whether the leader is present. Group members do so, according to Lewin, because their internal motivations are engaged by democratic processes and, as a result, they are motivated to act on behalf of the group (Gold 1999).

This advantage of democracy—that it engages the willing involvement of its members—is widely argued to be linked to the stability and effectiveness of democratic groups. As an example, the willingness to members to make sacrifices for the group is the advantage of democracies in times of war (Levi 1997; Reiter and Stam 2002). While democracies are generally less likely to go to war, and are particularly unlikely to start wars, once involved they are likely to prevail, due in particular to the morale of their publics. More broadly, the success of democratic government is traditionally viewed as lying in its ability to capture the loyalty of the populace.

What is the potential disadvantage of democracy? To achieve the advantages noted above, leaders must be constantly sensitive to the views of group members. They need to have legitimacy, and cannot simply rule via the use of power (Tyler 2006a). When they do, they lose the willing engagement of their followers who have the expectation that leaders will be chosen democratically and will use their authority appropriately.

The need to maintain legitimacy imposes real constraints upon the actions of authorities. They must obtain their positions and exercise their authority in ways that seem reasonable and appropriate to those they lead. In this section, I focus on the joint roles of (1) voting in elections on the willingness of group members to view as legitimate and to defer to their leaders in a democracy, and (2) the exercise of fair decision-making procedures on the part of these leaders once in power for engaging the commitment of the population they seek to govern.

First, I will focus on the manner in which leaders obtain their positions. One of the key features of democracy is the appropriateness of the manner in which leaders are chosen—typically by election, a procedure that legitimizes the leader's right to make decisions on behalf of the groups (Tyler 2006a). I will argue that voting is important symbolically because people want to have the opportunity to express their views about decisions that influence their lives. Furthermore, drawing upon research on procedural fairness, I argue that this is because being allowed to vote is an affirmation of one's good standing in the group; it signals that one is entitled to the rights and status associated with membership in a group (i.e., citizenship).

Second, I will extend the procedural justice argument to an examination of the relationship between perceptions of leaders' procedural fairness and the level of social inclusion or exclusion experienced by those affected by those procedures. Social psychological theory and research has recognized the general importance of this issue, and found strong evidence that people care deeply about their level of inclusion or exclusion in social groups, ranging from small interacting groups to large-scale membership in social collectives (Abrams, Hogg, and Marques 2005; Willliams, Forgas, and Von Hippel 2005). As a result, they readily read into treatment from authorities messages about their place within the social bodies that these leaders represent: the receipt of procedural fairness or unfairness contributes to one's sense of social inclusion or exclusion. Rather than just being the end product of appraisals of fairness, the extent to which people feel socially included or excluded also feeds into the extent to which procedural fairness matters to them. As a result, whether or not leaders exercise their authority fairly is more important to those who believe themselves to be socially excluded, peripheral, or marginalized, than to the socially included, central, and integrated.

The positive effects of perceived fairness are widely found in social psychological studies of political, legal, and social groups. And the sense that one is a member in good standing is central to the striking influence of fair procedures upon people's willingness to engage in, and cooperate with, the groups and institutions to which they belong. We argue that the fairness of leader selection procedures and the fairness of those leaders once in a position to exert authority is key to our understanding of how and why group members positively engage with, and perceive themselves to be included within, the groups to which they belong.

Although the classic work of Lewin does not focus on the political context, subsequent studies have supported its key suggestion about the value of having input into decisions. Bruno Frey (1997) has considered the opportunity to directly vote on referenda provided within Swiss cantons and argued that it builds support for democracy. Frey and Alois Stutzer (2002) have demonstrated this influence empirically by examining interviews with residents of Switzerland. They have shown that greater opportunities to participate in politics via voting in elections and via citizen-based initiatives elicited higher levels of subjective well-being.

Frey, Matthias Benz, and Stutzer (2004) have expanded upon this argument in a way consistent with the arguments in this volume, suggesting that there is a general utility to procedural attributes. In particular, they suggest that people are concerned about how they are treated by institutions and processes, because this influences their sense of themselves and how positively or negatively they feel about themselves. These arguments are consistent with those being made here, and suggest why participation matters.

The work of Frey also illustrates the importance of a consideration of social inclusion and exclusion in shaping reactions to participation in governmental decision making. Frey and Stutzer (2002) show that foreigners living in Switzerland who cannot participate in government experience a smaller positive effect of living in a democratic society. These foreigners lack voice in governmental processes and, as a consequence, do not receive the direct psychological benefits of participation in government. This finding is striking in two ways. First, there is some increase from being in a democratic state, despite being excluded from participation. Second, that increase is smaller than the increase for those who are entitled to participate.

Frey argues that the benefits of participation are not simply instrumental and in that way makes an argument similar to the conclusion which emerges from the work on dispute resolution begun by John Thibaut and Laurens Walker (1975). While participation is important because it allows for influence, and Frey argues that due to direct participation policies in Switzerland are more closely aligned with public preferences than elsewhere in Europe, participation also creates feelings of inclusion, identity, and a sense of self-determination because "the political sphere takes their wishes seriously into account in a fair political process" (Frey 1997, 387).

Experimental evidence suggests that procedural rights, such as the right to vote, are regarded as more central to the group than are monetary resources. Groups are more willing to deny outgroups resources than they are to deny them the right to participate in the political process (Huo 2002), viewing exclusion from participation as denying people a more important statement about group membership. Notably, Huo finds that the allowance for participative involvement in the group and the provision or denial of treatment with dignity and respect are both worse than denying people resources. These findings reinforce the argument that procedural protections, such as the right to participate in group decisions, are more than simple reflections of distributive justice conflicts over the allocation of goods and resources.

Voice effects are both instrumental and symbolic. People gain desirable outcomes from voice, and voice has value-expressive benefits. We suggest that the symbolic issue of enfranchisement, by providing voice in the political process via voting, is central to the way that people decide how to relate to government. By providing procedural justice in the form of participation in elections, the government recognizes people's inclusion in society and their entitlement to the status of group members. This allows people to link themselves to the attributes of the group and to define themselves in term of group membership. This, in turn, encourages the development of attitudes and values that support the group, as well as motivating voluntary cooperation.

Clearly, having the opportunity to give voice, and to be actively involved, in the leader selection process is valued by members of the population who are to be led. It is the aspect of fair treatment that links it to respect for rights that is especially relevant to our discussion. This act of acknowledgment of the person as a member of the group, who is entitled to address her concerns to authorities with the assurance that these will be taken seriously, is central to communicating to people that they have standing in the group. But once a leader has been chosen, how do his constituents respond to his methods of leading or governing them?

Underlying our policy analysis is the view that government depends upon the goodwill and buy-in of most of the members of the community most of the time. This means that government authorities must be sensitive to the appearance of fairness, as well as to its reality. They need to create and implement public policies with an awareness of how the public views those policies. Based upon empirical research it is clear that the public is very ethical in its evaluations of authorities, judging them against criteria of fairness and trustworthiness. In particular, the public is very sensitive to its assessment of whether the authorities are exercising their authority in ways that are fair.

The broader policy concern is with the question of how public views and public satisfaction or dissatisfaction should be considered. I would argue that any government program or policy should be viewed through the framework of how it influences or shapes the view that members of the public have of the legitimacy of government. This is equally true of local authorities with whom community residents have personal contact and national-level political and legal authorities.

The Importance of Voluntary Cooperation

The government depends heavily on voluntary cooperation from citizens (Tyler 2002). We want citizens to cooperate with government in many ways, including willingly obeying the law (Tyler 2006a), helping the police to fight crime and terrorism (Sunshine and Tyler 2003), being willing to assume duties such as fighting in wars (Levi 1997), paying taxes (Scholz and Lubell 1998; Scholz and Pinney 1995), and generally being engaged in their communities and in the political process (Putnam 1993). All of these behaviors are shaped by public views about the government and of its policies and actions. The key is that these views—attitudes, values, and identification—are guided by the social motivations of those holding the beliefs, and government policies and actions need to be viewed through a lens of how they shape the perceived legitimacy of government.

One key antecedent of assessments of the legitimacy of government—whether the U.S. Congress, the Supreme Court, the polity, or the law—is judgments about the fairness of the procedures the government uses to exercise governmental authority and of the trustworthiness of government authorities and institutions (Tyler and Mitchell 1994). This is important because the effectiveness of legal authorities, law, and government depends upon the widespread belief among its citizens that government is legitimate and entitled to be obeyed. Given the importance of these values, we need to understand how public views about legitimacy—that is, public trust and confidence—are created and maintained. If we understand the conditions under which supportive public values, such as legitimacy, play an important role in shaping public views, we can understand how to build a law-abiding society in which people take the personal responsibility and obligation to be good citizens onto themselves (Tyler and Darley 2000).

While both outcomes and procedural justice/trust in authorities are found to shape people's satisfaction with their outcomes when they are dealing with legal authorities (Casper, Tyler, and Fisher 1998), it is the procedural justice of government actions and trustworthiness of government authorities that generalizes to shape views about law and government (Tyler, Casper, and Fisher 1989). Hence, when it makes policies, the government needs to be cognizant of more than just the objective quality of those policies; it also needs to be aware of how their creation and implementation is viewed by the public at large. Moreover, it behooves these bodies to be aware that some constituents will be more sensitive to issues of procedural fairness than others when they have reason to doubt the quality of their connection to the government.

Overcoming Obstacles to Trust and Confidence

Issues of procedural justice and trust in authorities point to evidence of a potentially developing crisis in the relationship between citizens and the government of the United States. People today generally place less trust in authorities and institutions than they did in the past, and the current mistrust is often suggested to be centered upon political authorities. The General Social Survey, conducted by the National Opinion Research Center at the University of Chicago, asks people whether they have "a great deal of confidence" in social institutions. A comparison of views expressed in the period 1972–82 to results from 2004 shows declining confidence in banks and financial institutions (35 percent to 28 percent), major companies (26 percent to 17 percent), the press (24 percent to 9 percent), organized religion (35 percent to 24 percent), and education (36 percent to 27 percent). Political trust has been examined in the National Election Studies that are conducted by the University of Michigan. In 1964 about 76 percent of Americans indicated that they trusted the government in Washington, D.C., to do what is right "just about always" or "most of the time," while 64 percent percent indicated that they thought government was run "for the benefit of all the people." In the year 2000 the percentages of people agreeing with these answers had fallen to 44 percent and 35 percent, respectively. So the growing cynicism that one may feel reflects a broad and long-term decline in the public's belief that the people running its major national institutions are honest people who are sincerely concerned about the welfare of the average citizen.

Why is trust declining? Recent discussions by social scientists offer a variety of explanations. One set of arguments, made by Margaret Levi and Laura Stoker (2000), notes the importance of the procedural injustice of actions of authorities, who have lost public confidence by using unfair procedures and exhibiting untrustworthy behavior. Through actions such as misrepresenting the facts when seeking public support for their policies (e.g., the Vietnam War) and engaging in and sometimes covering up unethical and illegal conduct (e.g., the Watergate scandal), political authorities have presented the public with evidence that they are not acting sincerely and out of benevolence and concern for their constituents. Although all forms of trust are declining, the evidence suggests that trust in government is declining most dramatically.

Government authorities have not used transparent, fact-based procedures or allowed constituents to have input into policy decisions. For example, the ongoing discussion of the "facts" behind the invasion of Iraq illustrates a case in which accurate facts were not available for a discussion about the war. Similarly, a major escalation in the war in Vietnam occurred following misrepresentations to the American public about an incident in the Gulf of Tonkin in which U.S. forces were presented as having been attacked by North Vietnam. In a similar way in the corporate arena, through examples of corporate greed and excess such as self-serving misrepresentations of corporate profits and prospects, inflated CEO salaries, and a willingness to cut employee benefits and eliminate promised pensions, business leaders have presented an image of indifference to the welfare of their stockholders and employees.

Ironically, at the same time that the decline in institutional trust is reaching levels that attract attention in the mass media, recent developments in the social sciences of the type outlined in this volume point to the importance of public trust and cooperation to the success of social institutions, whether those institutions are businesses, communities, or societies (Tyler 2006a, 2006b).

Irrespective of whether our focus is on groups, institutions, or society in general, trust is an important antecedent of effectiveness because trust leads to high levels of engagement and motivation among group members. People feel connected to groups and do what is needed to help them succeed when they trust group authorities and institutions. This centrality of trust to effectiveness in the political arena is a troubling finding when coupled with the already outlined evidence that mistrust and cynicism is growing.

Mobilizing Support in Times of Threat

Issues such as citizen support are most likely to become central during periods of threat or emergency. The entire era in which we are living, of course, is a long "emergency" as we battle terrorism at home and abroad (Tyler 2006a, 2006b). Is it the case that these special circumstances change the dynamics of the relationship between citizens and the state? We could argue that, in these troubled times, the government is more than ever dependent on the goodwill and cooperation of its citizens, who are being asked to endure hardships and face risks as we battle to defeat terrorism.

In particular, terrorism depends for its success on finding support and safe havens within communities within the general population (Tyler 2006a, 2006b). The government needs the active cooperation of the members of these vulnerable and potentially stigmatizable minority groups to identify and capture terrorists. Hence it is now more than ever important that all citizens, whatever their background and history in America, feel loyal toward U.S. society and its institutions, and hence we could suggest that more than ever, this is a time when the government must both be and be seen to be exercising authority fairly.

The government needs to frame its actions in terms of what we know about how to create and sustain social motivations. In particular, the use of fair procedures and the establishment of trust in authorities encourage the development of supportive attitudes and values, identification with authorities and institutions, thus leading to voluntary cooperative behaviors. It is those behaviors that are central to sustaining the government and the society it supports and guides, especially during times of threat and crisis. Trust in authorities is especially key during times of scarcity and crisis, when collective resources are stressed and greater sacrifices are required from members for a society to be able to prevail. In such settings trust is a key antecedent of the willingness of the public to endure hardships and make sacrifices, as exemplified in the demonstrated link between trust in government and willingness to serve in the military during wartime (Levi 1997).

Across all types of organizations the core argument of legitimacy theory is that legitimacy provides a "reservoir of support" for institutions and authorities—something besides immediate self-interest that shapes reactions to their policies (Weatherford 1992). Such a reservoir is of particular value during times of crisis or decline, when it is difficult to influence people by appealing to their immediate self-interest, and when risks about the long-term gains associated with the group are salient.

Establishing or Reestablishing Social Order

Discussions of the stability of social and political systems have long emphasized the importance to effective governance of having widespread consent from those within the system (Tyler 2006a, 2006b). Such widespread consent enables the more effective exercise of social and political authority, since authorities can appeal to members based upon their shared sense of values. That is, effective governance depends upon the legitimacy of the state that is fostered by the presence of procedural fairness and the mitigation of social exclusion.

The many recent changes in the government within various societies around the world, including South Africa and the former Soviet republics, have provided additional field settings within which the underlying assumptions of legitimacy theory have been tested. These changes in government have also rekindled interest in understanding how to create and maintain institutional legitimacy, since issues of social disintegration and internal conflict become salient when governments collapse and new forms of social order must be created. This reemphasis on understanding how to legitimate new governments is consistent with the earlier "major preoccupation of political scientists and sociologists [with legitimacy] in the post-colonial, nation-building era after the Second World War" (Sears 2003, 323). That preoccupation with establishing legitimacy was fueled by the fear that, without legitimate authorities and institutions, societies would descend into anarchy, chaos, and communism.

This political perspective is that when a new government comes into being a key factor shaping its success is the degree to which it can establish legitimacy among the general populace. As James Gibson suggests, "In a new political system few resources are more coveted than political legitimacy. Legitimacy is an endorphin of the democratic body politic; it is the substance that oils the machinery of democracy, reducing the friction that inevitably arises when people are not able to get everything they want from politics. Legitimacy is loyalty; it is a reservoir of goodwill that allows the institutions of government to go against what people may want at the moment without suffering debilitating consequences" (2004, 289). Research on emerging governments supports the argument that political institutions, including courts, can legitimate and gain acceptance for unpopular decisions and policies (Gibson, Caldiera, and Baird 1998; Machura 2003). On the other hand, studies also raise questions about the breadth of such legitimation effects. Gibson and Gregory Caldiera (2003), for example, find that the Constitutional Court in South Africa has little power to legitimate unpopular decisions. In general, however, studies support the argument that legitimacy facilitates the effectiveness of authorities and institutions, making governance easier.

Summary

Governments have a great deal to gain by encouraging supportive attitudes and values and a great deal to lose from undermining the perceived value of inclusion either by individual disenfranchisement, which undermines the loyalty of particular individuals, or by evidence of procedural injustice in the process of enfranchisement, which diminishes the value of group membership for everyone.

Self-regulation as a General Model

Effective Group-based Design

What type of group-based design is needed? The specifics will vary depending upon the particular context. However, some general arguments can be made. First, consider the many people who are members of groups, organizations, and communities. What could be done to improve their experience with their group?

It is first important to provide people with information acknowledging their rights and giving them an authority to whom they can express concerns and/or complain if they feel mistreated. Respect for people's status is enhanced if this person has reasonably high status within the organization or if the organization has created someone to represent those who might have concerns (an ombudsperson, an ethics officer). People value seeing their rights and status acknowledged. The right to go to seek and receive justice is central to the meaning of membership in our society—even with work organizations, but especially in communities and political entities—and it is important to people to have those rights acknowledged. In general, it is important to remember that people react to whether they feel treated with politeness, dignity, and respect.

It is also important to explain procedures and account for decisions. Providing people with clear information explaining how the organization works in ways that make clear what they need to do and what is going to happen is central to creating trust. When authorities make decisions, they need to explain why they are deciding as they are, irrespective of whether the person "wins" or "loses." It is particularly helpful if people acknowledge the concerns of those involved, and indicate that they have considered those concerns when making their decision, irrespective of whether or not they can give people what they have asked for. Understanding how things work and why events are happening as they are is strongly associated with viewing procedures as fair.

One particularly important situation is one in which those involved are parties to a decision or dispute about which there are competing views. The issues already raised apply to those with cases before authorities when decisions that affect them are being made, since research suggests that fair procedures and trustworthy authorities are important antecedents of satisfaction with how decisions are handled. Those involved also want to have an opportunity to explain the concerns that are leading them to approach an authority. Studies suggest that people are much more willing to accept third-party decisions about how to resolve their dispute or make a policy decision that affects them if they feel they have had a chance to tell their story.

When a decision is being presented, authorities should emphasize that it accords with the ideas underlying the rules and procedures of the organization. In particular, they should explain the decision by reference to rules and organizational principles that show that the decision is not based upon personal prejudice or bias. People are more accepting of a decision if they can understand the principle that is behind it. When decisions go against the person, it is important to show that the decision was made by applying rules and using facts. Authorities should also communicate evidence that people's concerns were listened to and taken seriously. If possible, they should acknowledge valid issues that were raised by the parties, even when indicating that those concerns cannot be addressed. People focus heavily upon whether the authority considers the needs and perspective they have expressed, especially when the decision goes against them.

In general, the ideas underlying the procedural justice and trust literatures provide clear guidelines for how decisions should be made and explained. Those guidelines provide for rule-based decision making, respect for people's rights and for the standards and principles associated with moral principles of right and wrong. In addition, people are sensitive to respect for people, as reflected in treatment with dignity, courtesy, and respect. These elements of the exercise of authority both lead people to view decision-making procedures as just and to regard the authorities involved in making them as trustworthy.

The goal of organizational design is to produce groups, organizations, and communities that are effective, efficient, and satisfying to their members. When these goals are not being obtained one clear implication is that the structure of the group should be altered. This premise—that is, the suggestion that the structure of a group, organization, or community shapes the behavior of the people within it, and through that, influences the group—is a core assumption of social psychology, which both views human behavior as a response to the nature of the social institutions within which people are embedded and suggests that the viability of groups is linked to the behavior of the people within them.

A consequence of this argument is that when the design of groups is not consistent with the realities of human motivation, groups have difficulty achieving their objectives (Ferraro, Pfeffer, and Sutton 2005). For example, Tom Tyler (2007) suggests that the legal system has difficulty effectively motivating rule adherence because its model of human motivation does not encompass the primary factors that actually shape deference to rules. Research suggests that people's rule-related behavior is most strongly influenced by their sense of responsibility and obligation to defer to legitimate authorities and follow moral principles (Tyler 2006a; Tyler and Blader 2005; Tyler, Callahan, and Frost 2007). However, legal institutions are designed based upon the assumption that behavior is shaped by the instrumental risk of sanctioning. As a result, there is a fundamental misalignment of the group—in this case, the legal system and models of motivation—leading the system to be less efficient and effective than might potentially be the case.

This volume focuses on a microlevel exploration of the behavior of the people within groups. As noted, such an approach is premised upon the belief that the behavior of the people within them shapes the viability of those groups. The suggestion that there is linkage among the thoughts, feelings, and behavior of the people within groups and group viability is widely supported by studies within law (Tyler 1990), management (Allen and Rush 1998; Freund and Epstein 1984; Katz, Kochan, and Weber 1985; Koys 2001; Pfeffer 1994; Podsakoff, Ahearne, and MacKensie 1997; Shore, Barksdale, and Shore 1995), and government (Culpepper 2003; Harrison and Huntington 2000). In each area it has been shown that the beliefs, feelings, and behaviors of group members influence the functioning of the groups to which they belong.

This volume provides those in authority in groups, organizations, and communities with a perspective on how to motivate desirable behavior on the part of the members of the groups they manage. Management can potentially involve many tasks, and this discussion does not deal with all of them. It focuses, instead, on one concern that is common to many management situations—shaping the behavior of the people within a group, organization, or community—and is concerned with factors shaping people's motivation within such groups.

Within both work settings (for-profit organizations) and communities, one key question for group authorities is how to motivate the people within that group. One group that needs to be motivated is those who are members or participants: workers, teachers, police officers, community residents. A second group that authorities need to be able motivate are the members of other organizations that are partially or completely outside of the group, including semiautonomous branches, subsidiaries, and partners connected to the group as well as autonomous agencies and organizations. Finally, authorities must be able to motivate "clients" (e.g., customers, constituents). This volume is about strategies of motivation that apply to all of these groups.

This analysis does not dispute the suggestion of instrumental models that incentives and sanctions shape cooperation. Such effects are widely, but not universally, found. Rather, it argues that an exclusive focus on instrumental approaches is not optimal, since social motivations are the *primary* drivers of cooperative behavior. Hence, organizations that rely primarily or exclusively upon instrumental motivations are misaligned with human motivations and not optimally designed.

Instrumental Motivations

It is first important to acknowledge that, as noted, instrumental models have the advantage of being under the control of authorities, as long as those authorities can obtain and maintain the wherewithal to deploy them. Hence, they are a reliable way to motivate behavior, as least while times in a group are good. It may be this element of control that most strongly draws authorities to instrumental approaches. And with that control comes centrality, since when authorities use instrumental approaches they become the focus of attention, with employees shaping their behavior in response to what authorities are doing, rather than in response to their own needs and concerns.

One approach that might potentially be taken to the limits of the instrumental model is to shore up the effectiveness of such instrumental approaches. A strategy that is often used is to increase the magnitude of gains and losses. For example, law enforcement authorities often increase the severity of punishment for wrongdoing. Such strategies are shown by research to be generally ineffective, since the probability of punishment has a more important influence upon wrongdoing than does the severity of punishment. However, this implementation model may be viewed by authorities as desirable because, like the instrumental approach itself, increasing severity is something that is under the control of authorities. To increase the likelihood of punishment, authorities would need to be able to deploy more resources, which they may not be able to do.

Another approach is to more effectively deploy the available instrumental resources. In a work setting, resources can be deployed in response to productivity in a more direct manner than is commonly the case (Tyler and Blader 2000). Rather than deploying resources based upon nonperformance considerations, they can be deployed based upon actual evidence about productivity. Management models such as pay for performance may increase productivity by more directly linking productivity and the delivery of incentives. While it might seem obvious that that linkage would exist, one common critique of CEO compensation is that it is not linked to company performance, with social factors such as connections between the CEO and members of the board instead accounting for it.

Similarly, one common critique of policing resources is that they are not deployed in the most effective manner for reducing crime. Rather, those areas that pay higher taxes, while often low in crime, receive greater police protection.

Similarly, police prefer to work during the day, while more crimes occur late in the night. Again, the effectiveness of resources devoted to fighting crime depends upon whether those resources are actually deployed in ways that directly address the problems of crime. Of course, even when resources are optimally deployed, the inability to provide sufficient resources to enact a strategy of deterrence is a constant problem within instrumental approaches to social control.

Troubling Side Effects of the Deterrence Model

It is not possible to consider trying to modify the instrumental approach without also considering some of the social implications of this approach to maintaining order. These are particularly striking in the case of the deterrence model, which uses the threat of costs to shape behavior. The deterrence model has had dramatic effects on the nature of U.S. society. Consider the case of the American prison population (Haney and Zimbardo 1998). Because of the widespread belief that crime is deterred by the threat and/or the experience of punishment, a massive number of U.S. citizens have been convicted and sentenced to serve time in prisons. Today the United States is a world leader in the proportion of citizens it holds in prison. In 2000, there were over two million Americans in jail or prison (U.S. Department of Justice 2001), far surpassing incarceration rates in Europe and elsewhere (Garland 2001).

The heavy costs of imprisonment to individuals and communities have had a strong impact upon the communities of America, especially in urban communities and especially among members of racial and ethnic minority groups, which are overrepresented in the prison system. However, those costs are not only borne by the smaller ethnic group of low-income and largely minority men. Using the broken-windows version of deterrence, many people have been subjected to legal sanctions for minor lifestyle crimes such as drinking beer on the front steps of their homes, spending time in local jails or being fined for everyday illegal behavior.

Even when they are successful, the use of instrumental approaches requires the continual deployment of organizational resources. For example, employees whose work is motivated by pay do not, over time, become motivated by other factors. On the contrary, their internal motivations to work are undermined by an emphasis upon pay for performance. Hence, the organization must continually allocate resources to maintain performance and may, over time, gradually have to increase those allocations as other reasons for working are undermined.

The case of resource drain is especially striking with regulation. To prevent wrongdoing, authorities need to deploy a credible surveillance effort, such as a police or security force. And since the likelihood of apprehension is the primary determinant of behavior, that force needs to be of sufficient size and quality that it presents people with a reasonably high level of risk of being caught and punished for wrongdoing. Preventing rule-breaking is essential for viability, but it does not directly add value to the organization. Further, it is often out of the control of group authorities.

The September 11, 2001, terrorist attacks upon the United States forced a massive reallocation of resources to defense and policing within the nation at a time when authorities would have preferred to deploy those resources in ways that would be of greater benefit to our society—that is, to improve health care, lower the deficit, and so on. Hence, resources deployed for regulation cannot be optimally used to promote positive goals and are deployed reactively and out of necessity to combat security threats. While communities may gain economically by having a prison constructed and guards employed in their community, spending money to prevent and punish rule-breaking is not the optimal use of collective resources. Having a large standing army and/or police force may be necessary, but it is costly and, over time, drains resources from a society. Similarly, the resources that work organizations spend to monitor employees for theft and other types of rule-breaking are necessary to counter these serious organizational problems, but are not a desirable use of resources.

A further problem with instrumental approaches is that they are least effective when they are needed most. All groups have periods of difficulty and scarcity: a company may have a decline in market share and may need to reorganize and rebuild; a community may suffer drought or flooding and require sacrifices from its members to remain viable. It is at these times that the cooperation of group members is most essential to the survival of the group. But, ironically, this is when that cooperation is least likely to be obtainable via instrumental approaches.

A study by Peter Brann and Margaret Foddy (1988) is illustrative. In their study, members of a community were told that collective resources (fish in the pond) were being depleted too rapidly and might disappear. Those motivated by self-interest reacted to this information by increasing the number of fish they took from the pond. Those socially motivated took fewer fish. This study illustrates how instrumental motivations may often lead people to act against the group when the group is vulnerable rather than sacrificing on behalf of the group at the risk of their own self-interest. From the perspective of the group, its viability is more uncertain when it contains within it people primarily motivated by self-interest.

A derivative problem with deterrence is the pernicious social dynamic of severity of punishment. Because deterrence is marginally effective, authorities who are spending large sums of money typically find that their policies are at best minimally effective. One solution is to spend more money to deploy even larger forces of social control—more people to enforce the orders of judges and to ensure that laws are obeyed. However, there is a natural reluctance to commit high levels of resources, so the solution of increasing severity of punishment becomes politically attractive. While evidence suggests that increases in the severity of punishment have little impact upon behavior, there is political pressure to increase severity. An example, within the United States, is the constant increase in the number of offenses that receive the death penalty. The use of severe punishment offers the tantalizing prospect of low-cost deterrence.

Not surprisingly, resources must be deployed in strategic and cost-effective ways to maximize deterrence. As already noted (see Sherman 1998), within the United States policing services are typically used more in response to political pressures than to actual crime threat levels. As a result, police officers do not most heavily patrol the highest-crime areas, so the ability of the police to deter crime is typically suboptimal. Sherman suggests that a greater effort is needed to put surveillance where the crime problem lies. Current deployments reflect the reality that public resources are allocated in ways that respond to political pressures, and the effective implementation of social control strategies often conflicts with those pressures. Hence, many decisions by the legal system are politically motivated, and not dictated by effectiveness.

The use of surveillance systems also has deleterious effects on the social climate of groups. The use of surveillance implies distrust, which decreases people's ability to feel positively about themselves, their groups, and the system itself (see, e.g., Kramer and Jost 2002; Kramer and Tyler 1996). Furthermore, people may experience intrusions into their lives as procedurally unfair, leading to anger and other negative emotions often associated with perceptions of injustice (e.g., Gurr 1970; Tyler and Smith 1998). Whether surveillance works or not, it is often demotivating and introduces new costs in terms of distrust and perhaps even paranoia in subsequent social interaction. Such costs are borne by groups, organizations, and communities to which people belong, as they lose the gains that occur when people are willing to cooperate with each other. Research suggests that the increasing use of deterrence strategies and social control has exerted precisely this type of negative influence on the U.S. social climate. It has created an adversarial relationship between legal authorities and members of the communities they serve, especially with respect to racial and ethnic minority group members (Tyler and Huo 2002), leading the public to grow less compliant with the law and less willing to help the police to fight crime (Sunshine and Tyler 2003).

An analysis in terms of general principles of human motivation further suggests that if people comply with the law only in response to coercive power, they will be less likely to obey the law in the future because acting in response to external pressures diminishes internal motivations to engage in a behavior (Tyler and Blader 2000). This follows from the well-known distinction in social psychology between intrinsic and extrinsic motivation. Research on intrinsic motivation shows that when people are motivated solely by the prospect of obtaining external rewards and punishments they become less likely to perform the desired behavior in the absence of such environmental reinforcements (see, e.g., Deci 1975). On the other hand, if people are motivated by intrinsic reasons for behaving in a certain way, then their compliance becomes much more reliable and less context-dependent.

Studies of regulatory authorities indeed demonstrate that seeking to regulate behavior through the use of threat serves to undermine people's commitment to rules and authorities (Frey 1997). As has been noted, from a motivational perspective, instrumental approaches are not self-sustaining and require the maintenance of institutions and authorities that can keep the probability of detection for wrongdoing at a sufficiently high level to constantly motivate the public through external means (i.e., the threat of punishment). Over time it becomes more and more important to have such external constraints in place, for whatever intrinsic motivation people originally had is gradually "crowded out" by external concerns.

The undermining effects of deterrence do not only occur among the people being regulated. When authorities manage people by surveillance, they do not build up any basis for trusting them. For example, employees who have been given the opportunity to follow rules for internal reasons demonstrate to workplace authorities when they do so that they can be trusted. Subsequently, authorities are more comfortable allowing those individuals to work without supervision. However, when authorities are constantly present, they have no basis for trust and can suspect that the moment they leave people will stop following the rules. Hence, their very behavior of surveillance creates the conditions requiring future surveillance. And, as noted above, their suspicions are at least partially justified, since their surveillance has probably had the effect of undermining people's value-based motivations for obeying the law.

The inadequacy of instrumental models in general, and the deterrence model in particular, has led to widespread calls from legal authorities and scholars of social science to help in understanding how to secure the effective rule of law. Their concerns suggest that current models of the determinants of human behavior are not providing legal authorities with an adequate basis for effective social regulation. This presents an important opportunity for psychologists to put forward a new and more empirically grounded perspective on the relationship between the individual and society and the following of social rules. Taking psychology seriously means linking our understanding of motivation and social influence in legal contexts to a broader psychological understanding of the person (see, e.g., Cohn and White 1990; Krislov et al. 1966; Melton 1985; Tapp and Levine 1977).

In my experience, authorities acknowledge the problems I have outlined, but say that there is no better system available. Hence, they accept the high-cost/low-impact deterrence system by default, and then live with its troubling side effects. The difficulty over time has been that many of these side effects are cumulative. So the costs of incarceration are increasing as the prison population grows, while the undermining effects of deterrence on trust and confidence in legal authorities, as well as in intrinsic motivations for rule-following, grow over time. As these social dynamics unfold, the pressure to find other solutions increases. Nonetheless, instrumental approaches are widely used because they have the advantage of providing a reliable approach to motivation. Authorities do not need to seek to understand the people over whom they are exercising authority. They can deploy a system of incentives and sanctions that will generally shape behavior in directions that they desire.

Why Do Command-and-Control Models Persevere?

The arguments outlined in this volume suggest that command-and-control strategies are costly and ineffective. If so, why are these strategies so widely found? I propose several reasons. One reason is that concentrating resources at the top accords with the general finding that people, authorities or not, are overconfident about their abilities and believe that they are able to use those resources to effectively manage others, deploying them in ways that will solve problems. People's general overconfidence in their own abilities is widely noted (Lichenstein and Fischhoff 1977). Further, people have trouble correcting this bias, since they tend to understand events as being consistent with their expectations (i.e., they process events in ways that lead to self-fulfilling prophesies). Finally, this tendency to exaggerate competence and entitlement to resources and power is especially strong when people have linked their identity and feelings of self-worth to the idea that they can manage problems to a correct solution. These psychological tendencies are found to lead people to entrap themselves in escalating commitments, using ever greater resources to handle unmanageable problems rather than acknowledging an inability to effectively exercise control. Hence, command-and-control strategies accord well with human psychology, a psychology in which feeling able to control events is associated with positive well-being but can be linked to exaggerated views about wisdom.

Related to this problem of overconfidence is the general difficulty of trusting others. While the gains of a command-and-control strategy are minimal, they can be made to occur. The much greater gains in cooperation of a social motivation strategy require relinquishing control to others and hence are linked to trust. The authorities need to believe that people will do the right thing, rather than feeling the need to control others' behavior. Hence, there are social risks involved in the use of social motivations, risks that are not part of command-and-control strategies. That those risks are shown to pay off may not be sufficiently reassuring for many authorities.

Further, social motivations constrain leaders. Their actions have to be taken in ways that take account of the judgments of those over whom they exercise authority. In other words, their decision making has to involve some degree of consultation and consensus building. This limits the flexibility of authorities, who cannot simply change policy by reorganizing their incentive structures. And it requires a long-term approach, since social motivations take time to develop and internalize—to become part of the value and attitude structure of the members of their groups.

The idea of dispositions is that they are long-term in nature and shape people's behavior across situations and over time. The benefit of this is that the motivation for action is internal and does not require incentives or sanctions. The disadvantage is that the actions taken have to be consistent with people's beliefs and feelings. One of the reasons that procedural justice is so central to building supportive attitudes and values is that the elements of procedural justice and trust involve a joint effort by authorities and the members of groups to define needs and concerns and to address the issues that matter not just to leaders but to followers as well.

Finally, the influence of social motivations requires time for supportive attitudes and values to develop or be engaged. It is not possible to immediately shift behavior by redeploying resources. Hence, while more powerful when established, social motivations have a time element that requires a long-term perspective. Leaders have to anticipate and plan for the long term.

For all of these reasons, command-and-control strategies are widely used. And I would be the last person to say that they are never appropriate or reasonable. However, the goal of this volume is to highlight that they have downsides. An important finding of early research on social coordination—research involving negotiation in settings such as the prisoner's dilemma game (in which the player must take an action whose consequences can be good or bad depending upon the actions of another player) but whose findings extend beyond games to real-world negotiation—is that people often fail to reach Pareto optimum levels of outcomes. They often, in other words, fail to achieve the levels of outcome that could potentially be realized if they were able to effectively identify and divide the highest levels of possible outcome. Here, too, I am arguing that people leave potential gains uncapitalized upon. They accept a lesser, but sure, solution that they can impose by using incentives and sanctions, rather than a much greater solution.

One reason that legal authorities believe that there are no alternatives to deterrence is because of the conceptual framework used in research on compliance. Most studies approach this issue by defining the issue as whether or not deterrence "works." Typically this question then becomes whether it is possible to identify an effect of deterrence variables that is significantly different than zero. If such an effect is found, researchers conclude that deterrence "works," This approach has several problems. The first is that it does not consider how strongly deterrence works—that is, it does not examine the magnitude of the effects observed (Ziliak and McCloskey 2008). As has already been noted, one limit of experimental games is that they do not estimate how strongly something works in real settings. In addition, the testing of statistical hypotheses is problematic because it does not indicate how strong an effect is but only if it differs significantly from zero.

Second, it does not compare the effectiveness of deterrence to alternative models and approaches. As a consequence, it does not involve a cost-benefit analysis in which the gains and costs of differing policies are compared.

Because of the widespread availability of public records, there is a large literature examining the relationship between the risk of punishment, the severity of punishment, and criminal behavior. It is this literature that yields the conclusions already outlined, and which has generated a widespread effort to identify the circumstances under which deterrence is effective, as well as calibrating the magnitude of deterrence effects. And there is a parallel literature on perceptual issues and deterrence that examines the influence of the perceived risk of punishment.

What is often missing in these studies is an effort to compare deterrence to other factors, such as values. Tyler (2006b), for example, has compared the risk of deterrence to that of legitimacy and moral value congruence and found that both values were stronger predictors of compliance than was estimated risk. In other words, when alternative value-based models are compared to deterrence, these alternative models are found to be stronger. This is not, of course, a new finding. Consider the experimental studies of tax compliance conducted in the 1960s that showed that appeals to values were more effective than were threats of punishment in motivating compliance (Schwartz and Orleans 1967).

Further, one study finds that "consistent with a large body of research that shows that when other inhibitions are strong (such as those provided by one's moral beliefs), the deterrent effect of sanction threats are irrelevant [to whether adolescents and young adults engage in criminal behavior]" (Wright et al. 2004, 206). In other words, when people have values, such as legitimacy, risk calculations may become less relevant, or even irrelevant, to their behavioral calculations. Tyler (2005) has similarly found that values and risk perceptions interacted in shaping peoples' everyday law-related behavior, with risk calculations assuming a smaller role in behavioral choices when values were important.

One problem when deciding between these two approaches is that choices need to be made, and it is not possible to pursue one strategy without influencing the other. Earlier in this volume I mentioned the undermining influence of the use of incentives and sanctions upon attitudes and values. A command-and-control strategy undermines people's attitude- and value-based motivations. If people focus on working for money, they connect less fully with their liking for their job and group. Further, they are less motivated by their sense of responsibility and obligation. Incentives and sanctions "crowd out" these other motivations, lessening their role in shaping behavior. As a consequence, social motivations become less important. In other words, while it would be wonderful if we could imagine that these two strategies could be followed in parallel, in practice this is not feasible.

One potential approach is similar to that advocated in the pyramid model of Ian Ayres and John Braithwaite (1992). These authors address regulation, but their arguments have broader applicability. They suggest beginning by appealing to values through persuasion, and only targeting increasingly severe sanctions when persuasion fails. I advocate a similar approach here. The problem with a command-and-control approach is not that it may not been necessary with some people and in some settings. The difficulty occurs when this is the opening strategy so that everybody in the group is approached in this way, and led to highlight in their own minds the incentive and sanction elements in their relationship with the group. I would suggest the contrary approach: to begin by using procedurally fair policies and practices to focus people upon the attitudes, values, and identity elements that link them to the group in socially motivated ways. These would be emphasized, and command-and-control approaches would only be brought to bear when dealing with people or settings in which social motivations were failing to achieve their goals.

The Benefits of Social Motivation

Social motivations are distinct from instrumental motivations, conceptually, and as a consequence they have distinct strengths and weaknesses. A distinct strength is, as has been noted, that they do not require organizational authorities to possess the ability to provide incentives for desired behavior, or to be able to create and maintain a credible system of sanctions. At all times groups benefit from having more resources available that can be directed toward long-term group goals. If everyday group actions are shaped by self-regulating motivations, groups have more discretionary resources.

And, as the findings of this volume make clear, social motivations are important because they are more powerful and more likely to produce changes in cooperative behavior than are instrumental motivations. Hence, social motivations are both more powerful and less costly than are incentives and sanctions. Of course, this does not mean that social motivations can be immediately and automatically deployed in all situations.

A weakness of social motivations is that they cannot be quickly activated within any social context. A CEO with a million-dollar war chest can create an incentive system in order to motivate behavior in desired directions overnight. Conversely, a city can shift its police patrols around to vary the nature of the threat faced by community residents. Such flexibility is a major advantage of the instrumental system. Social motivations must be developed over time, as the culture of an organization is created. Hence, a long-term strategy is needed to build an organization based upon social motivations.

A strategy based upon social motivation also has the disadvantage of taking control away from those at the top of the social hierarchy. If a group relies on voluntary cooperation, its leaders need to focus upon the attitudes and values of the people in the group. For example, these leaders have to create work that people experience as exciting. Further, they have to pursue policies that accord with employee's moral values. These aspects of social motivation create constraints upon the actions of leaders.

It is natural that leaders would prefer a strategy in which they are the focus of attention, irrespective of its effectiveness, to one in which they focus their attention upon employees. Yet, within business organizations, a focus on the customer is a widely institutionalized value. Similarly, the concept underlying democratic processes is that, within communities, policies ought to be a reflection of the values of the members of those communities. Hence, it is hardly a radical suggestion that organizations benefit when they develop their policies and practices in consultative ways that involve all of the relevant stakeholders, including leaders, group members, and external clients.

Aspects of procedural justice and motive-based trust feed directly into the need to make group policies and practices consistent with the attitudes and values of group members. Participatory decision making and consultation at all levels are mechanisms through which people's views are represented. And one key element in trust is the belief that authorities are soliciting and considering people's views before making decisions. Procedures that are viewed as procedurally just and authorities judged to be trustworthy encourage input from employees to higher management.

Ironically, those constraints may often have additional value for groups. The era of corporate excess makes clear that, when left unchecked, the power of those in high management does not always end up serving the interests of the company. Hence, the need to be accountable to others within the organization may have valuable benefits for the group and may check the tendency of leaders to engage in unwise actions. Just as the notion of "checks and balances" is frequently held out as one of the primary desirable design features of the U.S. government, the balancing of policies and practices among stakeholders has the benefit of restricting any tendency toward excesses.

Building Identification, Creating Attitudes and Values

Why are social motivations important? They are important because they point a direction for future research into cooperation. In addition to exploring how to motivate cooperation via more effective systems of sanctioning, or by innovative incentive-based strategies, the findings outlined herein argue that we would benefit from outlining a framework for incorporating other motivations into our motivational models. This leads to a focus on understanding which social motivations shape cooperation.

In our analysis, dispositions emerge as a key antecedent of cooperation. How do we build dispositions? The findings outlined suggest that we create organizations in which people experience procedural justice in their dealings with authorities. If people work in a just social setting and deal with authorities whose motives they trust, their commitment to the group and to their jobs is higher; they identify with their group; they feel more obligation toward authority; and they view group policies as more consistent with their moral values.

Of course, it is not necessary to view these findings as only speaking to issues of group-based design. They also have implications for selection. To the degree possible, it makes sense to recruit and seek to retain those group members whose attitudes, values, and identity are already favorable toward the group. While group climate clearly shapes cooperation, it is not the only potentially relevant factor.

I have outlined the implications of a social motivational perspective in several areas, including ethical conduct in for-profit work settings, among employees who need high levels of discretionary authority (for example, agents of social control), and when a political authority is dealing with members of the public. Beyond these particular settings it is important to note that there is a broad emphasis in recent writing on regulation and motivation within many organizational settings that advocates various forms of self-regulation and self-motivation (Aalders and Wilthagen 1997; Coglianese 1997; Edelman and Suchman 1997; Gunningham and Rees 1997; Karkkainen 2002; King and Lenox 2000; Rechtschaffen 1998).

Recent discussions of the dynamics of organizations have focused on legitimacy in work organizations (Elsbach 2001; Elsbach and Sutton 1992, Haslam 2004; Kostova and Zaheer 1999; Suchman 1995). Like earlier work on political legitimacy, these discussions stress that organizational viability is enhanced when members share the view that organizational rules and authorities are legitimate and ought to be obeyed. Studies within work-based organizational settings show that, as predicted by legitimacy theory, employees are more willing to follow organizational rules and authorities when they believe that they are legitimate (Tyler and Blader 2005).

Studies suggest that legitimacy has an important role in securing support for work organizations. Pratima Bansal and Iain Clelland (2004) show, for example, that firms viewed as legitimate are more highly insulated from unsystematic variations in their stock prices; Timothy Pollock and Violina Rindova (2003) demonstrate that the legitimacy that companies acquire through media presentations of their initial public offerings shapes investor behavior; and research suggests that firms with legitimacy are generally more likely to survive (Baum and Oliver 1991; Human and Provan 2000; Rao 1994; Zimmerman and Zeitz 2002).

Moving beyond Regulation

There is an extensive literature on regulation. However, a goal of this volume is to emphasize that groups want more from people than restraint; they also want active effort. This has always been clear in the management literature, where productivity is a key issue. However, recent discussions of law and crime emphasize as well that we want community residents to be involved in policing their communities. And, of course, in political settings we want participation. Hence, we need to recognize a broader range of cooperative goals.

Societal Implications

The Lewinian approach to studying social settings developed following the Second World War and was directly influenced by the contrast between authoritarian and democratic styles of group leadership. In the aftermath of that war the dangers of autocratic leadership were apparent, and Lewin and his group of researchers sought to emphasize the virtues of democracy. The core such virtue is the ability to motivate voluntary action, because people are psychologically involved in groups and act based upon their own internal attitudes and values to assist those groups.

An argument in favor of the virtues of voluntary engagement does not fit well with the emphasis upon command-and-control strategies that is widely found within management settings, nor with the dominance of the deterrence approach to social control in the area of law. Hence, one benefit that is derived from adopting the broader framework of motivation articulated here is that it draws attention to the benefits of engaging people in groups in ways that support voluntary cooperation.

Such an argument fits well with the increasing recognition that groups, organizations, and communities benefit from more active engagement than can be motivated by incentives and sanctions. Within law and public policy the virtues of citizen participation are recognized, while in political science the importance of social capital is noted. In management, many studies focus on the need for extra-role behavior that moves beyond doing one's job. And in education the centrality of intrinsic motivation to active learning is a key issue. All of these literatures point to the value of having a broader conception of motivation.

Although the general point of this volume is to argue for the value of focusing on social motivations, each aspect of the social motivations considered can be treated as distinct, since each is making a distinct contribution to motivation.

Attitudes and Values

Attitudes and values are general predispositions, acquired over time, that broadly shape behavior. As a consequence, we expect to see a consistency of behavior over time and within different situations within the organization. Those who like their jobs ought to manifest this attitude in their behavior on a general basis across time and situations. Similarly, the motivation to act based upon values leads to consistency of behavior over time and across situations.[1] Employees who view theft as wrong ought not to steal office supplies, as well as not falsifying their expense accounts and time sheets.

Further, these consistencies in behavior ought to be distinguishable from the changes in behavior that occur due to variations in incentives and sanctions. It would be expected that people with values, for example, would steal less often even when the risks of sanctioning associated with theft are minimal or even nonexistent. In other words, it should be easier to predict what people are going to do knowing their attitudes and values than knowing the contingencies of the situation. And, of course, that is what the results of this study find to be the case.

Identity

The findings of this study further suggest that people are motivated by the desire to support groups with which they have identity-based and emotional ties. Since these groups are important to the development and maintenance of positive feelings about the self, it is important to people that the groups be viable. When someone has merged her sense of self with a group, the success or failure of that group is literally a personal success or failure. The person is the group, and the vicissitudes of the group influence a person's feelings about themselves. Under such conditions it is not surprising that people develop favorable attitudes toward a group, link their values to the group, and act cooperatively.

Procedural Justice and Motive-based Trust

Perhaps the central argument to emerge from the findings outlined is the importance of having an organizational structure in which people experience the procedures enacted as just and view the authorities involved as trustworthy. To understand the design implications of this finding, we need to consider what constitutes procedural justice and what leads to motive-based trust.

From an organizational perspective, procedural justice judgments are most useful to managers if those within the organization distinguish them from outcome judgments and rely on distinct procedural justice assessments when evaluating the actions of management. Based upon research in work settings, it is expected that views about the fairness of procedures will, in fact, be heavily influenced by distinct judgments about procedural fairness that are not linked to the favorability or fairness of the outcomes that result from those procedures (Tyler and Blader 2000). These include, for example, whether the procedures allow input into evaluations, whether they require that objective information be used, whether they try to control the influence of bias, and so on (Lind and Tyler 1988; Tyler and Lind 1992). Recent research draws upon the four-component model of procedural justice and tests the importance of four potential procedural justice criteria (see Blader and Tyler 2003a, 2003b).

Understanding the nature of procedural justice judgments is central to efforts to design a culture that encourages supportive values and that enhances rule adherence behavior. The argument advanced here is that the potential impact of these procedural issues lies in the ability of organizations to design systems of management that are sensitive to procedural concerns, even when they cannot or do not provide those within the organization with the outcomes they desire. Several such efforts have already been made in organizations by relying upon the ideas of total quality management, which include encouraging people's input into decision making and the use of objective data analysis in decision making (Couper and Lobitz 1991; Wycoff and Skogan 1993).

Images of Human Nature

The key argument in this volume is that people act based upon social motivations. This message emerges clearly from the analyses reported. Across variations in the form of the analyses, social motivations are consistently found to have an influence upon cooperation. Further, this effect is typically larger in magnitude than is the influence of instrumental factors. As a consequence, the effective design of organizations will be enhanced if that design is based upon an awareness of the organizational factors encouraging social motivations.

The value of social motivations emerges across the forms of cooperation considered. However, the value of social motivation is particularly relevant given the need for voluntary cooperation. Within the study of law and regulation, for example, it has been increasingly recognized that we want more from people than compliance. We also want active cooperation, with people working with both the police and others in their community to fight crime. In management, the virtues of voluntary extra-role behavior are touted in firms ranging from Silicon Valley start-ups to large corporations such as Apple and Microsoft. As work becomes less physical and more intellectual and social in nature, it is increasingly important that people move beyond simply doing their jobs to being creative and innovative in work settings. And in communities we recognize the need for people to work actively with others to develop consensual policies for their groups and to create the social capital to implement them. Given the problems that authorities are seeking to solve in modern organizations, social motivations are especially central, because those problems require voluntary cooperation on the part of the members of groups, organizations, and communities.

The primary implication of the findings of this research is that organizations gain when they can motivate the people within them through social, as well as instrumental, means. This argument has broad implications, and applies to all types of groups, organizations, and communities—legal, managerial, and political.

Models of motivation and the nature of organizational design are intertwined. Within the majority of U.S. organizational settings the primary model of design is that of command and control. This model concentrates resources at the top and encourages authorities to shape the behavior of their employees by using those resources to provide incentives for desired behavior while sanctioning undesired behavior. The use of this management model is linked to a model that views rewards and punishments as key drivers of two types of cooperative behavior: performance and rule adherence.

While the dominance of instrumental models is not confined to motivational examples focused on work settings, managerial models are important because their motivational roots are well defined. The roots of these approaches within management theory lie in the work of Frederick Winslow Taylor (1911), who argued for the need for clearly specified job tasks managed by highly structured lines of command and motivated by clear and specific systems of incentives and sanctioning. These models continue to dominate thinking within industrial settings (Braverman 1974; Haslam 2004; Merkle 1980; Thompson and Warhurst 1998; Waring 1991). They are widely found in discussions of pay for performance, reinforcement-based leadership, and many other instrumental management models (see, e.g., Lawler 2000).

The assumption underlying instrumental models is that the structure of the group, and of situations within it, affects the behavior of the people in the group by shaping the contingencies associated with various types of behavior. This leads to motivational strategies, which seek to change behavior within the group by altering the contingencies within particular situations. Reward-driven incentive systems encourage desired behaviors by rewarding those behaviors; they focus on the social facilitation of behavior that benefits the group, but may not benefit the individual, at least in the short term. Punishment-driven sanctioning systems discourage undesired behavior by punishing those behaviors; they focus on the social regulation of behavior that is individually beneficial but hurts the group.

From an organizational perspective, material motivations are a decidedly mixed bag. They have the virtue of being largely under the control of authorities; hence, they are a dependable way for the authorities to exert control. For example, because they can sanction people, legal authorities such as police officers and judges can control their behavior. Managers can do the same, even more effectively, since they also dispense incentives. However, such control only extends to situations in which sanctions and sanctions can be applied. Sanctions require observing rule violations, leading to the need for surveillance. Incentives motivate people to bring desirable behavior to the attention of the authorities.

The key difference between instrumentally and socially motivated behavior is that the behavior engaged in is motivated in a way that is distinct from environmental contingencies. Instead, it is shaped by internal forces. In that sense it is voluntary or self-regulating. People help their group because they feel personally committed to group success, and they follow group rules because they feel a responsibility to do so. In either case, the group does not need to shape behavior by creating environmental contingencies that create incentives or risks that have an impact on people's expected gains and losses.

The advantage of internally motivated behavior is that it is the result of motivational forces that are within the person rather than being linked to changes in the rewards and risks present in the environment. Hence, it is self-motivated. Self-motivated cooperation benefits the group, and it does so irrespective of mechanisms that come at a cost to the group, such as reward-driven incentive systems or punishment-driven sanctioning systems.

The findings of this volume support the argument that voluntary cooperative behavior can be most effectively encouraged by the activation of social motivations. These motivations supplement the incentive and/or sanction-based instrumental motivations that have been the traditional keystone of legal and managerial policies.

The framework for encouraging social motivation differs from the command-and-control model of management in that it focuses on the needs and concerns of those at the lower levels of the social hierarchy. Instead of concentrating power and decision making at the higher levels of organizations, a social motivation approach emphasizes the value of participatory decision making—that is, sensitivity to those at lower levels of the organization, and awareness of their needs and concerns.

The purpose of this volume is to advocate a particular model of management that motivates thoughts, feelings, and behaviors that support the functioning of groups. A social motivation–based management model as a style of management addresses two key management tasks that impact the effectiveness and viability of groups. These tasks are facilitating productivity and encouraging rule adherence.

If this model were accepted and used it would lead to several changes in the strategy used to motivate cooperation in group settings. One is the focus on the policies and practices of organizations. Building supportive attitudes and values via processes of exercising authority involves building structures that encourage input and collaboration from those at the lower levels of organizations. Those individuals are given opportunities to have input into decision making; to see how decisions are being made via transparent and factual, rule-based decision making; to feel respected and valued via treatment with courtesy and with recognition of rights; and to believe that authorities are sincerely seeking to do what is responsive to the needs and concerns of all members of the organization.

In addition, attitudes and values develop early in life and persist over time. Moral values, in particular, have roots in childhood and adolescence (Hoffman 1977). Hence, it is important to understand childhood socialization, extending into adulthood. Values do not develop, nor do they disappear, quickly in response to immediate events. But over time they become internal to the person and are motivating in and of themselves. As Martin Hoffman notes, "The legacy of both Sigmund Freud and Émile Durkheim is the agreement among social scientists that most people do not go through life viewing society's moral norms as external, coercively imposed pressures to which they must submit. Though the norms are initially external to the individual and often in conflict with his desires, the norms eventually become part of his internal motive system and guide his behavior even in the absence of external authority. Control by others is thus replaced by self-control [through a process labeled internalization]" (Hoffman 1977, 85). The key issue addressed by Durkheim and Freud is the personal taking on of obligations and responsibilities that become self-regulating, so that people feel personally responsible for deferring to society, social rules, and authorities.

Although the study of the early development of values has not been central to recent discussions of strategies of social regulation, during earlier eras there has been a strong emphasis on the importance of developing and maintaining positive social values toward political, legal, and social authorities (Easton 1965, 1975; Krislov et al. 1966; Melton 1985; Parsons 1967; Tapp and Levine 1977). This earlier focus on developing positive social values led to a number of studies of childhood socialization, since evidence suggests that the roots of social values lie in childhood experiences (Cohn and White 1990; Greenstein 1965; Hess and Torney 1967; Hyman 1959; Merelman 1966, 1986). This view of social regulation views groups as depending on the widespread existence of supportive attitudes and values among the members of the population—attitudes and values that develop during political and legal socialization. Focusing on mechanisms for developing these supportive attitudes and values is, therefore, a second implication of research on social motivations.

Conclusion

This volume began by pointing to the widespread recognition throughout the social sciences, as well as in law, management, and public policy of the importance of being able to secure reliable public cooperation with groups, organizations, and societies. Such cooperation aids authorities and institutions and increases the effectiveness and viability of groups.

The question raised is why such cooperation occurs. To address this question two broad categories of motivation were outlined and contrasted. The first was instrumental—the impact upon behavior of the material gains and losses associated with undertaking different types of behavior. The second type of motivation was social. Two types of social motivation were identified: (1) dispositions and (2) policies and practices. Dispositions are the general behavioral tendencies associated with attitudes, values, and identity. Policies and practices are the ways in which authorities and institutions exercise their authority, including their decision-making procedures, their interpersonal treatment of those over whom their authority is being exercised, and the trust in the benevolence and sincerity of their motivations that they create through their actions.

The influence of these two types of motivation upon cooperation was examined using research conducted in managerial, legal, and political settings. The results consistently suggested that social motivations exert a strong influence upon cooperative behavior. This was particularly true of two key voluntary forms of cooperation: deference to rules and extra-role behavior. This influence of social motivations was found to be distinct from, and typically stronger than, the influence of incentives and sanctions.

When social motivations were separated into dispositions and policies and practices, the findings suggest that two aspects of policies and practices were central to shaping dispositions: procedural justice and motive-based trust. Those authorities and institutions that exercised authority fairly and that communicated sincere and benevolent intentions encouraged their members to develop supportive dispositions. Those dispositions provided a reason for people to act on behalf of the organization that was distinct from whatever incentives or sanctions were deployed to motivate cooperation. Dispositions exerted a general influence upon behavior, encouraging cooperation of varying types in a wide variety of settings. They further provided a reason for people to cooperate during difficult periods or times of change when it is harder to motivate cooperation instrumentally because resources are scarce and any future instrumental gains and losses uncertain.

While the two sources of motivation—instrumental and social—were treated in parallel in this volume, it is argued that organizations gain when they create a structure in which social motivations are the primary motivational framework, because instrumental motivations undermine social motivations over time. In contrast, a pyramid of motivation in which people are generally treated through authority structures designed to encourage the development of supportive attitudes, values, and identities best captures the ability of most people to be motivated in this way. In such a framework those who are unable or unwilling to respond to the policies and practices associated with social motivations are then treated in more instrumental ways. This approach was shown to be the most likely to produce groups, organizations, and societies that both survive and flourish.

Notes

Chapter One
Why Do People Cooperate?

1. Because it is based upon interviews with individuals about their own behavior, the focus of this volume is on the microlevel. For a macrolevel comparison across societies see Culpepper (2003).

2. The importance of social motivations has been noted within the management literature. See Frey and Osterloh (2002); Meglino and Korsgaard (2004).

3. Government regulatory agencies have developed a variety of strategies for enlisting businesses and other stakeholders in the formulation and implementation of regulatory policy. These include negotiation to reach consensus on administrative regulations (Coglianese 1997), cooperative arrangements for delivering social services (Stewart 2003), and joint efforts to manage wildlife and wild lands (Karkkainen 2002; Lin 1996). These policies decentralize power to "enable citizens and other actors to utilize their local knowledge to fit solutions to their individual circumstances" (Dorf and Sabel 1998, 267). All of these efforts involve procedures for decision making that embody the values of participation, neutrality, and acknowledging the rights, needs, and concerns of people involved in the decision. This does not mean that they involve wide participation, but that they reflect the values inherent in social motivation-based perspectives.

4. Tyler and Blader (2000) focus upon identification as a key mediator between organizational policies and practices and attitudes, values, and cooperative behavior. This analysis simplifies the model by considering attitudes, values, and identity as one cluster of dispositions. It does so because the focus is upon actions that can be taken to motivate cooperation and such actions involve a concern with procedural justice and motive-based trust, not upon dispositions. Procedural justice and motive-based trust influence attitudes, values, and identity.

5. It is important to recognize that the range of goals that people find desirable is distinct from the study of how people pursue those goals. Hence, broadening the range of goals to include social motivations does not invalidate the finding of models of judgment and choice that argue that judgments and choices are linked to a multiplicative combination of likelihood estimates (expectancies about the consequences of actions) and how good or bad different consequences are judged to be (the value people place upon gains and losses). Rather, the same model operates, but it includes more potential gains and losses. What is changed is the range of goals that are considered in contrast to the traditional economic focus upon incentives and sanctions. While some economists have recognized the value of social motivations, the predominant focus of this literature has been upon material gains and losses. In other words, people are still viewed as acting based upon their judgments, as they do with material gains and losses.

6. It is important to acknowledge that prior social psychologists have recognized the importance of motivations of the type studied here. One example is the work of Foa and Foa (1974). However, discussions of motivation in organizational settings have focused largely on issues of incentives and sanctions.

7. They may also engage in behaviors targeted toward harming the group and its goals. However, this analysis is not focused on behaviors that undermine the group. Rather, it focuses on the degree to which people act in ways that help the group. It imagines a continuum from making minimal efforts on behalf of the group to making more extensive efforts. The question of when people actively sabotage or otherwise work against their group is important, but outside the scope of this analysis.

Chapter Two
Motivational Models

1. The difficulty of separating out instrumental and social motivations is illustrated by Podsakoff and colleagues' review. The authors find that incentives matter, but that a key issue is the justice of the manner in which incentives are delivered.

2. As already noted, other authors also recognize that possibility of nonmaterial motivations; see, e.g., Foa and Foa (1974). More recently this idea has been discussed by Tetlock (2000, 2002). More recent versions of social exchange theory also recognize that people care about more than material gains and losses. And, as with economic theory, a broader range of goals does not invalidate social exchange theory. Rather, it just says that the dynamics of social exchange occur over a broader range of potential gains and losses. Whatever people value from others, their behavior is shaped by their estimate of the gains and losses associated with exchanges.

3. Thibaut and Walker (1975) use a similar instrumental model to explain procedural justice. However, Tyler (1994) argues that procedural justice can best be understood as relational—that is, social—while distributive justice has both instrumental and relational elements. Hence, Tyler suggests that distributive justice is the form of justice most strongly shaped by instrumental concerns.

4. Tyler (1994) suggests that procedural justice is completely social (i.e., relational) in nature.

5. The discussion of attitudes about work should be distinguished from the more complex literature on commitment in the workplace. The multidimensional models of commitment that have been developed include several of the social motivations discussed here; see also Mayer and Allen (1997).

6. The results of this study also show that legitimacy—a social motive considered later—shapes deference.

7. Two arguments frame the suggestion that justice is a social motivation. The first is that procedural justice is distinctly relational. Tyler (1994) distinguishes procedural and distributive justice, arguing that procedural justice is uniquely framed by "relational motivations." These relational issues include concern about the quality of decision making and the quality of interpersonal treatment (Tyler and Lind 1992).

The original discussion of relational motivations included trust. In this analysis, trust in the motives of authorities will be treated separately in the analysis of policies and practices in chapter 6. Treatment of this issue has not always been the same. Tyler and Blader (2000) include indices of trust in their index of interpersonal treatment to create two factors, decision making and interpersonal treatment. On the other hand, in their analysis of personal experiences with authorities, Tyler and Huo (2002) treated both general procedural justice judgments and assessments of trust as distinct judgments from the justice of decision making and the justice of interpersonal treatment. This analysis follows the lead of Tyler and Huo in treating trust as an issue that is distinct from procedural justice.

8. Of course, trust is not completely distinct from procedural justice; see De Cremer and Tyler (2007).

9. As noted, the general focus of justice research has, until recently, been on negative reactions to injustice. In contrast, the focus of the literature on trust is on whether trust exists. The existence of trust is viewed as a condition that enables productive exchange among people. In law and business, for example, lack of trust is viewed as a barrier to the ability of individuals to engage in cooperative interactions. In contrast to the literature on justice, in which the absence of justice leads to outrage, in the literature on trust the absence of trust leads people to have a greater unwillingness to cooperate with others. In the absence of trust, people have trouble engaging in cooperative interactions in which they exchange resources and work together toward common goals.

10. People focus on their assessment of the motives of authorities for two reasons. The first is that they lack enough information to directly determine what actions the authority has taken. People are usually not in the position to know all that has been done in response to their problem or to understand whether the police or courts are doing everything possible to try to solve the problem in a reasonable way. The second is that they lack enough expertise to decide whether those actions are the most appropriate ones to have taken. Authorities are often in possession of special knowledge and training that allow them to make better professional decisions. Judges and police officers, like doctors, lawyers, and teachers, all spend significant time learning their roles and responsibilities, which allow them to make decisions that cannot easily be explained to an untrained member of the public. We expect a doctor to know, for example, about the appropriate way to treat an illness and we must to some degree trust that the doctor is acting in good faith.

The problem for people is to distinguish between situations in which cooperation with authorities is reasonable and situations in which exploitation is occurring. For example, we should cooperate with our doctor when that doctor is motivated by an interest in protecting our health. However, if our doctor is taking kickbacks from a drug company to prescribe ineffective or harmful drugs, our trust is being exploited, and we should not cooperate. The difficulty lies in determining which situation we are in, when we lack the expertise to independently evaluate the appropriateness of the drug or lack the knowledge of the fact that the doctor prescribes that same drug to all patients, regardless of their illnesses.

Chapter Three
Cooperation with Managerial Authorities in Work Settings

1. The panel used in this study is a sample of respondents who completed online surveys in exchange for free cable services. In addition, those respondents who completed the questionnaires received small cash incentives: $5 for completing the first-wave questionnaires, and $5 for completing the second-wave questionnaires. The sample can be weighted to approximate the demographics of the American population, but such weighting was not used in the analysis presented here. In this study only those members of this panel who work were allowed to participate in the study.

2. The study of employees was conducted with support from the Sloan Foundation Program on Business Institutions (Gail Pesyna, director). I would like to thank the foundation for its support and Gail for her commitment to this project.

3. Those who expressed interest were screened to ensure that they worked at least twenty hours per week, had a primary supervisor, and had worked at their current jobs for at least three months. Respondents meeting these criteria completed the survey in two parts, one week apart. Cooperative behavior was assessed in the first (week one) questionnaire and social motives in the second (week two) questionnaire. Respondents answered structured questions in their homes via the Internet (WebTV). The first wave of interviews yielded 4,430 completed interviews. It includes only those who completed both weeks of the study.

4. In comparison, the weighted first-wave sample was 53 percent male and 82 percent white; 32 percent had a college degree or postgraduate education; and 42 percent had a household income of over $50,000. The mean age was forty-one.

5. A four-item scale was created to measure in-role behavior (alpha = 0.80). Respondents were asked how often they engaged in the behaviors and the response scale ranged from (1) never to (7) always. The items were:

Fulfill the responsibilities specified for someone in your position.
Perform the tasks usually expected by your work organization as part of your job.
Complete your work in a timely, effective manner.
Meet the performance expectations of your supervisor.

6. Six items were used to measure how often respondents engaged in extra-role behavior (alpha = 0.81). Respondents were asked about frequency of behavior, and the response format was (1) never to (7) always. The items were:

Volunteer to do things that are not required in order to help your organization.
Volunteer to orient new employees to help your organization.
Help others with work-related problems as a way of helping your organization.
Put an extra effort into doing your job well, beyond what is normally expected.
Share your knowledge with others even when you will not receive credit.
Work extra hours even when you will not receive credit for doing so.

7. A seven-item scale was created to measure compliance (alpha = 0.86). Respondents were asked how often they engage in different behaviors, and the response format was (1) never to (7) always. The items were

Comply with organizational rules and regulations.
Use company rules to guide what you do on the job.
Seek information about appropriate company policies before acting.
Follow organizational rules about how you should spend your time.
Follow the policies established by your supervisor.
Carefully carry out the instructions of your supervisor.
Adhere to the directives of your supervisor.

8. Six items were used to measure voluntary rule adherence (alpha = 0.86). Respondents were asked about frequency with which they engaged in behaviors, and their format was (1) always to (7) never. The items were

Follow company policies even when you do not need to do so because no one will know whether you did.
Follow organizational rules and policies without questioning them.

Follow company rules and policies concerning how to do your job.

Implement your supervisor's decisions even when he will not know whether you did.

Do what your supervisor expects of you, even when you do not really think it is important.

9. Three items assessed the likelihood of receiving incentives/sanctions for good/bad work-related behavior (alpha = 0.66) on a scale of 1 to 5. The items were

How easy is it for your supervisor to observe whether you follow work rules? (1 = not easy, to 5 = very easy)

How often is your supervisor paying attention to whether you are follow work rules? (1 = never, to 5 = always)

How often do you think that you are closely monitored by your supervisor? (1 = never, to 5 = always)

10. Three items measured the magnitude of the relationship between behavior and rewards/costs. (alpha = 0.72) and the response format was (1) not much to (5) a great deal. The items were

If you do your job poorly, how much does it hurt your pay and benefits?

If you do your job well, how much does that improve your pay and benefits?

If you are caught breaking a work rule, how much does it hurt your pay or your chances for promotion?

11. Probability and strength were combined multiplicatively. The resulting scale was adjusted to range from 1 to 5 to maintain consistency with the range of the two main effects.

12. Four items assessed respondents' views about their long-term prospects for gain or loss in the organization (alpha = 0.76) on a scale of 1 to 5. The items were

How favorable are your opportunities for promotion? (1 = very unfavorable, to 5 = very favorable)

How favorable will your long-term financial benefits be if you stay with your company?" (1 = very unfavorable, to 5 = very favorable)

How favorable is the job security you have where you work? (1 = very unfavorable, to 5 = very favorable)

My company provides a level of rewards superior to what other companies offer. (1 = disagree strongly, to 5 = agree strongly)

13. Five items were used to assess the favorability of policies (alpha = 0.87). The response scale ranged from (1) favorable to (5) unfavorable. The items were

How favorable are the outcomes and resources you receive from the policies of your work organization?

How favorable are the resources that you are given to do your job?

Compared to what you expect, how favorable is your compensation?

How favorable is your pay?

How favorable are your benefits?

14. Three items measured the extent to which employees indicated working only for money (alpha = 0.69). The response scale was (1) agree strongly to (5) disagree strongly. The items were

How hard I work is directly related to how much I am financially rewarded.
I do not tend to do things at work that I do not think will be rewarded.
I only do what I need to do to earn my pay.

15. Five items measured whether people felt that they had to keep their jobs because they needed the money (alpha = 0.92). The response scale was (1) agree strongly to (5) disagree strongly. The items were

I depend heavily on the money I make where I work.
If I lost even one day's pay, I would have a difficult time making ends meet.
I really need every dollar I make.
Right now, staying in my company is a matter of necessity as much as desire.
It would be hard for me to leave my job, even if I wanted to.

16. Three items were used to assess organization-level distributive fairness (alpha = 0.82; mean = 2.83 [1.09]). The response scale was (1) agree to (5) disagree. The items were

In general, resources are fairly allocated among employees at my organization.
Employees receive the opportunities they deserve in my company.
The resources people receive are linked to how well they do their jobs.

Three items were used to assess personal outcome fairness (alpha = 0.76; mean = 2.97 [0.97]). The response scale was (1) agree to (5) disagree. The items were

I am fairly paid at work.
I receive the opportunities I deserve.
The resources I receive are linked to how well I do my job.

17. A six- item scale was created to measure instrumental trust (alpha = 0.89). The response scale was (1) disagree strongly to (5) agree strongly for the first five items, which were

I think that the management of my company will keep the company profitable in the future.
I think that management is making competent decisions about how to solve problems in our organization.
I trust management to make an effective plan that will keep our company competitive in the future.
I am generally able to anticipate the decision that management will make.
Management usually makes the policy decisions that I expect.

The response scale ranged from (1) very unfavorable to (5) very favorable for the sixth item:

How favorably would you rate the decisions that management makes about how to keep your company profitable in the future?"

18. Attitudes toward the organization were assessed using four items (alpha = 0.91). The response scale was (1) agree strongly to (5) disagree strongly. The items were

I am very happy where I work now.
I like my current employer.

I cannot think of another company for which I would rather work.

I think I have one of the best of all possible employers.

19. Six items were used to measure intrinsic motivation to work (alpha = 0.98). The response scale was (1) agree strongly to (5) disagree strongly. The items were

Compared to most jobs, mine is a great one to have.

All in all, I am satisfied with my job.

My job is a source of pleasure.

My job provides me with a sense of personal fulfillment.

My job teaches me new skills.

My job gives me the chance to do meaningful work.

20. Based upon a factor analysis of ten work-related affect items, two factors were identified—positive and negative. Positive emotion/affect during work was assessed by a five-item scale (alpha = 0.78). The items asked about the frequency with which employees felt particular affect during work and the response format was (1) never to (7) always. The respondents were asked how often at work during the last several weeks they had felt inspired, enthusiastic, excited, alert, or determined. Negative feelings were also assessed in the same manner, by asking how often employees had felt afraid, upset, nervous, scared, or distressed.

21. Twelve items were used to assess the legitimacy of workplace rules and authorities (alpha = 0.90). The response scale was (1) disagree strongly to (5) agree strongly. The items were

I feel I should accept the decisions made by my supervisors, even when I think they are wrong.

I think that it hurts my work group when I disagree with my supervisors.

I feel that it is wrong to ignore my supervisors' instructions, even when I can get away with it.

I feel that I should follow my companies' rules, even when I think they are wrong.

I think that it hurts my company when I break company rules.

I feel that it is wrong to break my company's rules, even when I can get away with it.

An employee should accept the decisions made by their supervisors, even when they think that their supervisors are wrong.

Disobeying one's supervisors is seldom justified.

Someone who disregards their supervisors hurts their work group.

People should follow organizational policies, even when they think that those policies are wrong.

It is wrong to break company rules, even if you can get away with it.

Companies are most successful when employees follow company policies.

22. Five items were used to measure obligation to perform well on the job (alpha = 0.86). The response scale was (1) disagree strongly to (5) agree strongly. The items were

I feel that any organization for which I work deserves my best work.

It is my responsibility to do a good job for my company.

I feel guilty when I do not do high-quality work on my job.

I respect those coworkers who give my employer their best effort.

I need to do a good job for my company in order to feel good about myself.

23. Four items measured the obligation to remain with the company (alpha = 0.75). The response scale was (1) disagree strongly to (5) agree strongly. The items were

I think that people move from company to company too often.
I think it is important to remain loyal to one's work organization.
Things were better in the days when people stayed with one organization for most of their careers.
I feel a moral obligation to keep working for my current company.

24. Five items measured moral value congruence (alpha = 0.88). The response scale was (1) disagree strongly to (5) agree strongly. The items were

I find that my values and the values where I work are quite similar.
What my company stands for is important to me.
I agree with the values that define the goals of my company.
I think that my employer acts very ethically.
I am seldom asked at work to do anything that goes against my personal moral values.

25. Six items indexed the degree to which respondents indicated that they felt respected by management (alpha = 0.94). The scale ranged from (1) not at all to (7) a great deal. The items asked how much managers

Respect the work you do
Respect your work-related ideas
Think highly of the quality of your work
Appreciate your unique contributions on the job
Think that you have valuable insights and ideas
Think it would be difficult to replace you

26. Five items assessed the degree to which respondents indicated feeling that they worked in a high-status organization (alpha = 0.91). The response scale ranged from (1) disagree strongly to (5) agree strongly. The items were

My company is one of the best companies in its field.
People are impressed when I tell them where I work.
My company is well respected in its field.
I think that where I work reflects well on me.
I am proud to tell others where I work.

27. Eight items indexed the degree to which respondents indicated merging their own identities with the group (alpha = 0.86). The response scale ranged from (1) disagree strongly to (5) agree strongly. The items were

Working at my company is important to the way that I think of myself as a person.
When someone praises the accomplishments of my company, it feels like a personal compliment to me.
I feel that the problems of my work group are my own personal problems.
When someone from outside criticizes my company, it feels like a personal insult.
The place I work says a lot about who I am as a person.
I think I am similar to the people who work at my company.

Most of those working at my company want the same things from their work that I do.
I have more in common with the people I work with now than I would at most other workplaces.

28. Tyler and Blader (2000) also identified a third component of pride—pride in shared moral values. In this analysis that variable—moral value congruence—will be treated as a parallel index of values and used together with legitimacy judgments.

29. A six-item emotional identification scale was created (alpha = 0.91). The scale ranged from (1) disagree strongly to (5) agree strongly. The items were

My company inspires me to do the very best job I can.
I would recommend to a close friend that they work in my company.
I feel emotionally attached to my company.
I feel like part of the family where I work.
I feel that I personally belong in my company.
My concern about what happens to my company goes beyond my just being an employee there.

30. Three items assessed views about the overall fairness or organizational procedures (alpha = 0.94; mean = 3.11 [1.14]). The response scale was (1) disagree strongly to (5) agree strongly. The items were

Decisions are usually made in fair ways in my company.
My company puts an effort into making decisions in fair ways.
Overall, people are treated fairly where I work.

31. Four items assessed respondents' views about the fairness of the procedures used with decisions involving them personally (alpha = 0.93; mean = 3.23 [0.99]). The response scale was (1) disagree strongly to (5) agree strongly. The items were

Decisions that affect me are usually made in fair ways in my company.
My company puts an effort into making decisions that affect me in fair ways.
Overall, I am fairly treated where I work.
Most of the issues involving me are handled in fair ways where I work.

32. Eight items were used to measure the fairness of the procedures used by the employee's supervisor (alpha = 0.93; mean = 3.36 [s.d. = 0.97]). The response scale was (1) agree to (5) disagree. The items were

Applies rules consistently
Does not act on biases
Uses accurate information
Explains actions
Respects rights
Treats people with dignity
Is polite
Acts ethically

33. The same eight items (see note 32), focused on the company, were used to create a scale indicating the fairness of company procedures (alpha = 0.96; mean = 3.25 [s.d. = 0.94]).

34. A two-item scale of motive-based trust was created (alpha = 0.91). The response scale ranged from (1) disagree strongly to (5) agree strongly. The items were

I trust management to do what is best for employees like myself.
I trust management to think about my needs as well as their own when making decisions.

35. A four-item scale of trust in management was created (alpha = 0.94). The response scale ranged from (1) disagree strongly to (5) agree strongly. Items asked the respondent whether or not management

Provides you with honest feedback about why decisions are made
Ensures that your views are considered
Makes sure your needs are taken into consideration
Reflects a desire by the company to do what is best for employees like you

36. A four-item scale was created to measure trust in one's supervisor (alpha = 0.93). The response scale ranged from (1) disagree strongly to (5) agree strongly. The same four items were used (see note 35), but focused on the behavior of the employee's immediate supervisor.

37. The complete correlation matrix suggests that there is a fairly high correlation within the cluster of social motivations (mean $r = 0.64$). The correlation across the five areas within the instrumental motivations is considerably weaker (mean $r = 0.27$). The most striking problem within instrumental motivations is that whether or not people indicate that they are mainly motivated to work by money is generally unrelated to other instrumental indices. This is probably the case because the instrumental indices generally describe the environment in which the employees work, while the motivation for working is external to the particular work environment.

38. In structural equation modeling, the indices of each type of motivation are allowed to load upon underlying factors that reflect each type of motivation. The program adjusts the strength of each link to maximize the ability to predict cooperation.

39. There are five instrumental and five social indices. In this analysis the error terms of each corresponding instrumental and social index were allowed to correlate.

40. The analysis presented up to this point is based upon the argument that instrumental and social motivations shape cooperation separately, as results suggest that they do. It is also possible to compare a model in which instrumental and social motivations are treated as two distinct, but correlated, influences on cooperation to models in which instrumental motivations are viewed as exercising their influence on cooperation through social motivations, or vice versa.

The model used in the analysis reported can be compared to two alternative models. One model argues that instrumental influences on cooperation only occur through an indirect influence on social motivations. The other model argues that social motivations only influence cooperation indirectly, by shaping instrumental motivations. A comparison of the fit of these models suggests that either is a significantly worse fit than a model suggesting that there are two correlated paths.

If the two are treated as distinct influences on cooperation, the model is found to fit better (chi-square [4 d.f.] = 44.8) than it does if instrumental factors are treated as exercising influence on cooperation only through social motivations (chi-square [7 d.f.] = 162.4) or social motivations are treated as exercising influence on cooperation only through instrumental motivations (chi-square [7 d.f.] = 275.9).

41. As has been outlined, the analysis also contains a panel component. This panel data can be used to test the validity of the arguments made by looking at change in the dependent variables. One way to test the validity of the conclusions is to use the panel data to conduct a panel analysis in which measures of cooperation noted in the first wave are controlled upon in an analysis of factors shaping second-wave cooperation. In this panel analysis the dependent variable is measured at the second wave, and is predicted using first-wave measures of the instrumental and social motivations. For each dependent variable, the first-wave measure of the same variable is included as a control.

The panel data shows that for required behaviors the average beta weight for instrumental factors was 0.06, and for social motivations 0.07. For voluntary behaviors the average beta weight for instrumental motivations was 0.04, and for social motivations 0.12.

42. For privacy purposes, salary information was not collected from respondents to the survey. The salary figures are based upon company records.

43. There were some minor variations in the questions used. For details see Tyler and Blader (2005).

44. And the correlation between social and instrumental motivations was similar to that found with corporate bankers ($r = 0.64$ for agents of social control).

Chapter Four
Cooperation with Legal Authorities in Local Communities

1. When people deal with legal authorities they could potentially deal with police officers or court officials, such as judges. This study focuses only on the police. It does so because Tyler and Huo (2002) have found that 85 percent of the direct contact that people have with legal authorities is with the police. Hence, the police are a much more direct presence in communities than are courts. Research on the courts suggests that the findings concerning the police and the courts are quite similar (Tyler and Huo 2002).

2. Another example of issues linked to deterrence is provided by Ross (1982), who focuses on the problem of drunk driving to outline some of the issues associated with using deterrence to shape law-related behavior. He suggests that raising risk estimates to a level that is high enough to lower the rate of lawbreaking behavior, while not necessarily impossible, involves prohibitively high costs in terms of police personnel and people's willingness to accept state intrusions into their personal lives. Notably, Ross finds that changes in laws can lead to short-term declines in lawbreaking because the high level of media exposure to police activities leads people to temporarily overestimate the risks of being caught and punished for such behavior. Ross further points out that even the intensive efforts of Scandinavian authorities to create high estimates of risk using random roadblocks and other similarly expensive and intrusive law enforcement measures are insufficient to create and maintain subjective risk estimates that are high enough to deter drunk driving over the long term.

3. The lack of a direct correspondence between objective and subjective risks leads to another problem with the psychology of the deterrence model—namely, its failure to take into account "threshold effects." That is, to influence people's behavior at all, risk esti-

mates need to be high enough to exceed some threshold of being psychologically mean-ingful (Ross 1982). In most situations the objective risk of being caught and punished is quite low. For example, the approximate objective risk of being caught, convicted, and imprisoned for rape is 12 percent; for robbery it is 4 percent; and for assault, burglary, larceny, and motor vehicle theft the incarceration rate is approximately 1 percent (Rob-inson and Darley 1997). Of course, psychologists know that subjective estimates of risk are stronger determinants of people's behavior than are objective risks. However, research suggests that subjective risk estimates for infrequent events are, if anything, even lower than are objective risks (see, e.g., Bazerman 2005). Furthermore, it is reasonable to as-sume that people's estimates of whether or not they will be apprehended by the police are subject to egocentric biases and the "illusion of invulnerability" (Kruger and Dunning 1999; Taylor and Brown 1988).

4. A grant from the National Institute of Justice funded the collection of interview data from the random sample of 1,653 of the residents of New York City. A grant from the National Science Foundation (NSF-0240938) funded the reinterviews. Any opinions, findings, or conclusions or recommendations expressed in this material are those of the author and do not necessarily reflect the views of the National Institute of Justice or the National Science Foundation.

5. To determine the degree to which respondents felt that the police created an effec-tive deterrent to rule-breaking, they were asked how likely they thought it was that they would be caught and punished if they broke each of the seven laws used to determine cooperation (alpha = 0.87). The seven items had a response scale ranging from (1) low to (4) high.

6. A four-item performance scale was created (alpha = 0.65). The items were

> How effective are the police in fighting crime in your neighborhood? (1 = very effec-tive, to 4 = not effective at all)
> When people in your neighborhood call the police for help, how quickly do they respond? (1 = very quickly, to 4 = not quickly at all)
> How effective are the police in your neighborhood at helping the people who ask for help? (1 = very effective, to 4 = not effective at all)
> You have confidence that the NYPD can do its job well. (1 = agree strongly, to 4 = disagree strongly)

7. Ten items evaluated the distributive fairness of the delivery of police services (alpha = 0.63). Respondents were asked whether each of the following seven groups received the quality of service and protection they deserved, using a three-point response scale: (1) received the service deserved, (2) received too much, and (3) received too little. The groups were

> The people who live in your neighborhood
> Minorities in your neighborhood
> Whites
> African Americans
> Latinos
> Poor people
> Wealthy people

The last three items used a response scale ranging from (1) agree strongly to (4) disagree strongly. The items were

Do the police treat all people equally, regardless of their race?
Do the police provide better service to the wealthy than to the average citizen?
Do the police sometimes give minorities less help than they give to others?

8. Respondents were also asked about the fairness of police service delivery to "people like you." The response scale ranged from (1) unfair to (4) fair.

9. The attitude scale (alpha = 0.63) contained three items, which were reverse scored:

The law represents the values of the people in power, rather than the values of people like you.
People in power use the law to try to control people like you.
The law does not protect your interests.

10. To assess legitimacy, respondents were first asked whether or not they felt that they ought to obey the police in situations in which the police told them how to behave and/or when there were relevant laws. There were seven items (alpha = 0.69), with a response scale ranging from (1) agree strongly to (4) disagree strrongly. The items were

Overall, the NYPD is a legitimate authority and people should obey the decisions that NYPD officers make.
You should accept the decisions made by police, even if you think they are wrong.
You should do what the police tell you to do even when you don't understand the reasons for their decisions.
You should do what the police tell you to do even when you disagree with their decisions.
You should do what the police tell you to do even when you don't like the way they treat you.
There are times it is okay for you to ignore what the police tell you to do (reverse scored).
Sometimes you have to bend the law for things to come out right (reverse scored).

11. The measure of moral value congruence respondents (alpha = 0.70) employed four items. The response scale ranged from (1) agree strongly to (4) disagree strongly. The items were

Your feelings about what is right and wrong usually agree with the law.
The police usually act in ways that are consistent with your own values about what is right and wrong.
The moral values of most police officers are similar to your own.
The law is generally consistent with the view of people in your neighborhood about what is right and wrong.

12. The identification with the police scale included nine items (alpha = 0.69). The response scale ranged from (1) low to (4) high. The items were

If you talked to most of the police officers who work in your neighborhood, you would find they have similar views to your own on many issues.

Your background is similar to that of many of the police officers who work in your neighborhood.

You can usually understand why the police who work in your neighborhood are acting as they are in a particular situation.

You generally like the police officers who work in your neighborhood.

You are proud of the work of the police department.

You agree with many of the values that define what the police department stands for.

If most of the police officers who work in your neighborhood knew you they would respect your values.

Most of the police officers who work in your neighborhood would value what you contribute to your neighborhood.

Most of the police officers who work in your neighborhood would approve of how you live your life.

13. The measure of police procedural justice featured two items (alpha = 0.75). The response scale ranged from (1) disagree strongly to (4) agree strongly. The items were

The police usually use fair procedures to decide how to handle the problems they deal with.

The police usually treat people in fair ways.

14. The fairness of police decision making was assessed using five items (alpha = 0.85; mean = 3.67; s.d. = 1.07). The response scale ranged from (1) disagree strongly to (4) agree strongly. The items asked whether the police

Usually accurately understand and apply the law

Make their decisions based on facts, not their personal biases and opinions

Try to get the facts in a situation before deciding how to act

Give honest explanations for their actions to the people they deal with

Apply the rules consistently to different people

15. Two items measured the quality of interpersonal treatment (alpha = 0.80), asking whether police

Treat people with dignity and respect

Respect people's rights

16. Motive-based trust (alpha = 0.71; mean = 2.65; s.d. = 1.14) was measured by asking respondents whether the police

Consider the views of people involved

Take account of the needs and concerns of the people they deal with

17. Details of this study are provided in Tyler and Degoey (1995).

18. Seventy-seven percent strongly agreed that they would conserve; 21 percent agreed; 2 percent disagreed; and 2 percent disagreed strongly.

19. The items were, "Government should determine water use" and "There should be mandatory water use rules."

20. Respondents were asked, "How much of an impact is the water shortage having on you and your family?" and "How much of an impact to you expect it to have in the future?"

21. The questions asked whether the commission made decisions favorable to the respondents, made decisions that gave them a fair amount of water, and allocated them enough water.

22. Procedural justice was measured using ten items (alpha = 0.89). The four-point response scale ranged from (1) disagree strongly to (4) agree strongly, asking about how the water commission made decisions and whether it was

Using fair procedures
Treating people fairly
Giving people an opportunity to be heard
Considering people's views
Giving people equal consideration
Being honest
Getting accurate information
Respecting people's rights
Treating people politely
Making decisions fairly

23. Respondents were asked whether the commission could be trusted to make decisions that were good for everyone and whether its rules were good for everyone in the community.

24. The legitimacy survey contained four items (alpha = 0.72). It used a four-point response scale ranging from (1) disagree strongly to (4) agree strongly and asked respondents whether government

Should have the authority to make water-use rules
Should have a great deal of authority to decide what the rules were concerning how much water homes could use, what they could use water for, and how much water should cost
Should be allowed to do whatever it felt was best to handle the problem

Chapter Five
Cooperation with Political Authorities

1. This data set was prepared by Paloma Bauer and Virginia Beard of Michigan State University and is available through the Interuniversity Consortium for Political and Social Research.

2. While eighteen countries were included in the study, conditions in Zimbabwe prevented many interviews from being conducted in that country.

3. The objective indicator of economic performance in both studies included World Bank indices of gross domestic product and of government consumption. The figures used in Round 1 were for 2002; in Round 2 they were for 2004–5. The quality of governance index for Round 1 included World Bank governance indicators of the rule of law (2002), political stability (2002), voice in government (2002), the Transparency International Corruption Perception Index (2001), and Freedom House indices of political rights (2002) and civil liberties (2002). Round 3 included the same indices for 2005.

4. Because of the conditions existing in Africa there were missing values on many variables for some respondents and, in some cases, for entire countries. The regres-

sion analysis was conducted using pairwise deletion. However, the same analysis was also performed using listwise and mean substitution approaches to ensure that errors did not occur due to the pattern of the missing values. Similar results were found using each approach.

5. In Round 1 the items on this index included attending community meetings, discussing political issues, going to rallies, and getting involved in campaigns.

6. People were asked how frequently they had gone without food, water, health care, electricity, and cash income.

7. There were three questions: "How satisfied are you with the state of the national economy?" "How satisfied are you with the state of the national economy compared to the past?" "How satisfied are you with the state of the national economy compared to the future?"

8. Respondents were asked whether they felt that democracy was preferable to any other form of government.

9. Legitimacy is measured through both institutional legitimacy ("The constitution expresses the values and aspirations of the people") and the obligation to obey ("The government has the right to make authoritative decisions").

10. This was measured using two items: "It makes you proud to be called [a citizen of the particular country]" and "You would want your children to think of themselves as [a citizen of the particular country]."

11. There were four items: "How honest are elections?" "Are all citizens treated equally?" "To what extent is your own group treated unfairly?" "Does the government represent all groups in society?"

12. People were asked how much they trusted four specific government institutions to "do what is right": the president, the police, the courts of law, and the electoral commission.

13. In Round 3 the items on this index included frequency of attending community meetings and joining others to raise issues, as well as how often respondents had contacted a local government councilor, a member of the parliament, an official of the government, a political party official, a religious leader, a traditional tribal leader, or some other influential person.

14. People were asked how frequently they had gone without enough food to eat, enough clean water for home use, medicines or medical treatment, enough fuel to cook with, a cash income, or school expenses for their children.

15. The questions were

How would you describe the economic situation?
How would you describe your own present living conditions?
How are your living conditions compared to those of others in your country?
How do economic conditions today compare to the past?
How are your own economic conditions, compared to the past?
How do you expect economic conditions in the country to change in the future?
How do you expect your own economic conditions to change in the future?
How has the availability of consumer goods changed?
How has the availability of job opportunities changed?
How has the gap between rich and poor changed?

16. Respondents were asked how likely it was that the authorities would enforce the law if a top government official (1) committed a serious crime, or (2) did not pay a tax on some of the income he had earned.

17. Respondents were asked three questions: "How much of a democracy is your country today?" "How satisfied are you with the way democracy works in your country?" "How likely is it that your country will remain democratic?"

18. First, institutional legitimacy was measured by responses to one item: "The constitution expresses the values and aspirations of the people." Second, obligation to obey was measured by three items:

The courts have the right to make decisions that people always have to abide by.
The police always have the right to make people obey the law.
The tax department always has the right to make people pay taxes.

19. Respondents were asked how free they felt they were to to say what they thought, to join any political organization they wanted, to avoid being arrested when they were innocent, to choose whom to vote for without feeling pressured, and to influence what government did. Additionally they were asked if they felt that all groups received equal and fair treatment from government.

20. Respondents were asked how much they trusted the president, the parliament or national assembly, the electoral commission, the local council, the ruling party, the military, the police, and the courts of law.

21. As noted, the analysis was conducted in two stages. First, country dummy codes, objective country level indices, and demographics were entered. The instrumental and social indices were then entered as a second stage. Step-up procedures were used to first test whether the addition of these variables in the second stage significantly raised the degree of variance explained. In Round 1 it did so for both variables. For participation the SS regression increased 36.88 (F [1, 20, 289]), $p < .001$; and for voting 73,77 (F [1, 18, 655]), $p < .001$. For Round 3 the participation SS regression increased 31.42 (F [1, 24005]), $p < .001$; and for voting 94.60 (F [1, 19940]), $p < .001$.

22. The correlation between the latent indicators of instrumental and social motivation was 0.56 for Round 1 and 0.59 for Round 3.

Chapter Six
The Psychology of Cooperation

1. Most of the models outlined consider trust as linked to procedural justice because trust is a key antecedent to procedural justice. However, it is also possible to view procedural justice and trust as two parallel processes, which is the approach taken by Tyler and Huo (2002).

2. On the other hand, it is important to recognize the possibility that these two motivations might interfere with one another. In particular, it has been argued that the use of instrumental motivations undermines or "crowds out" internal—intrinsic—motivations for behavior.

3. As in the prior analysis, instrumental judgments were treated as indicators of a single latent factor.

Chapter Seven
Implications

1. McCluskey notes that in street stops, "Regardless of police actions obedience to authority is near universal" (2003, 170).

2. McCluskey notes that when the police mention the possibility of arrest, compliance goes up. However, he views this effect as due not to coercion but to the greater legitimacy that the police have when their actions are seen as consistent with the law.

Chapter Eight
Self-regulation as a General Model

1. While legitimacy and morality are similar in many ways, they are also clearly differentiable. Legitimacy is a perceived obligation to societal authorities or to existing social arrangements. Moral values are personal standards to which people attempt to align their behavior. Often moral values and legitimacy work together. For example, with most everyday laws, people obey the law because they feel that they ought to obey legitimate authorities and because they believe that the conduct prohibited by law is also morally wrong (Tyler 2003). However, they do not always work in concert. In their work on obedience to authority Kelman and Hamilton (1989) argue that morality operates as a check against following immoral orders given by legitimate authorities. They find that when people deal with legitimate authorities they authorize those authorities to make decisions about what is right and wrong. Hence, people suspend their normal motivation to keep their behavior in line with their moral values. In settings of this type only legitimacy shapes behavior.

Recent studies suggest that people's moral values also shape their reactions to rules (Darley, Tyler, and Bilz 2003) and to public authorities such as the police (Sunshine and Tyler 2003). Past studies show that people follow rules when they think those rules accord with their moral values (Robinson and Darley 1995). Recent studies indicate that people's views about appropriate sentencing decisions in criminal cases are driven by their morally based desire to give wrongdoers the punishment they deserve. They are not driven by the instrumental goal of preventing future criminal activity either by the criminal themselves or by others whose actions might be shaped by the punishment the criminal receives. People punish based upon the moral wrong reflected by the level and type of crime committed (Carlsmith, Darley, Robinson 2002; Darley, Carlsmith, and Robinson 2000). The story traditionally told by psychologists is that moral values are learned early in life and are, thereafter, resistant to change. Hence, it is important to note that the findings of the studies outlined in this volume suggest that to a striking degree those studied view the authorities in their organization or community as acting in ways congruent with their personal moral values when those authorities use fair procedures and act in trustworthy ways. Hence, by acting in those ways authorities not only gain legitimacy but also engage the power of moral value congruence to support their actions.

References

Aalders, M., and T. Wilthagen. 1997. Moving beyond command and control: Reflexivity in the regulation of occupational safety and health and the environment. *Law and Policy* 19: 415–43.

Abrams, D. 1992. Processes of social identification. In *Social psychology of the self-concept*, ed. G. Breakwell, 57–100. London: Academic Press.

Abrams, D., K. Ando, and S. Hinkle. 1998. Psychological attachment to the group: Cross-cultural differences in organizational identification and subjective norms as predictors of workers' turnover intentions. *Personality and Social Psychology Bulletin* 24: 1027–39.

Abrams, D., M. Hogg, and J. M. Marques. 2005. *The social psychology of inclusion and exclusion*. Philadelphia: Psychology Press.

Akerlof, G. A. 2006. The missing motivation in macroeconomics. Presidential address, American Economics Association, Chicago.

Akerlof, G. A., and R. E. Kranton. 2000. Economics and identity. *Quarterly Journal of Economics* 115: 715–53.

———. 2002. Identity and schooling: Some lessons from the economics of education. *Journal of Economic Literature* 40: 1167–1201.

Albert, S. 1977. Temporal comparison theory. *Psychological Review* 84: 485–503.

Allen, T. D., and M. C. Rush. 1998. The effects of organizational citizenship behavior on performance judgments. *Journal of Applied Psychology* 83: 247–60.

Anand, P. 2001. Procedural fairness in economic and social choice: Evidence from a survey of voters. *Journal of Economic Psychology* 22: 247–70.

Anderson, T. L., and D. R. Leal. 2001. *Free market environmentalism*. New York: Palgrave.

Andrews, F. M., and S. B. Withey. 1976. *Social indicators of well-being*. New York: Plenum.

Angelis, J., and A. Kupchik. 2009. Ethnicity, trust, and acceptance of authority among police officers. *Journal of Criminal Justice* 37: 273–79.

Argyle, M. 1989. *The psychology of happiness*. New York: Routledge.

———. 1991. *Cooperation: The basis of sociability*. New York: Routledge.

Ayres, I., and J. Braithwaite. 1992. *Responsive regulation: Transcending the deregulation debate*. Oxford: Oxford University Press.

Baden, J. A., and D. S. Noonan. 1998. *Managing the commons*. 2nd ed. Bloomington: Indiana University Press.

Baier, A. 1986. Trust and antitrust. *Ethics* 96: 231–60.

Baker, G., R. Gibbons, and K. J. Murphy. 2002. Relational contracts and the theory of the firm. *Quarterly Journal of Economics* 117: 39–84.

Bansal, P., and I. Clelland, I. 2004. Talking trash: Legitimacy, impression management, and unsystematic risk in the context of the natural environment. *Academy of Management Journal* 47: 93–103.

Baron, J. 2000. *Thinking and deciding*. 3rd ed. Cambridge: Cambridge University Press.

Baron, J., and M. Spranca. 1997. Protected values. *Organizational Behavior and Human Decision Processes* 70: 1–16.

Barrett, L. F., B. Mesquita, K. N. Ochsner, and J. J. Gross. 2007. The experience of emotion. *Annual Review of Psychology* 58: 373–403.

Baum, J., and C. Oliver. 1991. Institutional linkages and organizational mortality. *Administrative Science Quarterly* 36: 187–218.

Baumeister, R. F., and M. R. Leary. 1995. The need to belong: Desire for interpersonal attachments as a fundamental human motivation. *Psychological Bulletin* 117: 497–529.

Bayley, D. 1998. *What works in policing.* Oxford: Oxford University Press.

Bazerman, M. 2005. *Judgment in managerial decision making.* 6th ed. New York: Wiley.

Beetham, D. 1991. *The legitimation of power.* Atlantic Highlands, NJ: Humanities Press International.

Beloff, D. E. 2007. Dignity, equality, and public interest for defendants and crime victims in plea bargaining. *Marquette Law Review* 91: 349–355.

Belvedere, K., J. L. Worrell, and S. G. Tibbetts. 2005. Explaining suspect resistance in police-citizen encounters. *Criminal Justice Review* 30: 30–44.

Benesh, S. C. 2006. Understanding public confidence in American courts. *Journal of Politics* 68: 697–707.

Bewley, T. 1999. *Why wages don't fall during a recession.* Cambridge, MA: Harvard University Press.

Bies, R. J., C. L. Martin, and J. Brockner. 1993. Just laid off, but still a "good citizen": Only if the process is fair. *Employee Responsibilities and Rights Journal* 6: 227–48.

Blader, S. L., and T. R. Tyler. 2003a. A four component model of procedural justice. *Personality and Social Psychology Bulletin* 29: 747–58.

———. 2003b. What constitutes fairness in work settings? *Human Resource Management Review* 12: 107–26.

———. 2009. Testing and expanding the group engagement model. *Journal of Applied Psychology* 94: 445–64.

Blair, M., and L. Stout. 2001. Trust, trustworthiness, and the behavioral foundations of corporate law. *University of Pennsylvania Law Review* 149: 1735–1810.

Blau, P. 1964. *Exchange and power in social life.* New Brunswick, NJ: Transaction.

Blumstein, A., J. Cohen, and D. Nagin. 1978. *Deterrence and incapacitation.* Washington, DC: National Academy of Sciences.

Bok, S. 1978. *Lying: Moral choice in public and private life.* New York: Pantheon.

Bolton, G. E., J. Brandis, and A. Ockenfels. 2005. Fair procedures: Evidence from games involving lotteries. *Economic Journal* 115: 1054–76.

Bommer, W. H., J. L. Johnson, G. A. Rich, P. M. Podsakoff, and S. B. MacKinzie. 1995. On the interchangeability of objective and subjective measures of employee performance. *Personnel Psychology* 48: 587–605.

Bottoms, Anthony E. 1999. Interpersonal violence and social order in prisons. In *Crime and Justice: An Annual Review* 26: 437–513.

Bouffard, L. A., and N. L. Piquero. 2008. Defiance theory and life course explanations of persistent offending. *Crime and Delinquency Online.* Retrieved January 19, 2010 from http://cad.sagepub.com/cgi/rapidpdf/0011128707311642v1.

Bourgois, P. 1996. *In search of respect: Selling crack in El Barrio.* Cambridge: Cambridge University Press.

Bradach, J. L., and R. G. Eccles. 1989. Price, authority, and trust. *Annual Review of Sociology* 15: 97–118.

Bradburn, N. M. 1969. *The structure of psychological well-being*. Chicago: Aldine.

Bradburn, N. M., and D. Caplovitz. 1965. *Reports on happiness*. Chicago: Aldine.

Bradford, B., J. Jackson, and E. A. Stanko. 2009. Contact and confidence: Revisiting the impact of public encounters with the police. *Policing and Society* 19: 20–46.

Braithwaite, J., and T. Makkai. 1994. Trust and compliance. *Policing and Society* 4: 1–12.

Braithwaite, V. 2003. *Taxing democracy*. Aldershot, England: Ashgate.

Brann, P., and M. Foddy. 1988. Trust and consumption of a deteriorating common resource. *Journal of Conflict Resolution* 31: 615–30.

Braverman, H. 1974. *Labor and monopoly capital*. New York: Monthly Review Press.

Brewer, M. 1991. The social self: On being the same and different at the same time. *Personality and Social Psychology Bulletin* 17: 475–81.

Brief, A. P. 1998. *Attitudes in and around organizations*. Thousand Oaks, CA: Sage.

Brocas, I., and J. D. Carrillo. 2003. *The psychology of economic decisions*. Oxford: Oxford University Press.

Brown, M. K. 1981. *Working the street: Police discretion and the dilemmas of reform*. New York: Russell Sage Foundation.

Bryan, P. E. 2006. *Constructive divorce: Procedural justice and sociolegal reform*. Washington, DC: American Psychological Association.

Burke, K., and S. Leben. 2008. Procedural fairness: A key ingredient in public satisfaction. *Court Review* 44: 4–25.

Burke, K. S., and R. D. Lefever. 2007. *Procedural fairness: The translation of the principles into practice*. Presentation, Superior Court of California.

Burt, R. S., and M. Knez. 1996. Trust and third-party gossip. In *Trust in Organizations*, ed. R. Kramer and T. R. Tyler, 68–89. Thousand Oaks, CA: Sage.

Calavita, K. 1998. *Inside the state*. New York: Routledge.

Callahan, P. E. 2006. *Membership has its privileges: Identity as social support benefits U.S. combat soldiers*. PhD diss., New York University.

Camerer, C., and E. Fehr, E. 2004. Measuring social norms and preferences using experimental games. In *Foundations of human sociality: Economic experiments and ethnographic evidence from fifteen small-scale societies*, ed. J. Henrich, R. Boyd, S. Bowles, C. Camerer, E. Fehr, and H. Gintis, 55–95. Oxford: Oxford University Press.

Carlsmith, K. M., J. M. Darley, and P. H. Robinson. 2002. Why do we punish? *Journal of Personality and Social Psychology* 83: 284–99.

Casper, J. D., T. R. Tyler, and B. Fisher. 1988. Procedural justice in felony cases. *Law and Society Review* 22: 483–507.

Choen, M. S., and B. B. Thompson. 2001. Training teams to take initiative: Critical thinking in novel situations. In *Advances in human performance and cognitive engineering research*, ed. E. Sales, 1:251–91. Oxford: Elsevier.

Coglianese, C. 1997. Assessing consensus: The promise and performance of negotiated rulemaking. *Duke Law Journal* 46: 1255–1349.

Cohen-Charash, Y., and P. E. Spector. 2001. The role of justice in organizations: A meta-analysis. *Organizational Behavior and Human Decision Processes* 86: 278–321.

Cohn, E. S., and S. O. White. 1990. *Legal socialization: A study of norms and rules*. New York: Springer-Verlag.

Coleman, J. 1990. *Foundations of social theory*. Cambridge, MA: Harvard University Press.

Collier, J. 2007. Corporate governance in the European context: Evolving and adapting. *Business and Society Review* 112: 271–85.

Colquitt, J., D. E. Conlon, M. J. Wesson, C. O. Porter, and K. Y. Ng. 2001. Justice at the millennium. *Journal of Applied Psychology* 86: 425–45.

Cornelius, W. A., and I. Salehyan. 2007. Does border enforcement deter unauthorized immigration? The case of Mexican migration to the United States of America. *Regulation and Governance* 1: 139–53.

Cosmides, L., and J. Tooby. 2000. Evolutionary psychology and the emotions. In *Handbook of emotions*, 2nd ed., ed. M. Lewis and J. M. Haviland-Jones, 91–116. New York: Guilford.

Cotterrell, R. 1999. *Emile Durkheim: Law in a moral domain*. Stanford, CA: Stanford University Press.

Couper, D. C., and S. H. Lobitz. 1991. *Quality policing: The Madison experience*. Washington, DC: Police Executive Research Forum.

Crawford, A. 2009. Criminalizing sociability through anti-social behaviour legislation: Dispersal powers, young people and the police. *Youth Justice* 9: 5–26.

Cropanzano, R., Z. S. Byrne, D. R. Bobocel, and D. E. Rupp. 2001. Moral virtues, fairness heuristics, social entities, and other denizens of organizational justice. *Journal of Vocational Psychology* 58: 164–209.

Cullen, F. T., T. C. Pratt, S. L. Miceli, and M. M. Moon. 2002. Dangerous liaison? Rational choice theory as the basis for correctional intervention. In *Rational choice and criminal behavior: Recent research and future challenges*, ed. A. R. Piquero and S. G. Tibbetts, 279–96. New York: Routledge.

Culpepper, P. D. 2003. *Creating cooperation: How states develop human capital in Europe*. Ithaca, NY: Cornell University Press.

Dahl, R. 1956. *A preface to democratic theory*. Chicago: University of Chicago Press.

Darley, J. M., K. M. Carlsmith, and P. H. Robinson. 2000. Incapacitation and just deserts as motives for punishment. *Law and Human Behavior* 24: 659–83.

Darley, J. M., T. R. Tyler, and K. Bilz. 2003. Enacting justice: The interplay of individual and institutional perspectives. In *The Sage handbook of social psychology*, ed. M. A. Hogg and J. Cooper, 458–76. London: Sage.

Dawes, R. M. 1988. *Rational choice in an uncertain world*. San Diego: Harcourt Brace Jovanovich.

DeAngelis, J., and A. Kupchik. 2009. Ethnicity, trust, and acceptance of authority among police officers. *Journal of Criminal Justice* 37: 273–79.

Deaux, K. 1996. Social identification. In *Social psychology: Handbook of basic principles*, ed. E. T. Higgins and A. W. Kruglanski, 777–98. New York: Guilford.

Deci, E. L. 1975. *Intrinsic motivation*. New York: Plenum.

———. 1980. *The psychology of self-determination*. Lexington, MA: Lexington Books.

Deci, E. L., R. Koestner. and R. M. Ryan. 1999. A meta-analytic review of experiments examining the effects of extrinsic rewards on intrinsic motivation. *Psychological Bulletin* 125: 627–68.

Deci, E. L., and R. M. Ryan. 2000. The what and why of goal pursuits: Human needs and the self-determination of behavior. *Psychological Inquiry* 11: 227–68.

De Cremer, D., M. Snyder, and S. DeWitte. 2001. The less I trust, the less I contribute (or not)? *European Journal of Social Psychology* 31: 93–107.

De Cremer, D., and T. R. Tyler. 2005a. Am I respected or not? Inclusion and reputation as issues in group membership. *Social Justice Research* 18: 121–53.

———. 2005b. Managing group behavior: The interplay between procedural justice, sense of self, and cooperation. *Advances in Experimental Social Psychology* 37: 151–218.

———. 2007. The effects of trust and procedural justice on cooperation. *Journal of Applied Psychology* 92: 639–49.

De Cremer, D., T. R. Tyler, and N. den Ouden. 2005. Managing cooperation via procedural fairness: The mediating role of self-other merging. *Journal of Economic Psychology* 26: 393–406.

De Cremer, D., and E. van Dijk. 2002. Reactions to group success and failure as a function of identification level: A test of the goal-transformation hypothesis in social dilemmas. *Journal of Experimental Social Psychology* 38: 435–42.

De Cremer, D., and D. van Knippenberg. 2002. How do leaders promote cooperation? The effects of charisma and procedural fairness. *Journal of Applied Psychology* 87: 858–66.

De Cremer, D., M. Zeelenberg, and J. K. Murnighan, eds. 2006. *Social psychology and economics: Interdisciplinary perspectives*. Mahwah, NJ: Erlbaum.

Demchak, Chris C. 1991. *Military organization, complex machines*. Ithaca, NY: Cornell University Press.

Denton, D. 2008. Procedural fairness in the California courts. *Court Review* 44: 1–10.

Diener, E., and M. Seligman. 2004. Beyond money: Toward an economy of well-being. *Psychological Science in the Public Interest* 5: 1–31.

Dillon, P. A., and R. E. Emery. 1996. Divorce mediation and resolution of child custody disputes: Long-term effects. *American Journal of Orthopsychiatry* 66: 131–40.

Dorf, M. C., and C. F. Sabel. 1998. A constitution of democratic experimentalism. *Columbia Law Review* 98: 267–371.

Durkheim, É. 1964. *The division of labor in society*. Translated by G. Simpson. Toronto: Collier-Macmillan.

Easton, D. 1965. *A systems analysis of political life*. Chicago: University of Chicago Press.

———. 1975. A reassessment of the concept of political support. *British Journal of Political Science* 5: 435–57.

Edelman, L. 1990. Legal environments and organizational governance. *American Journal of Sociology* 95: 1401–40.

Edelman, L. B., and M. Suchman. 1997. The legal environments of organizations. *Annual Review of Sociology* 23: 479–515.

Ellemers, N., D. de Gilder, and S. A. Haslam. 2004. Motivating individuals and groups as work: A social identity perspective on leadership and group performance. *Academy of Management Review* 29: 459–78.

Ellemers, N., P. Kortekaas, and J. W. Oewerkerk. 1999. Self-categorization, commitment to the group, and group self-esteem as related but distinct aspects of social identity. *European Journal of Social Psychology* 29: 371–89.

Ellemers, N., R. Spears, and B. Doosje, eds. 2002. *Social identity*. Oxford: Blackwell.

Ellsworth, P. C., and R. Mauro. 1998. Psychology and law. In *Handbook of Social Psychology*, 4th ed., ed. D. Gilbert, S. Fiske, and G. Lindzey, 2:684–732. New York: McGraw-Hill.

Elsbach, K. D. 2001. The architecture of legitimacy: Constructing accounts of organizational controversies. In *The psychology of legitimacy: Emerging perspectives on ideol-*

ogy, justice, and intergroup relations, ed. J. T. Jost and B. Major, 391–415. Cambridge: Cambridge University Press.

Elsbach, K. D., and R. I. Sutton. 1992. Acquiring organizational legitimacy through illegitimate actions. *Academy of Management Journal* 35: 699–738.

Emery, R. E., S. G. Matthews, and K. M. Kitzmann. 1994. Child custody mediation and litigation: Parents' satisfaction and functioning one year after settlement. *Journal of Consulting and Clinical Psychology* 62: 124–29.

Emler, N., and A. Hopkins. 1990. A social psychology of reputation. *European Review of Social Psychology* 1: 171–93.

Emler, N., and S. Reicher. 1995. *Adolescence and delinquency: The collective management of reputation*. Oxford: Blackwell.

Engel, R. S. 2005. Citizens' perceptions of distributive and procedural injustice during traffic stops with police. *Journal of Research in Crime and Delinquency* 42: 445–81.

Falk, F., and M. Kosfeld. 2004. *Distrust—The hidden cost of control*. IZA Discussion Paper 1203. Bonn, Germany: Institut zur Zukunft der Arbeit.

Fehr, E., and A. Falk. 2002. A psychological foundation of incentives. *European Economic Review* 46, 687–724.

Fehr, E., and U. Fischbacher. 2004. Social norms and human cooperation. *Trends in Cognitive Sciences* 8: 185–90.

Fehr, E. and Gächter, S. 2002. *Do incentive contracts undermine voluntary cooperation?* IZA Working Paper 1424-0459. Bonn, Germany: Institut zur Zukunft der Arbeit.

Fehr, E., and B. Rackenbach. 2003. Detrimental effects of sanctions on human altruism. *Nature* 422: 137–40.

Feld, L. P., and B. S. Frey. 2007. Tax compliance as the result of a psychological tax contract. *Law and Policy* 29: 102–20.

Ferraro, F., J. Pfeffer, and R. I. Sutton. 2005. Economics language and assumptions: How theories can become self-fulfilling. *Academy of Management Review* 30: 8–24.

Festinger, L. 1954. A theory of social comparison processes. *Human Relations* 7: 117–40.

Fischer, R., C. Harb, S. Al-Sarraf, and O. Nachabe. 2008. Support for resistance among Iraqi students. *Basic and Applied Social Psychology* 30: 1–9.

Fiske, A., and P. E. Tetlock. 1997. Taboo trade-offs: Reactions to transgressions that transgress the spheres of justice. *Political Psychology* 18: 255–97.

Foa, U. G., and E. B. Foa. 1974. *Societal structures of the mind*. Springfield, IL: Thomas.

Folger, R. 1977. Distributive and procedural justice: Combined impact of "voice" and improvement of experienced inequity. *Journal of Personality and Social Psychology* 35: 108–19.

Franke, D., D. Bierie, and D. L. MacKenzie. 2009. *Legitimacy in corrections: A randomized experiment of a boot camp and a prison*. Unpublished manuscript, University of Maryland.

Frazer, M. S. 2006. *The impact of the community court model on defendant perceptions of fairness: A case study of the Red Hook Community Justice Center*. New York: Center for Court Innovation.

Freund, W. C., and E. Epstein. 1984. *People and productivity*. Homewood, IL: Dow Jones/Irwin.

Frey, B. S. 1997. *Not just for the money: An economic theory of personal motivation*. Cheltenham, England: Edward Elgar.

Frey, B. S., M. Benz, and A. Stutzer. 2004. Introducing procedural utility: Not only what, but also how matters. *Journal of Institutional and Theoretical Economics* 160: 377–401.

Frey, B. S., and M. Osterloh. 2002. *Successful management by motivation: Balancing intrinsic and extrinsic incentives.* Berlin: Springer-Verlag.

Frey, B. S., and A. Stutzer. 2002. *Happiness and economics: How the economy and institutions affect human well-being.* Princeton, NJ: Princeton University Press.

Fuller, L. 1969. *Human interaction and the law. American Journal of Jurisprudence* 14: 1–36.

Gächter, S., and E. Fehr. 1999. Collective action as a social exchange. *Journal of Economic Behavior and Organization* 39: 341–69.

Gaertner, L., J. Iuzzini, M. Witt, and M. M. Orina. 2006. Us without them: Evidence for an intragroup origin of positive in-group regard. *Journal of Personality and Social Psychology* 90: 426–39.

Garland, D. 2001. *The culture of control.* Chicago: University of Chicago Press.

Gau, J. M., and R. K. Brunson. 2009. Procedural justice and order maintenance policing: A study of inner-city young men's perceptions of police legitimacy. *Justice Quarterly* 26: 1–25.

Geller, W. A., and M. Scott. 1992. *Deadly force—what we know: A practitioner's desk reference on police-involved shootings.* Washington, DC: Police Executive Research Forum.

Gibson, J. L. 2004. The legitimacy of the political institutions of the new South Africa. In *Overcoming apartheid: Can truth reconcile a divided nation?* 289–327. New York: Russell Sage Foundation.

———. 2008. Challenges to the impartiality of state supreme courts: Legitimacy theory and "new-style" judicial campaigns. *American Political Science Review* 102: 59–75.

Gibson, J. L., and G. A. Caldiera. 2003. Defenders of democracy? Legitimacy, popular acceptance, and the South African Constitutional Court. *Journal of Politics* 65: 1–30.

Gibson, J. L., G. A. Caldiera, and V. A. Baird. 1998. On the legitimacy of national high courts. *American Political Science Review* 92: 343–58.

Gibson, J. L., G. A. Caldiera, and L. K. Spence. 2003. The Supreme Court and the U.S. presidential election of 2000: Wounds, self-inflicted or otherwise? *British Journal of Political Science* 33: 535–56.

Gilson, R., and R. H. Mnookin. 1994. Disputing through agents. *Columbia Law Review* 94: 509–66.

Gintis, H., S. Bowles, R. Boyd, and E. Fehr. 2005. *Moral sentiments and material interests: The foundations of cooperation in economic life.* Cambridge, MA: MIT Press.

Gold, M. 1999. *The complete social scientist: A Kurt Lewin reader.* Washington, DC: American Psychological Association.

Goldstein, H. 1997. *Policing a free society.* Cambridge, MA: Ballinger.

Golembiewski, R. T., and M. McConkie. 1975. The centrality of interpersonal trust in group processes. In *Theories of group processes,* ed. C. L. Cooper, 131–85. New York: Wiley.

Gonzalez, C., and T. R. Tyler. 2008. The psychology of enfranchisement. *Journal of Social Issues* 64: 447–66.

Goodin, R. E. 1996. *The theory of institutional design.* Cambridge: Cambridge University Press.

Gottfredson, M. R., and D. M. Gottfredson. 1988. *Decision making in criminal justice: Toward the rational exercise of discretion.* New York: Plenum.

Grattet, R., and V. Jenness. 2005. The reconstitution of law in local settings: Agency discretion, ambiguity, and a surplus of law in the policing of hate crimes. *Law and society review* 39: 893–941.

Gray, Jameel. 2007. *Fair decision making and legitimacy: The effects of treatment on compliance and outcome satisfaction in a sample of incarcerated males.* PhD diss., Southern Illinois University.

Greacen, J. M. 2008. Social science research on procedural justice: What are the implications for judges and courts? *Judges' Journal* 47: 41–44.

Green, D. P., and I. Shapiro. 1994. *Pathologies of rational choice theory.* New Haven, CT: Yale University Press.

Greenstein, F. 1965. *Children and politics.* New Haven, CT: Yale University Press.

Grimes, M. 2006. Organizing consent: The role of procedural fairness in political trust and compliance. *European Journal of Political Research* 45: 285–315.

Gunningham, N., and J. Rees. 1997. Industry self-regulation. *Law and Policy* 19: 363–414.

Gürerk, O., B. Irlenbusch, and B. Rockenbach. 2006. The competitive advantage of sanctioning institutions. *Science* 312: 108–11.

Gurr, T. R. 1970. *Why men rebel.* New York: Basic Books.

Guzzo, R., R. D. Jette, and R. A. Katzell. 1985. The effects of psychologically based intervention programs on worker productivity: A meta-analysis. *Personnel Psychology* 38: 275–291.

Haney, C., and P. Zimbardo. (1998). The past and future of U.S. prison policy: Twenty-five years after the Stanford Prison Experiment. *American Psychologist* 53: 709–27.

Harrison, L. E., and S. P. Huntington, eds. 2000. *Culture matters: How values shape human progress.* Mahwah, NJ: Erlbaum.

Hartle, Anthony E. 1989. *Moral issues in military decision making.* Lawrence: University Press of Kansas.

Haslam, S. A. 2004. *Psychology in organizations.* 2nd ed. Thousand Oaks, CA: Sage.

Hastie, R., and R. M. Dawes. 2001. *Rational choice in an uncertain world.* Thousand Oaks, CA: Sage.

Hawkins, K. 1992. *The uses of discretion.* New York: Oxford University Press.

———. 2002. *Law as a last resort.* New York: Oxford University Press.

Heider, F. 1959. *The psychology of interpersonal relations.* New York: Wiley.

Henrich, J., R. Boyd, S. Bowles, C. Camerer, E. Fehr, H. Gintis, and R. McElreach. 2004. Introduction. In *Foundations of human sociality: Economic experiments and ethnographic evidence from fifteen small-scale societies,* ed. J. Henrich, R. Boyd, S. Bowles, C. Camerer, E. Fehr, and H. Gintis, 1–7. Oxford: Oxford University Press.

Hess, R. D., and J. Torney. 1967. *The development of political attitudes in children.* Chicago: Aldine.

Higgins, E. T., and A. W. Kruglanski. 2001. Motivational science: The nature and functions of wanting. In *Motivational science: Social and personality perspectives,* ed. E. T. Higgins and A. W. Kruglanski, 1–20. New York: Psychology Press.

Hinds, L. 2007. Building police-youth relationships: The importance of procedural justice. *Youth Justice* 7: 195–209.

———. 2009. Youth, police legitimacy and informal contact. *Journal of Police and Criminal Psychology* 24: 10–21.

Hinds, L., and K. Murphy. 2007. Public satisfaction with police: Using procedural justice to improve police legitimacy. *Australian and New Zealand Journal of Criminology* 40: 27–42.

Hinkle, S. W., and R. J. Brown. 1990. Intergroup comparisons and social identity: Some links and lacunae. In *Social identity theory*, ed. D. Abrams and M. A. Hogg, 48–70. New York: Springer-Verlag.

Hirschman, A. O. 1970. *Exit, voice, and loyalty: Responses to declines in firms, organizations, and states*. Cambridge, MA: Harvard University Press.

Hoffman, M. 1977. Moral internalization: Current theory and research. *Advances in Experimental Social Psychology* 10: 85–133.

Hogarth, R. 1980. *Judgment and choice*. New York: Wiley.

Hogg, M. A., and D. Abrams. 1988. *Social identifications*. New York: Routledge.

Hogg, M. A., D. Abrams, S. Otten, and S. Hinkle. 2004. The social identity perspective. *Small Group Research* 35: 246–76.

Hollander-Blumoff, R., and T. R. Tyler. 2008. Do nice guys finish last? Procedural justice and negotiation outcomes. *Law and Social Inquiry* 33: 477–500.

Hosmer, L. T. 1995. Trust: The connecting link between organizational theory and philosophical ethics. *Academy of Management Review* 20: 379–403.

Human, S. E., and K. G. Provan. 2000. Legitimacy building in the evolution of small firm multilateral networks: A comparative study of success and demise. *Administrative Science Quarterly* 45: 327–65.

Hunnington, S. P. 1957. *The soldier and the state: The theory and politics of civilian-military relations*. Cambridge, MA: Harvard University Press.

Huo, Y. J. 2002. Justice and the regulation of social relations: When and why do group members deny claims to social goods? *British Journal of Social Psychology* 41: 535–2.

Hurd, I. 1999. Legitimacy and authority in international politics. *International Organization* 53: 379–408.

Hyman, H. 1959. *Political socialization*. New York: Free Press.

Jackson, J., and J. Sunshine. 2007. Public confidence in policing: A neo-Durkheimian perspective. *British Journal of Criminology* 47: 214–33.

Jolls, C. 2004. *Behavioral law and economics*. Unpublished manuscript. Yale Law School.

Kahneman, D., J. L. Knetsch, and R. Thaler. 1986. Fairness as a constraint on profit seeking. *American Economic Review* 76: 728–41.

Kahneman, D., P. Slovic, and A. Tversky, A. 1982. *Judgment under uncertainty: Heuristics and biases*. Cambridge: Cambridge University Press.

Kahneman, D., and A. Tversky. 2000. *Choices, values, and frames*. Cambridge: Cambridge University Press.

Karkkainen, B. C. 2002. Collaborative ecosystem governance. *Virginia Environmental Law Journal* 21: 190–243.

Katz, H. C., T. A. Kochan, and M. R. Weber. 1985. Assessing the effects of industrial relations systems and efforts to improve the quality of working life on organizational effectivensss. *Academy of Management Journal* 28: 519–31.

Katz, J. 1988. *Seductions of crime*. New York: Basic Books.

———. 1999. *How emotions work*. Chicago: University of Chicago Press.

Kaufman, Herbert. 1960. *The forest ranger: A study in administrative behavior*. Baltimore: Johns Hopkins University Press.

Kelley, H. H., J. G. Holmes, N. L. Kerr, H. T. Reis, C. E. Rusbult, and P. A. van Lange. 2003. *An atlas of interpersonal situations*. Cambridge: Cambridge University Press.

Kelman, H. C. 1958. Compliance, identification, and internalization: Three processes of attitude change. *Journal of Conflict Resolution* 2: 51–60.

————. 1961. Processes of opinion change. *Public Opinion Quarterly* 25: 57–78.

————. 1969. Patterns of personal involvement in the national system: A social-psychological analysis of political legitimacy. In *International politics and foreign policy*, ed. J. Rosenau, 276–88. New York: Free Press.

———— 2006. Interests, relationships, identities: Three central issues for individuals and groups in negotiating their social environment. *Annual Review of Psychology* 57: 1–26.

Kelman, H. C., and V. L. Hamilton. 1989. *Crimes of obedience*. New Haven, CT: Yale University Press.

Kim, W. C., and R. A. Mauborgne. 1991. Implementing global strategies: The role of procedural justice. *Strategic Management Journal* 12: 125–43.

————. 1993. Procedural justice, attitudes, and subsidiary top management compliance with multinationals' corporate strategic decisions. *Academy of Management Journal* 36: 502–26.

King, A., and M. Lenox. 2000. Industry self-regulation without sanctions. *Academy of Management Journal* 43: 698–716.

Kitzman, K. M., and R. E. Emery. 1993. Procedural justice and parents' satisfaction in a field study of child custory dispute resolution. *Law and Human Behavior* 17: 553–67.

Kohn, A. 1993. Why incentive plans cannot work. *Harvard Business Review* 71: 54–63.

————. 1999. *Punished by rewards*. New York: Houghton Mifflin.

Komorita, S. S., and C. D. Parks. 1994. *Social dilemmas*. Madison, WI: Brown and Benmark.

Kopelman, S., J. M. Weber, and D. M. Messick. 2002. Factors influencing cooperation in commons dilemmas: A review of experimental psychological research. In *The drama of the commons*, ed. E. Ostrom, T. Dietz, N. Dolsak, P. C. Stern, S. Stonich, and E. U. Weber, 113–56. Washington, DC: National Academies Press.

Kostova, T., and S. Zaheer. 1999. Organizational legitimacy under conditions of complexity. *Academy of Management Review* 24: 64–81.

Koys, D. J. 2001. The effects of employee satisfaction, organizational citizenship behavior, and turnover on organizational effectiveness: A unit-level, longitudinal study. *Personnel Psychology* 54: 101–14.

Kramer, R. M. 1999. Trust and distrust in organizations. *Annual Review of Psychology* 50: 569–98.

Kramer, R. M., and J. T. Jost. 2002. Close encounters of the suspicious kind: Outgroup paranoia in hierarchical trust dilemmas. In *From prejudice to intergroup emotions: Differentiated reactions to social groups*, ed. D. M. Mackie and E. R. Smith, 173–89. New York: Psychology Press.

Kramer, R. M., and T. R. Tyler. 1996. *Trust in organizations*. Thousand Oaks, CA: Sage.

Krislov, S., K. O. Boyum, J. N. Clark, R. C. Shaefer, and S. O. White. 1966. *Compliance and the law*. Beverly Hills, CA: Sage.

Kruger, J. and Dunning, D. (1999). Unskilled and unaware of it. *Journal of Personality and Social Psychology* 77: 1121–34.

Lawler, E. E., III. 2000. *Rewarding excellence: Pay strategies for the new economy*. San Francisco: Jossey-Bass.

Lawsky, S. B. 2008. Fairly random: On compensating audited taxpayers. *Connecticut Law Review* 41: 161–209.

Layard, R. 2005. *Happiness: Lessons from a new science*. New York: Penguin.

Leary, M. R., and R. F. Baumeister. 2000. The nature and function of self-esteem: Sociometer theory. *Advances in Experimental Social Psychology* 32: 1–62.

Leben, S. 2000. Thoughts on some potential appellate and trial court applications of therapeutic jurisprudence. *Seattle University Law Review* 24: 467–75.

Levi, M. 1988. *Of rule and revenue*. Cambridge: Cambridge University Press.

———. 1997. *Consent, dissent, and patriotism*. Cambridge: Cambridge University Press.

Levi, M., and L. Stoker. 2000. Political trust and trustworthiness. *Annual Review of Political Science* 3: 475–507.

Lewis, J. D., and A. Weigert. 1985. Trust as a social reality. *Social forces* 63: 967–85.

Lichtenstein, S., and B. Fischhoff. 1977. Do those who know more also know more about how much they know? *Organizational Behavior and Human Performance* 20: 159–83.

Lin, A. C. 1996. Participants' experiences with habitat conservation plans and suggestions for streamlining the process. *Ecology Law Quarterly* 23: 369–437.

Lind, E. A. 2001. Thinking critically about justice judgments. *Journal of Vocational Behavior* 58: 220–26.

Lind, E. A., Y. J. Huo, and T. R. Tyler. 1994. And justice for all: Ethnicity, gender, and preferences for dispute resolution procedures. *Law and Human Behavior* 18: 269–90.

Lind, E. A., R. Kanfer, and P. C. Earley. 1990. Voice, control, and procedural justice: Instrumental and noninstrumental concerns in fairness judgments. *Journal of Personality and Social Psychology* 59: 952–59.

Lind, E. A., C. T. Kulik, M. Ambrose, and M. de Vera Park. 1993. Individual and corporate dispute resolution. *Administrative Science Quarterly* 38: 224–51.

Lind, E. A., and T. R. Tyler. 1988. *The social psychology of procedural justice*. New York: Plenum.

Lind, W. S. 1985. *Maneuver warfare handbook*. Boulder, CO: Westview.

Lipset, S. M. 1959. Some social prerequisites of democracy: Economic development and political legitimacy. *American Political Science Review* 53: 69–105.

Lipsey, M. W., and F. T. Cullen. 2007. The effectiveness of correctional rehabilitation: A review of systematic reviews. *Annual Review of Law and Social Science* 3: 297–320.

Locke, E. A., and G. P. Latham. 1991. *A theory of goal setting and task performance*. Englewood Cliffs, N.J.: Prentice-Hall.

Lott, A. J., and B. E. Lott. 1965. Group cohesiveness as interpersonal attraction: A review of relationships with antecedent and consequent variables. *Psychological Bulletin* 64: 259–309.

MacCoun, R. J. 1993. Drugs and the law: A psychological analysis of drug prohibition. *Psychological Bulletin* 113: 497–512.

MacCoun, R. J., E. A. Lind, D. R. Hensler, D. L. Bryant, and P. A. Ebener. 1998. *Alternative adjudication: An evaluation of the New Jersey Automobile Arbitration Program*. Santa Monica, CA: RAND.

Machura, S. 2003. Fairness, justice, and legitimacy: Experiences of people's judges in South Russia. *Law and policy* 25: 123–50.

MacKenzie, D. L. 2002. Reducing the criminal activities of known offenders and delinquents: Crime prevention in the courts and corrections. In *Evidence-based crime prevention*, ed. L. W. Sherman, D. P. Farrington, B. C. Welsh, and D. L. MacKenzie, 330–404. London: Routledge.

Mael, F., and B. E. Ashforth. 1992. Alumni and their alma mater: A partial test of the reformulated model of organizational identification. *Journal of Organizational Behavior* 13: 103–23.

Maroney, T. A. 2006. Law and emotion: A proposed taxonomy of an emerging field. *Law and Human Behavior* 30: 119–42.

Martinson, B. C., M. S. Anderson, A. L. Crain, and R. De Vries. 2006. Scientists' perceptions of organizational justice and self-reported misconduct. *Journal of Empirical Research on Human Research Ethics* 1: 51–66.

Mastrofski, S. D., J. B. Snipes, and A. E. Supina. 1966. Compliance on demand: The public's responses to specific police requests. *Journal of Crime and Delinquency* 33: 269–305.

May, P. J. 2005. Regulation and compliance motivations: Examining different approaches. *Public Administration Review* 65: 31–44.

McCluskey, J. D. 2003. *Police requests for compliance: Coercive and procedural just tactics*. New York: LFB Scholarly.

McCluskey, J. D., S. D. Mastrofski, and R. B. Parks. 1999. To acquiesce and rebel: Predicting citizen compliance with police requests. Police Quarterly 2: 389–416.

McCullough, D. 2005. *1776*. New York: Simon and Schuster.

McGuire, W. J. 1969. The nature of attitudes and attitude change. In *Handbook of social psychology*, 2nd ed., ed. G. Lindzey and E. Aronson, 3:136–314. Reading, MA: Addison-Wesley.

McNeil, C. B. 2009. Perceptions of fairness in state administrative hearings. *Judicature* 92: 160–64.

Meares, T. L. 2000. Norms, legitimacy, and law enforcement. *Oregon Law Review* 79: 391–415.

Meglino, B. M., and M. A. Korsgaard. 2004. Considering rational self-interest as a disposition: Organizational implications of other orientation. *Journal of Applied Psychology* 89: 946–59.

Melton, G. B., ed. 1986. *The law as a behavioral instrument: Nebraska Symposium on Motivation, 1985*. Current Theory and Research in Motivation 33. Lincoln: University of Nebraska Press.

Merelman, R. J. 1966. Learning and legitimacy. *American Political Science Review* 60: 548–61.

———. 1986. Revitalizing political socialization. In *Political psychology*, ed. J. Knutson, 279–319. San Francisco: Jossey-Bass.

Merkle, J. 1980. *Management and ideology*. Berkeley and Los Angeles: University of California Press.

Meyerson, D., K. Weick, and R. M. Kramer. 1996. Swift trust and temporary groups. In *Trust in organizations*, ed. R. M. Kramer and T. R. Tyler, 166–95. Thousand Oaks, CA: Sage.

Miller, Dale T. 1999. The norm of self-interest. *American Psychologist* 54: 1053–60.

Mitchell, L. E. 1995. Trust, contract, process. In *Progressive corporate law: New perspectives on law, culture, society*, ed. L. E. Mitchell, 187–217. Boulder, CO: Westview.

Moore, M. H. 1997. Legitimizing criminal justice policies and practices. *FBI Law Enforcement Bulletin* 66: 14–21.

Moorman, R. H. 1991. Relationship between organizational justice and organizational citizenship behaviors: Do fairness perceptions influence employee citizenship? *Journal of Applied Psychology* 76: 845–55.

Moorman, R. H., B. P. Niehoff, and D. W. Organ. 1993. Treating employees fairly and organizational citizenship behavior. *Employee Responsibilities and Rights Journal* 6: 209–25.

Murphy, K. 2004. The role of trust in nurturing compliance: A study of accused tax avoiders. *Law and Human Behavior* 28: 187–210.

———. 2005. Regulating more effectively: The relationship between procedural justice, legitimacy, and tax non-compliance. *Journal of Law and Society* 32: 562–89.

Murphy, K., L. Hinds, and J. Fleming. 2008. Encouraging public cooperation and support for the police. *Policing and Society* 18: 136–55.

Murphy, W. F., and J. Tanenhaus. 1968 Public opinion and the United States Supreme Court. *Law and Society Review* 2: 357–84.

Murphy, K., T. R. Tyler, and A. Curtis. 2009. Nurturing regulatory compliance: Is procedural justice effective when people question the legitimacy of the law? *Regulation and Governance* 3: 1–26.

Myers, D. G. 1992. *The pursuit of happiness*. New York: Morrow.

Nagin, D. S. 1998. Criminal deterrence at the onset of the twenty-first century. *Crime and Justice* 23: 1–42.

Nagin, D. S., and R. Paternoster. 1991. The preventive effects of the perceived risk of arrest. *Criminology 29*: 561–85.

National Research Council. 2004. *Fairness and effectiveness in policing: The evidence*, ed. W. G. Skogan and K. Frydl. Washington, DC: National Academies Press.

Newman, K. S. 1999. *No shame in my game: The working poor in the inner city*. New York: Russell Sage Foundation.

Niehoff, B. P., and R. H. Moorman. 1993. Justice as a mediator of the relationship between methods of monitoring and organizational citizenship behavior. *Academy of Management Journal* 36: 527–56.

Nisbet, R. A. 1974. *The sociology of Emile Durkheim*. Oxford: Oxford University Press.

Nisbett, R., and L. Ross. 1980. *Human inference: Strategies and shortcomings of social judgment*. Englewood Cliffs, NJ: Prentice-Hall.

Oaker, G., and R. Brown. 1986. Intergroup relations in a hospital setting: A further test of social identity theory. *Human Relations* 39: 767–78.

O'Hear, M. M. 2007. Plea bargaining and victims: From consultation to guidelines. *Marquette Law Review* 91: 323–47.

O'Reilly, C., and J. Chatman. 1986. Organizational commitment and psychological attachment. *Journal of Applied Psychology* 71, 492–99.

Ostrom, E., T. Dietz, N. Dolsak, P. C. Stern, S. Stonich, and E. U. Weber, eds. 2002. *The drama of the commons*. Washington, DC: National Academies Press.

Paine, L. S. 1994. Managing for organizational integrity. *Harvard Business Review* 72: 106–17.

Parsons, T. 1967. Some reflections on the place of force in social process. In *Sociological theory and modern society*, ed. T. Parsons, 139–65. New York: Free Press.

Paternoster, R. 1987. The deterrent effect of the perceived certainty and severity of punishment: A review of the evidence and issues. *Justice Quarterly* 4: 173–217.

Paternoster, R. 1989. Decisions to participate in and desist from four types of common delinquency: Deterrence and the rational choice perspective. *Law and Society Review* 23: 7–40.

Paternoster, R., R. Brame, R. Bachman, and L. W. Sherman. 1997. Do fair procedures matter? *Law and Society Review* 31: 163–204.

Paternoster, R., and L. Iovanni. 1986. The deterrent effect of perceived severity: A reexamination. *Social Forces* 64: 751–77.

Paternoster, R., L. E. Saltzman, G. P. Waldo, and T. G. Chiricos. 1983. Perceived risk and social control: Do sanctions really deter? *Law and Society Review* 17: 457–79.

Petersilia, J. 2003. *When prisoners come home: Parole and prisoner reentry.* Oxford: Oxford University Press.

Pfeffer, J. 1994. *Competitive advantage through people.* Cambridge, MA: Harvard University Press.

Plous, S. 1993. *The psychology of judgment and decision making.* New York: McGraw-Hill.

Podsakoff, P. M., M. Ahearne, and S. B. MacKenzie. 1997. Organizational citizenship behavior and the quantity and quality of work group performance. *Journal of Applied Psychology* 82: 262–70.

Podsakoff, P.M., W. H. Bommer, N. P. Podsakoff, and S. B. MacKenzie. 2006. Relationships between leader reward and punishment behavior and subordinate attitudes, perceptions and behaviors. *Organizational Behavior and Human Decision Processes* 99: 113–42.

Pollock, T. G., and V. P. Rindova. 2003. Media legitimation effects in the market for initial public offerings. *Academy of Management Journal* 46: 631–42.

Proudstone, W. 1992. *Prisoner's dilemma.* New York: Doubleday.

Pruitt, D. G., R. S. Peirce, N. B. McGillicuddy, G. L. Welton, and L. M. Castrianno. 1993. Long-term success in mediation. *Law and Human Behavior* 17: 313–30.

Pruitt, D. G., R. S. Peirce, J. M. Zubek, G. L. Welton, and T. H. Nochajski. 1990. Goal achievement, procedural justice, and the success of mediation. *International journal of conflict management* 1: 33–45.

Putnam, R. D. 1993. *Making democracy work.* Princeton, NJ: Princeton University Press.

———. 2000. *Bowling alone.* New York: Simon and Schuster.

Rao, H. 1994. The social construction of reputation: Certification contests, legitimation, and the survival of organizations in the American automobile industry: 1895–1912. *Strategic Management Journal* 15: 29–44.

Ratner, R., and D. T. Miller. 2001. The norm of self-interest and its effects on social action. *Journal of Personality and Social Psychology* 81, 5–16.

Rechtschaffen, C. 1998. Deterrence vs. cooperation and the evolving theory of environmental enforcement. *Southern California Law Review* 71: 1181–1272.

Reisig, M. D. 1998. Rates of disorder in higher-custody state prisons. *Crime and Delinquency* 44: 229–44.

Reisig, M. D., J. Bratton, and M. G. Gertz. 2007. The construct validity and refinement of process-based policing measures. *Criminal justice and behavior* 34: 1005–28.

Reisig, M. D., and M. Chandek. 2001. The effects of expectancy disconfirmation on outcome satisfaction in police-citizen encounters. *Policing* 24: 88–99.

Reisig, M. D., and C. Lloyd. 2009. Procedural justice, police legitimacy, and helping the police fight crime: Results from a survey of Jamaican adolescents. *Police Quarterly* 12: 42–62.

Reisig, M. D., and G. Mesko. 2009. Procedural justice, legitimacy, and prisoner misconduct. *Psychology crime and law* 15: 41–59.

Reiss, A. 1971. *The police and the public.* New Haven, CT: Yale University Press.

Reiter, D., and A. C. Stam III. 1998. Democracy and battlefield military effectiveness. *Journal of Conflict Resolution* 42: 259–77.

———. 2002. *Democracies at war.* Princeton, NJ: Princeton University Press.

Reus-Smit, C. 1999. *The moral purposes of the state: Culture, social identity, and institutional rationality in international relations.* Princeton, NJ: Princeton University Press.

Robinson, P. H., and J. M. Darley. 1995. *Justice, liability, and blame: Community views and the criminal law.* New Directions in Social Psychology. Boulder, CO: Westview.

———. 1997. The utility of desert. *Northwestern University Law Review* 91: 453–99.

Ross, H. L. 1982. *Deterring the drinking driver: Legal policy and social control.* Lexington, MA: Lexington Books.

Rottman, D. 2005. *Trust and confidence in the California courts: A survey of the public and attorneys. Part 1: Findings and recommendations.* Williamsburg, VA: National Center for State Courts.

Rusbult, C. E., and P.A.M. van Lange. 1996. Interdependence processes. In *Social psychology: Handbook of basic principles,* ed. E. T. Higgins and A. W. Kruglanski, 564–96. New York: Guilford.

———. 2003. Interdependence, interaction, and relationships. *Annual Review of Psychology* 54: 351–75.

Samet, D. D. 2004. *Willing obedience: Citizens, soldiers, and the progress of consent in America, 1776–1898.* Stanford, CA: Stanford University Press.

Sampson, R. J., and D. J. Bartusch. 1998. Legal cynicsm and (subcultural?) tolerance of deviance. *Law and Society Review* 32: 777–804.

Sampson, R. J., S. W. Raudenbush, and F. Earls. 1997. Neighborhoods and violent crime. *Science* 277 : 918–24.

Sarat, A. 1977. Studying American legal culture: An assessment of survey evidence. *Law and Society Review* 11: 427–88.

Scherer, K. R., A. Schorr, and T. Johnstone. 2001. *Appraisal process in emotion.* Oxford: Oxford University Press.

Schminke, M. 1998. *Managerial ethics.* Mahwah, NJ: Erlbaum.

Schmitt, J. F., and G. A. Klein. 1998. Fighting in the fog: Dealing with battlefield uncertainty. *Human Performance in Extreme Environments* 3: 57–63.

Scholz, J. T. 1998. Trusting government: Fear, duty, and trust in tax compliance. In *Trust and Governance,* ed. V. Braithwaite and M. Levi, 135–66. New York: Russell Sage Foundation.

Scholz, J. T., and M. Lubell. 1998. Trust and taxpaying. *American Journal of Political Science* 42: 398–417.

Scholz, J. T., and N. Pinney. 1995. Duty, fear, and tax compliance: The heuristic basis of citizenship behavior. *American Journal of Political Science* 39: 490–512.

Schwartz, R. D., and S. Orleans. (1967). On legal sanctions. *University of Chicago Law Review* 34: 274–300.

Sears, D. O. 2003. The psychology of legitimacy. *Political Psychology* 25: 318–23.

Sedikides, C. 2002. Self and identity: Social psychological perspectives. *Revue Internationale de psychologie sociale* 15: 3–4.

Sedikides, C., and M. B. Brewer, eds. 2001. *Individual self, relational self, collective self.* Philadelphia: Psychology Press.

Sedikides, C., and A. Gregg. 2003. Portraits of the self. In *The Sage handbook of social psychology,* ed. M. A. Hogg and J. Cooper, 110–38. London: Sage.

Sedikides, C., and M. J. Strube. 1997. Self-evaluation: To thine own self be good, to thine own self be sure, to thine own self be true, and to thine own self be better. *Advances in Experimental Social Psychology* 29: 209–69.

Selznick, P. 1969. *Law, society, and industrial justice.* New York: Russell Sage Foundation.

Senden, L. 2005. Soft law, self-regulation and co-regulation in European law: Where do they meet? *Electronic Journal of Comparative Law* 9. Retrieved June 1, 2007, from http://www.ejcl.org/91/art91-3.pdf.

Shackleton, R. 1961. *Montesquieu: A critical biography.* Oxford: Oxford University Press.

Shapiro, M. 1988. *Who guards the guardians? Judicial control of administration.* Athens: University of Georgia Press.

Sherman, L. W. 1993. Defiance, deterrence, irrelevance: A theory of the criminal sanction. *Journal of Research in Crime and Delinquency* 30: 445–73.

Shore, L. F., K. Barksdale, and T. H. Shore. 1995. Managerial perceptions of employee commitment to the organization. *Academy of Management Journal* 38: 1593–1615.

Shute, S., R. Hood, and F. Seemungal. 2005. *A fair hearing? Ethnic minorities in the criminal courts.* Cullompton, England: Willan.

Simmons, B. A. 1998. Compliance with international agreements. *Annual Review of Political Science* 1, 75–93.

Skogan, W. G. 2006. Asymmetry in the impact of encounters with the police. *Policing and Society* 16: 99–126.

Skogan, W. G., and T. Meares. 2004. Lawful policing. *Annals of the American Academy of Political and Social Science* 593: 66–83.

Skolnick, J. H., and J. J. Fyfe. 1993. *Above the law: Police and the excessive use of force.* New York: Free Press.

Smith, C. A., D. W. Organ, and J. P. Near. 1983. Organizational citizenship behavior: Its nature and antecedents. *Journal of Applied Psychology* 68: 653–63.

Smith, H. J., and T. R. Tyler. 1997. Choosing the right pond: How group membership shapes self-esteem and group-oriented behavior. *Journal of Experimental Social Psychology* 33: 146–70.

Smith, H. J., T. R. Tyler, Y. J. Huo, D. J. Ortiz, and E. A. Lind. 1998. The self-relevant implications of the group-value model: Group membership, self-worth, and procedural justice. *Journal of Experimental Social Psychology* 34: 470–93.

Smithson, M., and M. Foddy. 1999. Theories and strategies for the study of social dilemmas. In *Resolving social dilemmas: Dynamic, structural and intergroup aspects,* ed. M. Foddy, M. Smithson, S. Schneider, and M. Hogg, 1–15. Philadelphia: Psychology Press.

Sondak, H., and T. R. Tyler. 2007. How does procedural justice shape the desirability of markets? *Journal of Economic Psychology* 28: 79–92.

Sparks, R., A. Bottoms, and W. Hay. 1996. *Prisons and the problem of order.* Oxford: Clarendon.

Stewart, R. B., 2003. *Administrative law in the twenty-first century.* Paper presented at the New York University Law School, February 10.

Stutzer, A., and R. Lalive. 2001. *The role of social work norms in job searching and subjective well-being.* IZA Discussion Paper 300. Bonn, Germany: Institut zur Zukunft der Arbeit.

Suchman, M. C. 1995. Managing legitimacy: Strategic and institutional approaches. *Academy of Management Review* 20: 571–610.

Suls, J., and R. J. Miller, eds. 1977. *Social comparison processes: Theoretical and empirical perspectives*. Washington, DC: Hemisphere.

Suls, J., and T. A. Wills. 1991. *Social comparison*. Hillsdale, NJ: Erlbaum.

Sunshine, J., and T. R. Tyler. 2003. The role of procedural justice and legitimacy in shaping public support for policing. *Law and Society Review* 37: 555–89.

Swedbert, R. 2006. Max Weber's contribution to the economic sociology of law. *Annual Review of Law and Social Science* 2: 61–81.

Tajfel, H. 1978. Social categorization, social identity and social comparison. In *Differentiation between social groups*, ed. H. Tajfel, 66–76. London: Academic Press.

Tajfel, H., and J. C. Turner. 1979. An integrative theory of intergroup conflict. In *The social psychology of intergroup relations*, ed. W. G. Austin and S. Worchel, 33–47. Monterey, CA: Brooks-Cole.

———. 1986. The social identity theory of intergroup behavior. In *Psychology of intergroup relations*, ed. S. Worchel and W. G. Austin, 2–24. Chicago: Nelson-Hall.

Tankebe, J. 2008. Police effectiveness and police trustworthiness in Ghana: An empirical appraisal. *Criminology and Criminal Justice* 8: 185–202.

Tapp, J. L., and F. Levine. 1977. *Law, justice, and the individual in society*. New York: Henry Holt.

Taylor, F. W. 1911. *Principles of scientific management*. New York: Harper.

Taylor, S. E., and J. D. Brown. 1968. Illusion and well-being. *Psychological Bulletin* 103: 193–210.

Tenbrunsel, A. E., and D. M. Messick. 1999. Sanctioning systems, decision frames, and cooperation. *Administrative Science Quarterly* 44: 684–707.

Terrill, W. 2001. *Police coercion: Application of the force continuum*. New York: LFB Scholarly.

Tetlock, P. E. 2000. Cognitive biases and organizational correctives. *Administrative Science Quarterly* 45: 293–326.

———. 2002. Social functionalist frameworks for judgment and choice: Intuitive politicians, theologians, and prosecutors. *Psychological Review* 109: 451–71.

Thaler, R. H. 1991. *Quasi-rational economics*. New York: Russell Sage Foundation.

Thibaut, J., and H. H. Kelley. 1959. *The social psychology of groups*. New York: John Wiley.

Thibaut, J., and L. Walker. 1975. *Procedural justice: A psychological analysis*. Hillsdale, NJ: Erlbaum.

Thompson, P., and C. Warhurst, eds. 1998. *Workplaces of the future*. Houndmills, England: Macmillan.

Tice, D. M., and H. M. Wallace. 2003. The reflected self: Creating yourself as (you think) others see you. In *Handbook of self and identity*, ed. M. R. Leary and J. P. Tangney, 91–105. New York: Guilford.

Trevino, L. K., and K. A. Nelson. 2007. *Managing business ethics*. 4th ed. New York: Wiley.

Trevino, L. K., G. R. Weaver, D. G. Gibson, and B. L. Toffler. 1999. Managing ethics and legal compliance: What works and what hurts. *California Management Review* 41: 131–51.

Tversky, A., and D. Kahneman. 1974. Judgment under uncertainty: Heuristics and biases. *Science* 185: 1124–31.

Tversky, A., and D. Kahneman. 1981. The framing of decisions and the psychology of choice. *Science* 211: 453–58.

Tyler, T. R. 1987. Conditions leading to value expressive effects in judgments of procedural justice: A test of four models. *Journal of Personality and Social Psychology* 52: 333–44.

———. 1989. The psychology of procedural justice: A test of the group value model. *Journal of Personality and Social Psychology* 57: 830–38.

———. 1990. *Why people obey the law.* New Haven, CT: Yale University Press.

———. 1991. Using procedures to justify outcomes: Testing the viability of a procedural justice strategy for managing conflict and allocating resources in work organizations. *Basic and Applied Social Psychology* 12: 259–79.

———. 1994a. Governing amid diversity: Can fair decision-making procedures bridge competing public interests and values? *Law and Society Review* 28, 701–22.

———. 1994b. Psychological models of the justice motive. *Journal of Personality and Social Psychology* 67: 850–63.

———. 1997. Citizen discontent with legal procedures. *American Journal of Comparative Law* 45: 869–902.

———. 1998. Public mistrust of the law: A political perspective. *University of Cincinnati Law Review* 66: 847–76.

———. 2000a. Multiculturalism and the willingness of citizens to defer to law and to legal authorities. *Law and Social Inquiry* 25: 983–1019.

———. 2000b. Social justice. *International Journal of Psychology* 35: 117–25.

———. 2001. Public trust and confidence in legal authorities: What do majority and minority group members want from the law and legal institutions? *Behavioral Science and the Law* 19: 215–35.

———. 2002. Leadership and cooperation in groups. *American Behavioral Scientist* 45: 769–82.

———. 2003. Procedural justice, legitimacy, and the effective rule of law. *Crime and Justice* 30: 431–505.

———. 2005. Promoting employee policy adherence and rule following in work settings: The value of self-regulatory approaches. *Brooklyn Law Review* 70: 1287–1312.

———. 2006a. Legitimacy and legitimation. *Annual Review of Psychology* 57: 375–400.

———. 2006b. Social motives and institutional design. In *The evolution and design of institutions,* ed. G. von Wangerheim, 56–76. Oxford: Blackwell.

———. 2006c. What do they expect? New findings confirm the precepts of procedural fairness. *California Court Review* (Winter): 22–26.

———. 2006d. *Why people obey the law.* 2nd ed. Princeton, NJ: Princeton University Press.

———. 2007. *Psychology and the design of legal institutions.* Nijmegen, Netherlands: Wolf Legal.

———. 2008. Psychology and institutional design. *Review of Law and Economics* 4: 801–87.

———. 2009. Legitimacy and criminal justice: The benefits of self-regulation. *Ohio State Journal of Criminal Law* 7: 307–59.

Tyler, T. R., and R. Bies. 1990. Interpersonal aspects of procedural justice. In *Applied social psychology in business settings,* ed. J. S. Carroll, 77–98. Hillsdale, NJ: Erlbaum.

Tyler, T. R., and S. L. Blader. 2000. *Cooperation in groups.* Philadelphia: Psychology Press.

———. 2001. Identity and prosocial behavior in groups. *Group Processes and Intergroup Relations* 4: 207–26.

———. 2002. The influence of status judgments in hierarchical groups: Comparing autonomous and comparative judgments about status. *Organizational Behavior and Human Decision Processes* 89: 813–38.

———. 2003. Procedural justice, social identity, and cooperative behavior. *Personality and Social Psychology Review* 7: 349–61.

———. 2005. Can businesses effectively regulate employee conduct? The antecedents of rule following in work settings. *Academy of Management Journal* 48: 1143–58.

———. 2007. *The identity mediation of cooperative behavior*. Unpublished manuscript.

Tyler, T. R., R. J. Boeckmann, H. J. Smith, and Y. J. Huo. 1997. *Social justice in a diverse society*. Boulder, CO: Westview.

Tyler, T. R., A. Braga, J. Fagan, T. Meares, R. Sampston, and C. Winship, eds. 2007. *Legitimacy and criminal justice in global perspective*. New York: Russell Sage Foundation.

Tyler, T. R., and A. Caine. 1981. The role of distributional and procedural fairness in the endorsement of formal leaders. *Journal of Personality and Social Psychology* 41: 642–55.

Tyler, T. R., P. Callahan, and J. Frost. 2007. Armed, and dangerous(?) Can self-regulatory approaches shape rule adherence among agents of social control? *Law and Society Review* 41: 457–92.

Tyler, T. R., J. D. Casper, and B. Fisher. 1989. Maintaining allegiance toward political authorities: The role of prior attitudes and the use of fair procedures. *American Journal of Political Science* 33: 629–52.

Tyler, T. R., and J. Darley. 2000. Building a law-abiding society: Taking public views about morality and the legitimacy of legal authorities into account when formulating substantive law. *Hofstra Law Review* 28: 707–39.

Tyler, T. R., and R. Dawes. 1993. Justice in organized groups: Comparing the self-interest and social identity perspectives. In *Psychological perspectives on justice*, ed. B. Mellers, 87–108. Cambridge: Cambridge University Press.

Tyler, T. R., and D. De Cremer. 2006a. Cooperation in groups. In *Social psychology and economics: Interdisciplinary perspectives*, ed. D. De Cremer, M. Zeelenberg, and J. K. Murnighan, 155–70. Mahwah, NJ: Erlbaum.

———. 2006b. How do we promote cooperation in groups, organizations, and societies? The interface of psychology and economics. In *Bridging social psychology*, ed. Paul van Lange, 427–36. Philadelphia: Psychology Press.

Tyler, T. R., and P. Degoey. 1995. Collective restraint in social dilemmas. *Journal of Personality and Social Psychology* 69: 482–97.

———. 1996. Trust in authorities. In *Trust in organizations*, ed. R. Kramer and T. R. Tyler, 331–56. Beverly Hills, CA: Sage.

Tyler, T. R., P. Degoey, and H. Smith. 1996. Understanding why the justice of group procedures matters: A test of the psychological dynamics of the group-value model. *Journal of Personality and Social Psychology* 70, 913–30.

Tyler, T. R., J. Dienhart, and T. Thomas. 2008. The ethical commitment to compliance: Building value-based cultures that encourage ethical conduct and a commitment to compliance. *California Management Review* 50: 31–51.

Tyler, T. R., and J. Fagan. 2008. Why do people cooperate with the police? *Ohio State Journal of Criminal Law*, 6, 231–75.

Tyler, T. R., and Y. J. Huo. 2002. *Trust in the law*. New York: Russell Sage Foundation.

Tyler, T. R., and J. T. Jost. 2007. Legal psychology. In *Handbook of social psychology*, 2nd ed., ed. E. T. Higgins and A. W. Kruglanski, 807–25. New York: Guilford.

Tyler, T. R., and E. A. Lind. 1992. A relational model of authority in groups. *Advances in Experimental Social Psychology* 25: 115–91.

Tyler, T. R., and G. Mitchell. 1994. Legitimacy and the empowerment of discretionary legal authority. *Duke Law Journal* 43: 703–814.

Tyler, T. R., K. Rasinski, and N. Spodick. 1985. The influence of voice on satisfaction with leaders: Exploring the meaning of process control. *Journal of Personality and Social Psychology* 48: 72–81.

Tyler, T. R., and D. Rottman. 2009. *Public perspectives on the courts*. Unpublished manuscript, Department of Psychology, New York University.

Tyler, T. R., L. W. Sherman, H. Strang, G. C. Barnes, and D. J. Woods. 2007. Reintegrative shaming, procedural justice, and recidivism: The engagement of offenders' psychological mechanisms in the Canberra RISE drinking-and-driving experiment. *Law and Society Review* 41: 553–86.

Tyler, T. R., and H. J. Smith. 1998. Social justice and social movements. In *Handbook of Social Psychology*, 4th ed., ed. D. Gilbert, S. Fiske, and G. Lindzey, 2:595–629. New York: McGraw-Hill.

———. 1999. Sources of the social self. In *The psychology of the social self*, ed. T. R. Tyler, R. Kramer, and O. John, 223–64. Hillsdale, NJ: Erlbaum.

Tyler, T. R., and C. Wakslak. 2004. Profiling and the legitimacy of the police: Procedural justice, attributions of motive, and the acceptance of social authority. *Criminology* 42: 13–42.

U.S. Army. 1994. *Leaders' manual for combat stress control*. U.S. Army Field Manual 22-51. Washington, DC: Office of the Army.

———. 1999. *Army leadership: Be, know, do*. U.S. Army Field Manual 22-100. Washington, DC: Office of the Army.

U.S. Department of Justice. 2001. *Prisoners in 2000*. Bureau of Justice Statistics Bulletin NCJ 188207. Washington, DC: Department of Justice, Office of Justice Programs.

U.S. Sentencing Commission. 2009. *U.S. Sentencing Commission guidelines*. Manual 8B2.1(a)(2). Washington, DC: U.S. Sentencing Commission.

Vandenbergh, M. P. 2003. Beyond elegance: A test of social norms in corporate environmental compliance. *Stanford Environmental Law Journal* 22: 55–143.

Van Lange, P.A.M. 2006. *Bridging social psychology: Benefits of transdisciplinary approaches*. Mahwah, NJ: Erlbaum.

Van Lange, P.A.M., D. De Cremer, E. Van Dijk, and M. Van Vugt. 2007. Self-interest and beyond: Basic principles of social interaction. In *Social psychology: Handbook of basic principles*, ed. E. T. Higgins and A. W. Kruglanski, 540–61. New York: Guilford.

Van Vugt, M., M. Snyder, T. R. Tyler, and A. Biel, eds. 2000. *Cooperation in modern society: Promoting the welfare of communities, states and organizations*. New York: Routledge.

Wakin, M. M. 1979. *War, morality, and the military profession*. Boulder, CO: Westview.

Wakslak, C. J., J. T. Jost, T. R. Tyler, and E. Chen. 2007. System justification and the alleviation of emotional distress. *Psychological Science* 18: 267–74.

Walster, E., G. W. Walster, and E. Berscheid. 1978. *Equity*. Boston: Allyn and Bacon.

Waring, S. P. 1991. *Taylorism transformed: Scientific management since 1945*. Chapel Hill: University of North Carolina Press.

Wasserstrom, Richard A. 1970. *War and morality*. Belmont, CA: Wadsworth.

Weatherford, M. S. 1992. Measuring political legitimacy. *American Political Science Review* 86: 149–66.

Weber, J. M., S. Kopelman, and D. M. Messick. 2004. A conceptual review of decision making in social dilemmas. *Personality and Social Psychology Review* 8: 281–307.

Weber, M. 1968. *Economy and society*. Trans. and ed. G. Roth and C. Wittich. Berkeley and Los Angeles: University of California Press.

Weitzer, R., and S. A. Tuch. 2006. *Race and policing in America*. Cambridge: Cambridge University Press.

Whetten, D. A., and P. C. Godfrey, eds. 1998. *Identity in organizations: Building theory through conversations*. Thousand Oaks, CA: Sage.

Wiley, M., and T. Hudik. 1974. Police-citizen encounters. *Social Problems* 22: 119–27.

Williams, K., J. P. Forgas, and W. von Hippel. 2005. *The social outcast: Ostracism, social exclusion, rejection and bullying*. Philadelphia: Psychology Press.

Williamson, O. 1993. Calculativeness, trust, and economic regulation. *Journal of Law and Economics* 34: 453–502.

Winter, S. C., and P. J. May. 2001. Motivation for compliance with environmental regulation. *Journal of Policy Analysis and Management* 20: 675–98.

Wissler, R. 1995. Mediation and adjudication in the small claims court. *Law and Society Review* 29: 323–58.

Wortley, S., J. Hagan, and R. Macmillan. 1997. Just de(s)serts? The racial polarization of perceptions of criminal injustice. *Law and Society Review* 31: 637–76.

Wright, B.R.E., A.Caspi, T. E. Moffitt, and R. Paternoster. 2004. Does the perceived risk of punishment deter criminally prone individuals? Rational choice, self-control, and crime. *Journal of Research in Crime and Delinquency* 41: 180–213.

Wyatt, T. C., and R. Gal. 1990. *Legitimacy and commitment in the military*. New York: Greenwood.

Wycoff, A., and W. G. Skogan. 1993. *Community policing in Madison: Quality from the inside out*. Washington, DC: Police Foundation.

Yamagishi, T. 1986. The provision of a sanctioning system as a public good. *Journal of Personality and Social Psychology* 51: 110–16.

Yamagishi, T., K. Cook, and M. Watabe. 1998. Uncertainty, trust, and commitment formation in the United States and Japan. *American Journal of Sociology* 104: 165–94.

Zak, P. J., ed. 2008. *Moral markets: The critical role of values in the economy*. Princeton, NJ: Princeton University Press.

Zelditch, M., Jr. 2001. Theories of legitimacy. In *The psychology of legitimacy*, ed. J. T. Jost and B. Major, 33–53. Cambridge: Cambridge University Press.

Ziliak, S. T., and D. N. McCloskey. 2008. *The cult of statistical significance: How the standard error costs us jobs, justice, and lives*. Ann Arbor: University of Michigan Press.

Zimmerman, M. A., and G. J. Zeitz. 2002. Beyond survival: Achieving new venture growth by building legitimacy. *Academy of Management Review* 27: 414–31.

Index

Akerlof, George, 41–42

altruism, 155–156

attitudes: as affective or emotional predisposition, 33; toward group or organization, 32–33; identity and, 40–41, 101, 112, 143, 145, 161, 169n4; measuring, 172–173, 179; procedural justice and, 112, 128, 135, 136, 143, 155, 169n4; process-based approaches and, 102, 128, 136–140; as social motivation, 53, 73, 161–162, 165–166; toward tasks, 32–33; *vs.* values, 32

authority: abuses of, 118; and appeals to social motivations, 6; command-and-control model of, 100, 129–130; instrumental motivations and, 6; justice and legitimacy of, 102–105, 146–147; morality and legitimacy of, 186n1; process-based approaches and cooperation with, 101–102, 106–107; regulation and cooperation with, 12; social status or reputation and legitimacy of, 146; trust in, 105–107, 142. *See also* legal authorities; managerial authority; political authorities

Baron, Jonathan, 21

Baumeister, Roy, 41

Benz, Matthias, 139

Bewley, Truman, 41–42

Blader, Steven, 93, 108, 109, 111

Blau, Peter, 43

Caldiera, Gregory, 145

Casper, Jonathan, 135

Chatman, Jennifer, 41

cognition or cognitive models: of decision making, 14–15, 16, 30–31; of instrumental trust, 30–31

command-and-control models: abuses of authority in, 121; cost/benefit inefficiencies of, 154; and erosion of intrinsic motivation, 157; and extrinsic motivation, 122 (*see also* sanctions/incentives); organizational structures and, 60; persistence of, 154–157; *vs.* process-based approaches, 100–101; psychology of, 154; Sarbanes-Oxley Act and, 115, 117; *vs.* self-regulatory

approaches, 122–123; *vs.* values-based approach, 109–111, 114–116; in workplace environments, 109–110

compliance, 61; contrasted with deference, 26, 52; crime prevention and punishment, 6–7; as instrumentally motivated change, 28, 125–126; with legal authorities, 67–68, 126, 129–130; measuring voluntary, 172nn7–8; organizational design and, 147–148; procedural justice and, 128–130; process-based regulation and, 124–128; respect and, 129

cooperation, defined, 21

cooperative regulation, 116

corporate misconduct, 108–118

culture, organizational, 110–114

Curtis, Amy, 136

Darley, John, 36–39

DeAngelis, Joseph, 133

death penalty, 152

decision making: biases and errors during, 16; cognitive models of, 14–15, 16, 30–31; procedural justice and, 102–107, 112, 133, 146–147; self-interest and economics of, 15–18; transparency of and legitimacy of authority, 146–147; in work organizations, 112–114

deference, 7, 37, 61–62, 64, 65, 67–68, 117–118, 125, 127–128, 147–148, 170n6; *vs.* compliance, 26, 52; procedural justice and, 129

Degoey, Peter, 44

democracy, 2–4, 129, 137–138, 160–161, 184n8, 185n17

dependence: as instrumental motivation, 27, 29, 53

deterrence: cost-effectiveness of, 71–72, 150–152, 154, 179n2; criminal justice system and, 72–73, 126, 134, 150–154; measuring, 156–157, 178; sanctions and, 7, 24, 27, 70, 127, 179n2; self-interest and, 70; surveillance and, 71–72; threshold effects, 179–180n3; undesirable side effects of, 150–154